LOVING LIFE
CAN BE YOURS

"The purpose of this book," the author comments, "is to share a path out of the spiritual dark ages for womankind and humanity, into the light of the glorious adventure of equality and beyond, into the world of Mastery. . . . To be a Master is to face, be responsible for, and to overcome one's problems, challenges, and self-imposed limitations. I have found that my greatest challenges have taught me my greatest lessons, and, in the overcoming of these, I have become wiser and stronger in more loving and understanding ways."

Here Terry Cole-Whittaker generously shares her experience and insight so that we too may be inspired to love and be loved, to empower others and be empowered, and to create a world that is truly without limits.

LOVE AND POWER IN A WORLD WITHOUT LIMITS

A Woman's Guide to the Goddess Within

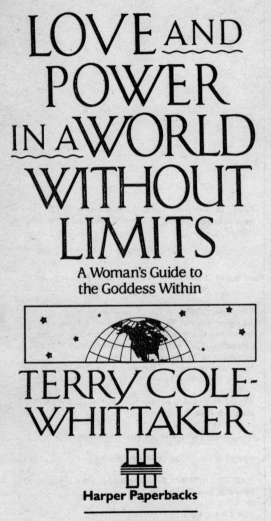

TERRY COLE-WHITTAKER

Harper Paperbacks

Harper & Row, Publishers, New York
Grand Rapids, Philadelphia, St. Louis, San Francisco
London, Singapore, Sydney, Tokyo, Toronto

Terry Cole-Whittaker can be contacted by writing to Adventures in Enlightenment, P.O. Box 528, Rochester, Washington 98579.

Harper Paperbacks a division of Harper & Row, Publishers, Inc.
10 East 53rd Street, New York, N.Y. 10022

A hardcover edition of this book was published in 1989 by Harper & Row, Publishers, Inc.

First Harper Paperbacks printing: September, 1990

Printed in the United States of America

HARPER PAPERBACKS and colophon are trademarks of Harper & Row, Publishers, Inc.

10 9 8 7 6 5 4 3 2 1

I dedicate this book to
the ancient Goddess Sussistanako
(Spider Woman) and her daughters.

Contents

PART II. LIVE YOUR VISION!

PART III. GETTING WHAT YOU WANT IN RELATIONSHIPS

Acknowledgments

NO ONE DOES ANYTHING ALONE, YET EACH OF US MUST in our aloneness commit to our lives and our dreams. I'm grateful to all those that have loved and supported me for many years, for your love has helped me recognize and know my value, discover my gifts, and live my dream.

Reuben Zeigler, thank you for your precious love and depth of courage and strength. You took the chance of being my lover, friend, partner, and pal, which helped me to come to balance and wholeness. Because of men such as yourself women can be who they are. Rebecca Wiesehan, my daughter, thank you, for in your willingness at such a young age to trust yourself, be a mother, wife, and friend, I know that I have succeeded in my mothering. I am so proud of you and of who you have created yourself to be. David Wiesehan, my son-in-law, I am proud of you and your willingness to love my daughter, yourself, and your children. You are an example of someone whose masculine and feminine nature is balanced, and I am grateful for the opportunity to grow with you. Suzanne Cole, my daughter, thank you for being true to yourself and for opportunities to love and grow.

My Goddess friends Nancy Devereaux and Barbara Mastro—I have found in you the friends I have been seeking to align with, share with, create with, and love. Nancy, words fail to express to you my eternal gratitude and excitement about our love and support. Together we get to be girlfriends, pals, confidants, and sisters. Your commitment to go through this work, word for word, to ensure the integrity of what I intended has allowed for the birth of this child of my desires. I am blessed that you are my friend.

Bobey Thompson, thank you for putting the book in the computer and for your commitment to yourself and to the completion of this project. Beth Backman, my faithful literary agent, I am eternally grateful to you and your trust and faith in me when I was going through such enormous changes and didn't even believe in myself. We all need a friend like you.

Clayton Carlson and Yvonne Keller of Harper & Row, I'm so glad we connected. Yvonne, I have been empowered by you in ways you don't know and when I needed it most. Your insight and professionalism in working with me on this book have made it a work of which I am proud.

Introduction: A User's Guide to Love and Power in a World Without Limits

I OFFER THIS BOOK TO ALL WOMEN AND TO THOSE MEN who are willing to recognize their feminine as well as their masculine nature, and who join with the women in creating their lives from love, peace, joy, health, passion, and abundance. Writing a book for women has long been my dream. I love women and have wanted to make a contribution that would make a major difference in their lives. Having come through so many tests, lessons, and challenges myself, I offer my experience so that women may be inspired to love and let themselves be loved, empower others and be empowered, and learn to create for themselves a world that is truly without limits. This book is an opportunity for you to transcend any fears you may have, so that we as women may arise and take our rightful place in the world once again.

Our world has been in chaos, conflict, and war since the fall of women. In this book my energy is focused on trying to redress that balance, to help women reach their own natural potential. When women are restored to wholeness men will also be restored, and balance and harmony will prevail once again. This world of balance will be our Golden Age, and then we can welcome the return of the Goddess Mother in our lives.

It is my deepest desire that this book be a tool for those of us who seek wholeness and balance in our own lives. This book is for you if you desire to know and reaffirm who you are, without the constraints of any fear-based cultural, religious, or moral controls. We have the opportunity to create our lives and our world. We can start from a new foundation of love and personal responsibility that will open us up to the realities beyond fear. The ultimate, inescapable truth is this: What you give out comes back to you. When you give love, you get love back. When love and this law of reciprocity are understood and applied, we will be living in the Golden Age.

As I travel the world and meet people, I know that everyone isn't ready or even willing to bring forth the Golden Age at this time—but you and I are. So let's begin. There aren't many role models here, so whatever is to be is up to you and me. We can create whatever we want through our thoughts, feelings, and actions.

The first chapter of this book has some historical references, but do not be put off by them—this is primarily a how-to book. On the other hand if you want more historical material there is a new and increasing supply of valuable books on women's history available at your local bookstore. This is a book that will help you discover and nurture your own love and power. It relies on my personal experiences and the experiences of others. You do not need to agree with me, and I challenge you to dig deep to uncover the treasures you are seeking within yourself. Without challenge and impact from new ideas there is no growth.

You are not alone. There are others like you who are on the leading edge as pioneers. Use the support that is available; if there isn't much support for you and the way you desire to live, create it for yourself and others. Support is the key, for without it, it is difficult to make sustained gains, and with it you have synergy. Synergy is the name for what happens when two or more people come together with a common purpose. The whole of what you experience in this interaction is greater than the sum of the parts.

I'd suggest you read this book through and then read it again and do the exercises at the end of each chapter. Read the book over and over, and each time you'll become closer to and be clearer on who you are, what you desire, how you choose to live, and what your gifts are to others.

I'm excited about the possibilities this book offers, and I'm excited by the possibilities you yourself bring to the book. Your future and the future of our children and our precious earth are in your hands. You and I can no longer afford to be passive and submissive and afraid of being alone. You are never alone. To become what you are capable of being you must take a stand for what you feel in your heart, what you believe and what you desire. There are no limits except those that are self-imposed. This book is about solutions, possibilities, opportunities, and the steps to take to bring our highest aspirations into this world. Our earth is ready to come of age through you as the awakened, enlightened, loving, and powerful Goddess.

LOVE AND
POWER
IN A WORLD
WITHOUT
LIMITS

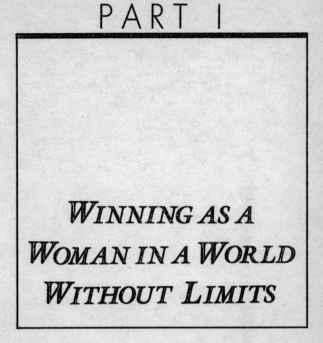

PART 1

WINNING AS A WOMAN IN A WORLD WITHOUT LIMITS

CHAPTER 1

The Fall and Rise of God the Mother

HUMANITY IS AT AN OBVIOUS CROSSROADS AT THIS time, wondering what is coming next. Actually, we are continuously at crossroads, but this is unlike any other time. We can't go back technologically, and we can't continue to pollute our environment, drain our natural resources, or push our planet to extinction. Many aspects of our lives are at the point where we must choose a new way of being that contributes to all people and to our earth in a way that brings about love, peace, happiness, health, wealth, and enlightenment. By enlightenment I mean the awareness of making one's decisions and choices consciously in the highest interest of all concerned.

We'll be able to choose our careers based on our

talents, abilities, and desire for self-expression. We'll flourish in every aspect of our lives. Instead of polluting, we will be able to handle our trash in a biodegradable, organic manner that actually benefits all life forms. Our world will be a beautiful garden in which we explore, discover, create, play, learn, invent, express, share, and participate in a new adventure unlike anything we have ever known.

In order for us to leave our warrior, fear-based reality behind and move into the spirit of the adventurer, women and men must heal their relationship with each other so that we can join hands and walk as whole people into our future together.

What can we as individuals do?

"Well, what do you want?" asks the fairy godmother!

What each of us wants is the most basic of all questions, and it is we ourselves who must answer it. Another way of asking the question is, "What is the outcome that I want?" This becomes a process of self-discovery, for you must consult with all the parts of yourself for the answer.

Whatever the answer is, you must do what it takes to have what you have decided you want. It is time to discover what is possible for us beyond our fear-based belief system. We have put our planet and the very survival of the species called human in jeopardy. Why? We have been living out of balance and in opposition to our nature.

There are many names that could be given to this time we are entering. I like to call it the Golden Age.

It feels like a rich time, a time that marks our entrance into a relationship with the universe, galactic in its scope.

God the Mother has returned and is now bringing herself fully into existence at every level of life on earth. God the Father has been the predominant energy in motion, and it is now time for balance.

Everything in life seeks balance. If the pendulum swings far to the left, it must also swing far to the right to balance itself. For every action there is an equal and opposite reaction. This is a definition of cause and effect. One causes the other as well as itself and co-creation is what is occurring.

This book is about a vision many of us have about a partnership, a family whose name is humanity. We live on a tiny planet that travels through the galaxy going nowhere fast, and we are along, enjoying the ride. The vision of which I speak is the answer to the question, "What do I want, and just what is the outcome I desire?" We are co-creating our vision for ourselves, each other, and Mother Earth. The key to this vision is the recognition and rise of the feminine energy into its full power and glory once again. This vision encompasses the feminine as she joins in a cosmic dance of ecstasy with the masculine energy.

Ecological balance is what is needed to keep our planet in a constant state of regeneration. Female-male balance is needed to keep each person and humanity in a continual state of aliveness, passion, love, happiness, and growth. Life either grows or it dies.

We can see a great example of this principle of balance in how we've cut down trees all over the world without replanting. Little by little we've raped the land without being aware of the consequences. We are now experiencing the effects of our ignorance. This is how we learn and correct imbalances. Less oxygen and less rain change the ecosystem. The lack of rain creates a drought and eventually a desert. Starvation results, which produces government games of food and people control. No water, no crops, no farming, no education, no people. Why? No trees! The earth is an intricately balanced ecological system, just as we ourselves are. One small part affects the whole. Your body too is a whole system; you can't treat one part without affecting the whole body.

THE FEMALE ENERGY IN HISTORY

The female energy is at least one-half of the creative essence of life. The female is the womb, the feeder, the nurturer, and the mother of her children. She is the cradle of civilization, the fertility goddess, the enchantress, the wise crone, the hag witch conjuring up visions and magical potions. She is the creator of the universe.

Her children are her thoughts, her visions, and her feelings projected from the center of the universe out into the vastness of the darkened void as sparks and waves of light. Without "Her" the "He" does not exist, nor can He create without the She being in operation. The He without the She can only use force, fear, and control to produce his vision of a supreme male universe devoid of the feminine influence. The male energy, separate, afraid, and alone, has maneuvered itself onto the throne to be worshiped.

Each of the current major Western and Eastern religions makes the male supreme ruler. Some offer the female a token support role. Some pretend to elevate the female only to silence her and harness her power. Most place the man as the head of household, church, temple, business, and government. The woman is still a property with a separate set of rules and standards by which to live if she is to be sought after by the male. Female virginity is recognized as a gift to the male, and wars have been fought over sexual favors. But any religion that has a female bow down to a male figure is not in the best interests of women or men.

In the Judeo-Christian and Moslem traditions there was a fall, a moment when humanity fell out of favor with God. Jews and Christians believe that happened when the female, Eve, ate from the tree of knowledge of good and evil, against God's rules. The punishment for eating from the tree of life and attempting to obtain physical immortality was to be cast out of the Garden of Eden forever and to live in pain and hardship working the land to merely survive. Women were not to be trusted and became the property of men. Women became seen as the tool of the devil, enticing the otherwise virtuous,

God-favored male into sin. God became a singular male, favoring men, who became the womb of civilization by giving birth through a bone called the rib. Religion became a flesh cult, and sex, money, and power became the game. Eternal life was the prize for the believers, and eternal damnation went to the nonbelievers. It's such a simple, obvious game, and we've played it for thousands of years.

Whenever and however it happened in our history, God the Father decided to upset the balance of power and be all-powerful without God the Mother. The thought appeared, floated by, and was absorbed by both the male and female, and a nightmare of fear, competition, jealousy, disease, death, loss, and scarcity began. Without women's agreement to and acceptance of this mad thought, the imbalance could never have happened.

THE DANGER OF TRUSTING IN HISTORY

I'm not a historian in the academic sense. I am an explorer and adventurer. I'm not here to prove or disprove the equality of women or to gather the facts from what's left of our recorded—and much-changed and tampered-with—history. It is said that the one who can change history can control the future. Why? Because we place so much faith in what *was* rather than what can be *now* and may be *in the future.*

Our history books have all been written, as have our religious and historical documents, to elevate the male and the masculine supreme creator and to degrade and deny the Goddess, the female as the womb and cradle of civilization. It doesn't take long to obliterate an entire value system. It didn't take long for Russia or China to erase a previous government, religion, and way of life. We've seen it in our own century. Consider our drug-tranquilized "me" culture. We change quickly; our children don't know a world without pollution, for example.

There is a great danger in using history to validate your own divinity or the divinity of your God. You really don't know what the people who wrote it were up to or if any of it happened anywhere except in the minds of the artists, historians, and rulers. If you use your family tree to prove or disprove your right to live and flourish, you run the risk of never knowing who you are on your own. The masters of life are those who step out from the crowd and are arrogant enough to trust and validate themselves without the need for outside approval; they own their own power. A master controls and is responsible for his or her own life and destiny in harmony with others.

Many religions, however, use history as proof of their absolute truth. When each person, woman or man, is whatever she or he decides to be, we're in a completely different ballpark. In a moment, with a change of mind, a whole new person will emerge.

This just makes sense to me, and that is all the proof I need. I anoint myself. I elevate myself. I proclaim my own mastery and my own godliness. It takes "chutzpah." It takes arrogance, and it takes a strong sense of oneself to make no excuses, to need no proof, and to have no reasons or justifications other than "I am!"

USING LOGIC ON HISTORY

We'll look back into history from time to time, for there is value there in remembering where we've been, but we cannot use it as a map of our present and future. History is his-story, and there is a her-story that is yet untold, but equally important. The two are the One and the Many.

Shining our light back into the far corners of our memory called his-story, we find a point at which female and male became significant in their differences and the course of history was altered. The fall in Judeo-Christian legend was the point at which male and female fell from God's grace, and since that point earthlings have lived in darkness. The snake was the first representative of evil and the forces of the dark and created the "fall" of human beings from heaven. Somewhere along the way after the fall, a devil and hell were created. Hindus call this dark period the Kali Yuga, the outflow of Krishna's breath. Scientists would name this period the outward motion of the big bang. There are many legends, myths, and dogmatic beliefs about what it all meant. Some call this the Lucifer rebellion and a point at which the governing body of the earth rebelled against the structure of the universe.

As a result, the earth was cut off from its connection with the center of the universe at our request, and we've been struggling ever since. Lucifer is called the fallen angel, the one who went astray.

It was woman in the Judeo-Christian legend who enticed man into eating the apple, the fruit of good and evil. Whatever the story (and there are hundreds of different stories about what happened and how we as a people and planet have come to be where we are), we are here, now!

My story, and perhaps a her-story for many, is this: God the Mother and God the Father lived together as one within all beings. These two energies in harmony did the dance of creation and the result, their offspring, was the material world. Their thoughts, feelings, and desires expressed their marriage and blendings, and infinite creation was set in motion. God the Mother is the creative aspect, the womb, the gestalt, the whole within which the Father is the messenger, the seed, the doer who goes out to plant and manage the seeds. She creates a home, the earth, as a greenhouse in which her seeds can be loved and nurtured and grow into their full glory. In this perfect, ecologically balanced greenhouse, playground, and laboratory, She and He would play together—She loving and worshiping her greatest creation, Him, and He basking in the radiance of Her love, satisfied, joyful, and feeling that all is well as both perform according to their true function and purpose.

There are a few remnants of Goddess cultures here on earth, but most of that part of our earth history has been destroyed since God the Father decided to be the almighty without God the Mother. In that instant, a separation in consciousness took place that placed the male energy upon the throne and the female energy into prison as his servant. The fear-based ego machinery set itself in motion, and away we went into an adventure of separation and fear. But the ultimate fear of both men and women is now being found out, and this game is being uncovered and the male being dethroned.

But the whole cannot be run by a single part. The single aspect that makes itself the whole must, to stay in power, deny all the other parts. The other parts must deny themselves, their intuition, and direct knowing, in order to play this game. "Absolute power corrupts absolutely" is a well-known theory. I've found this tendency in my own life, for without feedback, without balance and the partnership of equals, we are tyrannical dictators who can only create destruction.

Civilization has been on a path of death, sickness, suffering, stagnation, competition, jealousy, poverty, war, crime, greed, violence, and sexual abuse ever since that moment of separation. Step by step the old consciousness of unity and oneness was exchanged for a belief in one male God with male representatives to ride herd on generations of people, animals, and plants, and the inanimate world. This new Supreme Being elevated and worshiped by all became a tyrant, and the feminine energy, newly made lowly, was thrown out of heaven into hell. This act upset the system of balance and harmony, and the result is work, struggle, stress, conflict, and dysfunction.

Our planet was now cut off from the feelings and thoughts of God the Mother; creation became a struggle and no longer an effortless joy. Scarcity, war games, power struggles, and limitations became the way of life, and life itself was exchanged for survival. Survival became the purpose. The values, ideals, and standards for one's life were now dictated by a new set of rules and agreements whose function was to keep the male energy supreme and to keep the female energy from remembering who she was and what had happened.

For years, I thought death was the number-one fear in all people. Bur now I feel the greatest fear and the base of all other fears and anxieties is that *this game has been found out and is now going to have to end.* Why are men so nervous and fearful of women owning their power? Why are the most secure men unwilling to think about the female energy as the creator of life? Why do women teach their boys and girls to continue the game of inequality and separation? Why do the majority of churches and temples disempower women and some, even to this day, make the female the property of the male, giving him the right to use her body and her possessions for his own purposes? Why do we make emotion, tenderness, love, compassion, and peace signs of emasculation and weakness? Why do so many women not own their own power and instead give over to men the power to validate themselves? Why do men, in order to punish, withhold love, sexual intimacy, communication, and support from the women who love them? Why do some men seek out powerful, talented, and able women and then attempt to cripple them emotionally, spiritually, mentally, and physically? Why do many women who are angry disempower their husbands through devious, nondetectable means? Why do we make men leaders even though they have failed to bring peace, love, and light to the world as a whole? Why do women not come forth, use their immense power, and put in the correction to bring the world back into balance once again? We're afraid to live from love.

What I am proposing is that women and men alike awaken to the female and male energies within themselves and return to the pre-separation state of oneness. I feel it is possible to awaken the feminine and the masculine within all of us and return to the cosmic dance of passion and play.

HOW TO AWAKEN TO WHOLENESS

Wholeness begets wholeness. Wellness creates wellness, just as illness results in illness. There are a few balanced men and women who have recognized their multiple levels of self and consciously focus and direct these energies to create and experience themselves as they want to be.

Separation demanded that the She within the He be hidden and denied. If a woman was to be powerful, she needed also to hide the She within herself and become masculine. The most popular way in which women could have more options in this new male game was to serve the male and use their great creative powers to bring about *his* dreams, wants, and needs. He could not have done any of it without the feminine, yet the feminine had to pretend that there could be a He without a She.

Without the balance of female and male energy, all we've done is take, not knowing that we can give. Without the awareness of sufficiency, sharing, and love, all we've had are enemies who threaten our existence rather than sisters and brothers with whom we can play and create.

Mother Earth gives to us far more than we give, yet she eventually receives back all she has given so that the recycling process can continue. Why obstruct nature and use force and might to build for oneself physical illness as well as emotional distress, economic extremes, and governmental insanity? The male energy wants to do something, the female energy simply is. To be and to do creates having. One without the other is imperfect.

When the female embraces her male self, she can focus her energy, take action, and carry through her visions and desires. When the male accepts his feminine self, he reconnects himself through intuition to the heart of the universe, allows himself to feel, to love, and to express his most magical and creative self.

Fear is what keeps us living in separation, crippling ourselves and negating the very qualities, abilities, and talents that would solve our problems and move us into the twenty-first century as whole people ready to create a new and beautiful world for all. Our past is filled with shattered dreams; now it is time to pick up the pieces, put our most precious dreams back together, and go forward. It will take courageous men and women to transcend the fear of awakening to this new reality. Awakening only takes a moment, and in that moment there is a union within made in heaven, heaven being the experience of no fear, only wholeness and love.

Our fear-based belief system of the past is no longer appropriate or even possible as we move into this Golden Age. The warrior age is finished, and the adventure is here. It is no longer even a question of whether or not we are ready to say good-bye to the warrior. We must. We can keep the passion without the force, violence, violation, and attack. It is no longer appropriate for us to envision and generate a victim-victimizer society in which the female is the victim.

This book is for women and the feminine within all of us. All it takes to change is for us to no longer play the old game, take back what we believe we have lost, love ourselves and others, and get on with the new game.

Let the rediscovery of ourselves begin!

EXERCISES

To receive the most value use a journal or separate piece of paper and write out your answers.

1. List at least twenty-five objectives you intend to achieve for yourself from reading this book (spiritual, mental, emotional, physical, and material).

2. What does "owning your power" mean to you?

3. List fifteen religious beliefs that you allow to keep you unequal and less powerful than men and subservient to the church or temple.

4. Fill in the blank: The greatest fear I have that prevents me from being responsible for and creating my own life as I want it is _____.

5. List the people and organizations you make greater than yourself and thus make yourself answer to.

6. The greatest benefit I receive from being controlled by others is _____.

7. Why do you play by others' rules? I allow myself to be controlled by another's rules because _____.

8. How much of the time do you feel good about yourself? What situations, people, or events do you react to by lowering your feelings of self-esteem and self-worth? For each answer

also write down why you devalue yourself. What is the payoff or benefit you get from doing it?

9. Recall the times when you have felt wonderful, beautiful, loved, and valuable. Why did you feel that way? Notice the workings in your mind that determine how you are feeling about yourself.

10. Remember how you feel when you feel confident, certain, loved, and worthy. Anchor in the feelings by breathing in deeply and on the exhalation, relaxing into more of these pleasant feelings. Create a new habit of feeling wonderful within yourself as often as you want.

11. If you aren't feeling loved, wonderful, beautiful, and worthy, it's because you don't want to. Why don't you want to have high self-esteem and feelings that signify personal worth?

12. Write out a description of the way you believe you should be in order for you to be worthy of your own respect and the respect of others. Why not pass these conditions and go straight to self-love? Notice the motivation self-hate and self-condemnation create.

13. Write out twenty-five fears or thoughts you have that prevent you from respecting and loving yourself all the time. What's the payoff or the

imagined benefit? What's the cost to you, and is it worth it?

14. How would you feel if you were equal to men? What would you be doing and having that's different from what you are doing and having now?

15. What would you be doing if you felt equal, powerful, beautiful, loving, peaceful, and unlimited? (This question may not pertain to you if you already feel equal, powerful, beautiful, loving, peaceful, and unlimited!)

16. What is it in your past or present that you use to blame yourself, blame others, and in any way prevent yourself from being 100 percent alive, living your vision and dream for yourself?

17. What, if anything, do you do to keep a relationship that denies you or your desires and abilities in any way?

AFFIRMATIONS

Write these statements about your desired reality a few times each day. Say these words out loud to yourself, and as you do feel that the words are true about yourself. Remember, the subconscious doesn't know the difference between fact and fantasy. With these affirmations you are creating your ideal as reality.

1. I, ___(your name)___, respect and value myself.

2. It's safe for me, _____, to respect and love myself under any and all circumstances.

3. I, _____, forgive myself for not placing a high value on myself.

4. I, _____, accept my equality now and forever.

5. The more I, _____, love myself and value who I am, the more I respect others.

CHAPTER 2

The Power of Your Thoughts and Beliefs

HOW YOU THINK ABOUT YOURSELF IS MORE IMPOR-
tant than how others think about you. Each of us
is affected by our own thoughts. "No one's beliefs
affect you but your own" is a thought I love to contemplate. Imagine how freeing that thought is!

"Men are superior to women. They are blessed
in the sight of God, and he has given men dominion
over women, children, and nature itself." This
thought, believed at any level as truth, upsets the
balance of nature and generates untold hardships
and inequalities. Change this to, "All people as
valuable and divine are meant to live in harmony,
balance, and love with each other and nature." This

thought creates an entirely different world than the first one. Thought is creative!

Thoughts are bubbles of consciousness, like tiny worlds floating in space complete in themselves. Thoughts believed become truths, laws, and rules through a built-in system called self-fulfilling prophecy. Thoughts are received, given, and generated within the individual. A thought agreed upon by two or more people is called collective reality.

We hold a thought and project it outward. What we see is our projection. The process goes like this: First, we think a thought or perhaps latch onto a thought as it floats by. Second, we project the thought on the screen of life. Third, a reality is created from that thought with proof and validation to justify the truth of the thought on that screen. Absolutism is the belief of a lot of people that some thoughts are not just thoughts but eternal facts about an unchanging reality. It is a belief that thoughts are not just projections reflecting back to us. It is what we are taught, but it is a mistaken belief. Herein lies the problem!

WE ARE PROGRAMMED FROM BEFORE BIRTH

We take in beliefs, values, opinions, ideas, and ideals from the moment of conception and perhaps before. The moment we enter our bodies we are affected by the consciousness of those around us. We are programmed just as a computer is programmed, by our parents, other family members, our friends and our teachers, by religion, the government, and television and other media. The moment you are born you are a customer, a citizen, a potential voter, taxpayer, client, enemy, and member of the same or opposite sex. We are programmed on multiple levels of consciousness, mind, emotions, and body. We are open, vulnerable, impressionable beings of pure love, ready to jump into the game of life and play.

Who you believe yourself to be at this moment is the result of that programming unless you have found and begun to deprogram yourself. This programming is both an unconscious, nondeliberate action by some people and a conscious, purposeful action by others. A child is 60 percent imprinted with his or her beliefs and values by the age of two. Yet all that can be changed at will.

Whatever we accept as true, absolute, unchanging, real, and valid is simply a thought believed. If we change our minds, it's all different. To not know this is to be a conditioned robot asleep to one's greater self, known as Spirit. It's all made up in our minds and projected onto the bigger screen of life so that we may experience our movie. We climb into the movie to increase the impact.

Personally, I like happy movies that motivate me and stimulate my intellect, artistic abilities, genius, and inner beauty. I don't pay money to see violence in movies. Some say, "Be realistic, it's life!" I say we create life by what we think, feel, believe, fantasize, and act upon. If I want beauty, I live in beauty, and I allow others to create whatever they want as long as it doesn't interfere with my desire for love, peace, and beauty in my own life.

Mental movie themes that depict women as less than men or as whores, drunks, bitches, sex toys, dummies, hags, witches, or as Satan's handmaidens are relics of a civilization programmed with superstition and fears. As a matter of fact, the words hag and witch were once beautiful, sacred terms of respect and holiness earned by women who proved themselves wise counselors and proficient healers in ancient times. Through religious persecution and the intent of some to rob the female of her immense power, these terms now conjure up fear, devil worship, negativity, and ugliness. Mind movies that mainly portray men as criminals, tyrants, "Rambos," as violent, macho, aggressive, insensitive sex machines and warlords keep humanity stuck in these ancient, worn-out games. Our role models are a major part of our programming. I used a process called rebirthing to change my programming.

During rebirthing the person being rebirthed lies down in a relaxed and comfortable position and inhales and exhales in a connected breathing pattern for at least one hour. Through my rebirthing process I recalled my first experience of programming at birth. I felt my father's and mother's feelings, I heard their words, I smelled them, and I saw them. I loved them immediately and I felt their fears, needs, and desires. I believe babies communicate telepathically and so pick up the real emotions and actual communication going on, not the words or smoke screens. A baby is a fully operational spacecraft, and having just landed on earth, she opens herself to the game called being human. If born into a loving, nurturing family environment, a child can blossom into a multifaceted gem. If born into a family full to overflowing with fears, neuroses, psychoses, doubts, and insecurities, a child has a tremendous amount to overcome. Ignorance of the process of creation through imprinting consciousness and of the power to change this imprinting keeps people enslaved.

We are sponges absorbing data—light, color, sound, feelings, thoughts, and beliefs. In the first few months of human life, we learn language, motor control, humor, games, and emotion, just to name some of what happens. We learn this mostly from others, but I also believe we come in with a highly developed consciousness depending on how advanced we were before we entered the earth plane for another "go-round." We have our soul and our past experiences, which join with the genes of our mother's and father's ancestral lineages. We have our parents', siblings', and family's consciousness package to affect us.

Genetically speaking, we are the sum total of all life before us. Our bodies as machines are imprinted with beliefs and controlled through our glandular systems as activated, I believe, by the hypothalamus gland. The pineal gland, about which little is known, is probably the instrument of our particular consciousness called "self." Heredity can be a help or a hindrance depending on the awareness of the self in the body. I feel we are powerful enough to transcend any limits and to reprogram our entire energy system through intention, love, and will. This is my opinion, and it's a part of what I call the Divine Experiment, my concept of the exploration of the possibilities of the self in all dimensions. The Divine Experiment is the name I give to life and its process. Instead of looking at life as something that has a destination or goal, hold it as an opportunity to explore, discover, and experiment. If your relationship, for example, is an experiment, you are exploring the possibilities available in *relating*. You are not stuck in a box of preconceived ideas or the beliefs of your ancestors. To explore the possibilities of anything gives one the freedom to "fail" or "succeed." Both are aspects of the Experiment. You, the research scientist and creative artist, can then take what is of benefit, and discard the rest. The Divine Experiment has no end in sight and the greatest opportunity it presents is that you and I can seek our highest aspirations, desires, and revelations and bring them into our lives at whatever level is appropriate. This earthly life is a limitless opportunity to realize who we are and what we can co-create with the Source of life.

THE FIRST THING TO DO: TAKE RESPON-
SIBILITY

What I've done is to travel into the depths and heights of my thought and belief system, cleansing myself of those thoughts and beliefs that limit, sabotage, or harm me and others in any way. In this place, I can program any feelings, thoughts, attitudes, and beliefs I choose, and I always choose the most beautiful, alive, limitless thoughts and feelings possible. I combine this action with appropriate words, behavior, nutrition, life-style, and so on. This I call self-imprinting or self-programming.

What thrills me is the discovery and experience of what is possible for me and others. What brings me pleasure is the elation of knowing and proving my most loving thoughts as they are manifest in my self, my relationships, my body, and my activities. I enjoy feeling myself an artist with life as my canvas. I am fascinated by what could happen if all people knew who they were and we created our lives, technology, and earth from love and joy.

I'm not interested in being "accepted" into heaven or escaping from the clutches of hell. I'm in heaven, and I've been in hell, survived, and moved on. Logically, any Supreme Being would just love me, so I have no fear. You and I are star children, the seeds of a new generation of brilliant lights playing together in our earth paradise, bringing a new awareness to our planet.

To do this requires us to take responsibility for our past, release what we don't want, and program what we do. You and I are being programmed constantly, even through the vibrations of other people's attitudes and emotions. Either we're victims and contented with our sentence or we shake off the cloak of unconsciousness and create ourselves in our own image and likeness. We set our vision as high as we can in the ethereal and celestial planes, link up with spirit, ask for the help of spirit, and blossom. What we have to shake off is whatever we decide is unwanted or not valuable to us and how we choose to be.

The first thing to do is to think about how you want to feel about yourself, how you want to be, what you want to do. The second thing is to question every thought, belief, value, ideal, custom, law, rule, concept, principle, and truth by which you live your life. Look at each one as it presents itself in your day-to-day life, and notice how each has affected aspects of your life. The third step is to create the thoughts and values that you most want to have as part of you and imprint them on all levels. The fourth step is action. Bring those deepest desires and dreams into this world through your behavior and actions. (Since I use the word desire often, I thought I'd explain my preference for the word. Desire is a word that describes a feeling of passion, excitement, intention, and certainty. "Desire" to me is a much more empowering term than the word "want." It describes an inner urging to be, do, or have. "Want" is fine. Too much "want" disempowers you because "want" is a word that speaks of lack.)

We're used to being stimulus-response machines, programmed from the outside and simply following the program without challenge. The vast majority of people in the world cope and survive by following other people's examples. A master, one who *knows* that she is divine, selects what she wants; if there is nothing that suits her, she simply creates what she wants.

As a child, I picked up people's concepts and values, through mostly nonverbal communication, and believed each one, because after all, these were the "big people." "Big people" are right and know everything; "little people" don't know anything. I picked up my family's beliefs and values about God, men, women, money, bodies, sex, work, and so on. Cross-messages were common. I spent one summer with my great-grandmother when I was fifteen, and she allowed my boyfriend to stay at her house for a couple of weeks. I knew that sex was a "no-no," but because she liked this boy who came from a family of "means," she let him sleep in the single bed beside her and me. I was confused and angry at her, feeling the pain of yet another mixed message. What I learned later was that Nanny believed that sex was okay if it got you somewhere, but it was not just for enjoyment. Nanny was the matriarch of my mother's family. She was a stout woman of pioneer stock who always provided a home, food, and money for her children, grandchildren, and great-grandchildren when they needed it. Nanny was of Irish peasant stock with a slight touch of German aristocracy, which gave her an erect stance, a twinkle in her eye, a royal tilt to her head, and a passion for hard work. She married three men that I knew of, and there were tales of another two or three in her lifetime. She was a liberated woman before her time and also a product of her environment.

Nanny was the one I could count on for love and support, yet she was a strict taskmaster. When Nanny had me do a job, she made sure I was thorough and complete. I'd scrub her kitchen floor, and she'd watch me to make certain it was cleaned in the corners and on the sidewall. I had to rinse it carefully, not leaving a trace of soap, which Nanny said "ate at the floor." To this day, I rinse and rinse as if she were still watching me!

My great-grandmother gave me values, ideas, and beliefs, many of which I still hold today. She taught, "If you are going to do a job, be thorough and do it well," and she taught me how to do that by her example. I learned basic lessons about how to take care of myself by my own efforts. Nanny earned a good living for herself and provided for her family even in times of depression and war. She did what she wanted and made her dreams real. Glacier Lodge was her resort complex, high in the rugged and beautiful Sierra Nevada. She was a pillar of her community, even though a nonconformist in many ways. Her beliefs about men and women greatly affected what I came to believe and therefore prove in my relationships. I learned from Nanny, my mother, and their friends that men were weak, irresponsible women chasers, prone to addictions and incapable of being equal partners in a relationship. I now know this isn't true unless I choose that type of man. But Nanny also helped me realize women could support themselves. She never took "guff" from any man except Scotty, her last husband. She loved him dearly, but she eventually had to leave him because his anger and greed drove him to fits of violence and she feared for her life. Imagine how difficult it was for her to be a woman who was strong and able yet who wanted love and intimacy with a man she cared about. Most of her women friends stayed married to the same man until they died. She didn't.

I was her most precious and fulfilling love, for in me she could live the dreams the women of her generation couldn't, wouldn't, and didn't. Just as she was my past, I was her future. She was my first teacher of metaphysics and strong female role model. (Incidentally, I feel she is now once again in a body and in my life as my granddaughter. In the moment this came to me I felt a rush of energy, tears of joy, and a deep and profound sense of knowledge. Of course, Nanny and I had been so close and so loving, why wouldn't she choose the same family again? One night at the dinner table my granddaughter Austin looked around and said, "Well, we're all here!" Her family was together again.)

My precious mother, Barbara, lived through the twenties, the depression, the war, and the postwar years. In those times, women were wives and mothers. The women who seemed to be having fun were the movie stars and singers. She was torn between being a "sit-at-home" wife and mother and her desire to be a glamorous party girl and professional singer. Married at sixteen, by twenty she had four little girls and a husband who shirked the responsibilities of being a father and provider. He left, and she carried on with the care and feeding of the young. Mom worked as a waitress, and after work we'd sit on the bed together and count her tips for the day. That was our grocery money. My mom has a great sense of humor, loves us dearly, and never felt truly loved by her man, my father. She has a loving and supportive husband now.

My sweet father, Adam, blessed me with a tall, strong body. He was tall, dark, and handsome. Dad loved his girls and did his best. But he found himself weighed down by an insecure wife, four dependent babies, and a set of strong-willed, complex in-laws. He once told me he never felt wanted, probably something he felt since early childhood; he was the ninth of twelve children.

I watched the adults play their games. Even as a small child I could see through them and knew what they were doing. A child absorbs everything. Little by little, I forgot to remember that I was spirit, and little by little, I slipped into unconsciously playing the games the adults were playing. I was born into this world choosing these people as my caretakers, teachers, and eventually friends and equals. These were the people I first looked to for clues about what it meant to be female and human playing in the challenging game of life. No one gives us any of the predetermined rules at birth, so by trial and error we pattern ourselves after others unless we learn we can step out from the crowd, look within, and cut a new path.

BECOMING FEMININE

Other role models I found in books, movies, television, school, and the society columns. I would admire and envy these women I saw in the hopes they could somehow show me how to become a "successful," happy woman. Envy, jealousy, and competition began to surface as I sought my identity and tried to create a life for myself. Should I be a blonde, or should I keep my hair brown? Why doesn't the boy I like like me? Why didn't that teacher compliment me on my nice work? Why are those girls laughing at my clothes? Why don't the girls have an athletic program as costly and extensive as the boys'? It seemed that men had it made; life belonged to them. It appeared that my only hope for happiness was to have one of my own who loved me and gave me whatever I wanted and needed. And to do that I had to achieve the elusive quality I thought was femininity. The feminine ones got the men and received the gifts.

I tried everything to become feminine. I read books on the subject. I studied the rules, roles, and thoughts I had to subscribe to. I played games; I became a master of manipulation, denial, and people pleasing but mostly at fooling myself.

I labeled and classified men and women. Women were gentle, loving, understanding, graceful, intuitive, giving, sharing, psychic, and nurturing. They were also petty, bitchy, pushy, whining, emasculating, undirected, helpless, victimized, smothering, frustrated, and self-pitying. Men were strong, forceful, goal-oriented, and intelligent; they were leaders and initiators. They were also aggressive, overpowering, tyrannical, violent, and selfish. I didn't like women; I much preferred men. Men were going somewhere; men had dreams. Women had casseroles. I also hated men; they had so much power over me. Men could hurt me, and women could steal these "prizes" away from me. Women's magazines for the most part don't deal with the genius of woman and her available power. Instead they deal with the trivia: "How to Dress" or "How to Get a Powerful (Man's) Job" or "Which Diet Will Keep You Marketable."

The church taught me through its stories, threats of hell, and rewards of heaven to be subservient to men. It subtly and continually programmed me to sit in front of a male minister week after week and allow him to tell me how to live if I wanted a male God to love me. If I failed, a male God sent me to hell to live with a male devil and shovel coal in a red-hot fire.

My folks weren't involved in church. In fact, they discouraged us from going, which made church even a little more special. As I write I can smell the church, clean and pristine. What I remember is all the women there were in church, many more than men. Their objective was to be religious and serve the men and their male God. If you did, you were a good woman. If not, you were bad. What I did like in church were the very few Bible stories and parables that gave me a clue about how I could love myself and others and plant and grow the seeds of my dreams.

All this started to change when I entered the world of metaphysical teachings. I learned I could be a divine person. Finally I had found a teaching that permitted me to be a whole person, someone who could create a life for herself. I began to wake up to another way of living my life, but it was hard fighting the programming deep in my soul of the inferiority of women and the Goddess.

Women are the work force and the backbone of religions that don't even accept them as equals or elevate them to the status of God/Goddess. In the Judeo-Christian approach, the sought-after females are virgins and breeding stock for the "king's" seeds or they are considered slaves or corrupt, treacherous destroyers of men and God's rules. Considering how deeply imprinted beliefs affect every aspect of our innermost selves, is it any wonder women are still falling in love with their ministers and doctors, thus setting them up to be saviors, sex symbols, and gods who control life and death, heaven and hell?

Why do we keep trying to "get into the club"? Why do we continue to fall prey to threats of rejection or hell? We need to examine the values that create these patterns and if they are not *our* values, we need to find our own answers within. We need to anoint ourselves and get on with life! We'll never know who we are if we have to keep asking men for validation. It is about challenging every thought and finding our own answers within. If the values and ideals are yours, keep them. If not, discard them and select others.

HERESY

The programming and conditioning of minds has been thorough, even to the point of making it fundamentally evil to question, disbelieve, or challenge the dogma. Her-esy—I just realized it begins with "her." Even now, if you as a woman question the programming of a male system, you are put back in "your place," punished in some way, labeled radical, separatist or even man-hater!

Because of our long and sorry history of acting out and proving these beliefs about women's inequality to be real, women tend to hold back. And it's no wonder when we remember that the programming has been reinforced by such stimulus-response methods as burning witches. During the Inquisition, it was mostly women, rich and poor, young and old, who were tortured and forced to confess to being heretics and partners with the devil or dark forces. Their money and property was taken, and they were tortured and killed. We have those memories of torture, death, pain, and suffering within our very bodies through soul memory. Men's soul memory includes the belief that they are the chosen ones, the keepers of truth and faith, the rulers, the much-desired prize, and therefore in charge. Men are preprogrammed to deny the feminine within themselves and the masculine in women. With such a history, it's easy to see why we believe our thoughts are more than just thoughts, which can be changed, but real, true, and eternal *facts*.

Go back only a few thousand years, and you'll find that women were the landowners and their property was passed to their youngest daughter. *Husbandman* was the term given to the men who were the caretakers of the land, the livestock, and the crops. Marriage was an institution created by men so that a man could be certain a woman's children were his in order to control the property. Before the patriarchal system, the woman was synonymous with the earth and therefore the power and source of life through her energy and womb. Now, in an age in which male children are still preferred, baby girls are still sometimes killed in China to give the parents another opportunity to have a son. (In China, couples are permitted only one child.)

RELEASING OURSELVES

You and I stand here in this moment, the product of yesterday, programmed to our teeth by everyone and everything for their own purposes and survival needs. Thoughts and beliefs that empowered the female and her divine nature as the Mother Creator of life were methodically beaten out of her. The process continues today if we allow it. Why are you and I so important that others want to control our minds, bodies, thoughts, beliefs, values, actions, jobs, relationships, money, feelings, and ideals and our past, present, and future?

Why are men interested in what you do with your body, while their bodies are theirs to do with as they choose? Why are women jealous, petty, fearful, insecure, and fiercely and covertly competitive? Why do women continue the programming process with their little girls and boys who'll one day be women and men? Why do women stay loyal to religious, cultural, and business organizations that deny them and suppress their genius, divinity, and leadership? Why are women so angry and men so afraid that they have to play their little war games, even in sex?

In a couple of my marriages, the marriage began to deteriorate the night I opened up the subject of sex. Why? Why is sex so critical an area? Could it be we have made it the sole reason for the relationship? The sexual energy that flies between two people is glorious but our value to each other needs to be greater than one aspect. We have made that one aspect the complete reason for a relationship, and it costs us our full self-expression.

The awakening of the spirit is a process of releasing ourselves from the material, physical realm and floating upward and outward to find space and perspective. We bring spirit down to earth and raise earth into heaven. To raise earth up into a new frequency that offers us greater freedom to explore the possibilities of a love-based reality is to shake off the grogginess of a deep unconscious sleep. When your head is full of clutter, cross-purposes, denial, unworthiness, fear, doubt, guilt, and judgments, you are confused about whether to follow your own inner needs or to conform to the program, course, and agenda that has been prearranged. There is an almost overwhelming push to become part of the herd, not make waves, and follow the "party" line. But being labeled an eccentric certainly has its rewards. It can mean you have the freedom to be who you are as a unique person, free of the limiting, fear-based programming.

The cells of our bodies are programmed. The DNA/RNA system holds the code of that programming pattern and sends its messages to the rest of the body. I believe that the essence or etheric body of the person takes on the body complete with its genetic code. We bring with us the memory of all our prior lives. I feel that we are able to alter that programming through our will, emotions, attitudes, desires, and nutrition. We are controlled by our bodies, the memory of our ancestors, and our past incarnations until the "awakening" takes place. The point of power is in the moment. In this moment, now, you are actually affecting your future. We are all programmed mentally, emotionally, intellectually, visually, and physically by the past. Unless we are aware of that programming we can victimize ourselves. Once we are aware, we can keep what benefits us, release what doesn't serve us and our purpose, and imprint our highest, most loving thoughts, feelings, beliefs, and visions into our lives. To consciously impact your own system is to choose your present and future and to bring it about. Loving yourself and your body is one of the best ways to guarantee a healthy body and life.

We can, as individuals and as a collective, weed out the programming that causes sickness, crime, low self-esteem, war, premature death, and mental illness, and through love we can program the qualities of joy, health, happiness, peace, and wealth.

When a person has support for her genius and for who she is as a talented, valuable, and important person, she blossoms. It is a shame that all of us aren't supported in blossoming and unfolding in our radiance. I believe we will be if you and I are committed to it.

What a blessing to have created a family as a support base of genius! Those who are slow, through improper nutrition, unkind treatment, and negative programming were reinforced to remain slow and unfulfilled. We are conditioned-response machines and can be much, much more when we know what makes us tick. Any seed must be watered and fertilized and receive plenty of light to grow. We need to create more love and support for ourselves and our families.

EXERCISES

To assist you in moving on, here are some thought-provoking questions to "exorcise" your demons.

1. What are the thoughts and beliefs that we as women hold within us that keep us outside of paradise? I've listed some. Look them over, and notice if any are yours. Use a separate piece of paper to list any others that come to you.

God is a man, it is God the Father.
Men are afraid of love.
Man gave birth to woman from his rib.
Woman is evil because she tempted Adam with the apple.
Women are not allowed to be religious leaders.
Women are not capable of running their lives.
Those who are born into money are the beautiful people.
A woman's place is in the home.
Those who have "old" money are better than others.
Women represent the dark side.
If a woman is really good in this life, God may accept her back again.
Women with power are dangerous.
Jesus, Buddha, Mohammed were men; God must be a man.

Women who are powerful are lonely.

No man would love a woman who can take care of herself.

I need a man to make me whole.

If I'm not pretty, no man will marry me.

Women have to pump up a man's ego, or he'll leave.

Men leave me.

I'm only valuable if a man wants to marry me.

Women are too emotional.

If I'm not careful, another woman will steal my man.

It's God's will that women serve men.

A woman needs to be pretty, slender, and dumb.

Women aren't as smart as men.

All the spiritual masters were men.

If I'm old, my man will trade me in for a younger woman.

It's a man's world.

Men can handle more stress than women.

Men are frightened by strong, intelligent, powerful women.

Men aren't nurturers.

Men need many women to satisfy them.

Men are superior to women.

A man is head of the household.

A husband is a wife's spiritual leader.

Men aren't intuitive and spiritual.

Women are meant to be wives and mothers only.

Men aren't caring and loving.

Women can't get along with and support other women.

A woman can't get into the celestial kingdom without a husband.

Women are without souls and are evil temptresses of righteous, good men.

Men are cold and unfeeling.

Men want war and violence.

Women are not allowed by God to be ministers and preach the gospel.

Women are flighty.

Write out your own list.

2. Are any of these standards and values yours?

You must be married to be accepted into society.

A woman without a man is an old maid.

A successful business woman is tough, ruthless, and cold.

A woman who has sex with more than one man is a whore.

Women who play around and are sexually free are loose trash.

The man is always right.

You can't raise children alone. They'll become emotionally unstable delinquents.

Women are to mind their husbands and do what they say.

It's okay for men to keep a harem. It's biologically natural.

A man's role is to take care of the woman and children.

The man is the provider.

You have to fight for what you believe in.

All men are the same, no good.

There is a double standard that's real.

A woman's body is not her own.

If I am a good wife, my husband will provide for me.

"Till death do us part" is the measuring stick of a good relationship.

You made your bed, now lie in it.

Divorce is a sin and a sign of failure.

Write out your own list.

All of these values, standards, and beliefs may not have been yours, but you have others. Search them out. Release them. Set yourself free!

AFFIRMATIONS

1. I, _____, now release any past negative judgments on myself as a woman.

2. As a woman I, _____, now love myself and appreciate who I am.

3. I release men from any negative judgments and allow them to be where they are.

4. I, _____, now open myself to the thoughts, feelings, and beliefs I need to have a beautiful life.

5. I, _____, let myself accept myself as valuable, worthwhile, and able right now!

CHAPTER 3

Transcending Your Personal History

KNOWING THAT YOUR THOUGHTS ARE CREATIVE AND that you create your own reality is one thing; doing something about it is something else. Creating a consciousness reality takes work!

Here at the beginning of the Golden Age, we're at a point in our evolution where we've cast aside many of the values, morals, ideals, myths, and legends of our ancestors. Much of what we are casting aside is in fact no longer valid—if it ever was valid. But we are also set adrift from some values, myths, and stories that have great value. They give us guidelines that lead into the earth, into ourselves, and out into the vastness of the cosmos.

You and I are way-showers, visionaries and role

models for a new way of being, seeing, sensing, touching, knowing, and living. It is easy when you are transforming to throw away everything. You feel you are finished with the past and want to get rid of anything related to it. I've noticed that about every nine years I have an upheaval, invalidate myself and my past, and become a fanatic about another point of view or life-style. I give away my dreams and goals as well as my clothes, furnishings, and beliefs that represented my past. I start all over again, rebuild my empire, get stuck in my ego, and then trash it all again.

Now that I am aware of this pattern, I can grow in my awareness, keep what is valid and valuable, and leave behind what isn't. I always believed that I had to burn my bridges so that I'd never go back. Sometimes it is important to burn bridges, and sometimes it is important to keep them in good repair.

In the early days of the women's movement we thought it was important to emulate men if we were to succeed in a man's world, and we denied our feminine, nurturing nature. Some men who wanted to develop and bring forth their feminine nature have disowned their masculine aspect. It is important for us to keep what is useful and valuable to us and release what isn't. We don't have to throw away what gives us joy or hold onto what causes us pain. We decide what we want to keep from our past and release the rest.

KEEP THE BEST, DUMP THE REST

We live in a time when everyone has rules that they believe *you* need to follow. A powerful woman takes what she finds worthwhile and uses and applies it. If it doesn't work, she dumps it and uses something else. What worked at one time may not apply today, so there really aren't any absolute principles or rules for all times and all situations.

Finding some values, ideals, and standards either from ancient mythology, legends, and teachings or your own experience can give you a home base and a stable anchor from which you can move off in any direction. I feel they are essential to keep you from getting lost or disoriented. Just what those ideals, values, and morals are is up to you to discover.

When I left the Terry Cole-Whittaker Ministries I dumped practically everything I had believed and taught so that I could explore other aspects of myself. After I felt anchored in those other parts of myself, the earth, and the cosmos, I selected bits and pieces of my past philosophy and teachings and merged those old values, beliefs, and thoughts with the new ones. Now as I evolve, I won't toss everything, as has been my pattern, but will keep what is working, release what isn't, and bring in what is new.

You are on your own. You are also one with the all. It is up to you to know how to access the guidance, power, and wisdom of the higher realms. Have some "truths" or basics, such as, "Who I am is love," "I am one with the infinite," or "Whatever

I do always brings me and others love, joy, and wealth." I have two truths that always, always support me, open doors, and create opportunities for me to flourish in love. The first one is, "I am the creator and cause of whatever I am experiencing." The second is, "I am unlimited love and joy; therefore, I can create whatever I desire, forever."

I see my life, relationships, activities, and situations as a reflection of what I believe about myself and the Goddess/God of the totality. I can then make my corrections and also validate and acknowledge what is flourishing. The garden gives me the lessons of nature, and nature is in harmony with the nature spirit energy. There is a constant need to prune, pull weeds, water, pick off the dead leaves, plant, fertilize, and harvest. The plant reflects its state of health. If it is sick, we heal it. If it doesn't heal, it returns to the earth and becomes fertilizer for the next year's crop. When you rise above your past, present, and future you can be the overseer, the caretaker who has a plan for her garden. The garden also becomes your reflection, teacher, lover, friend, and nourishment.

ON GOING SKIING

To transcend your personal past requires that you first know that who you are is greater than the pieces of your life or the garden. Next, you must realize that after you change your thoughts and design for yourself and your creations, you need to take action and do whatever is required. This commitment, backed with the change in your thinking, feeling, and imagination, is carried through in all of your actions. The universe aligns with you out of your action, and miracles occur. You are then in alignment on all levels with your deepest, most cherished desires. What I am saying is illustrated in this story I love to tell about what I learned during a recent skiing vacation.

Skiing has always been a teacher, a very intense mirror, for me, as it reflects the way I live my life. I can discover a great deal about myself when I observe my skiing. I can discover, for example, how I have approached my career and the fulfillment of my purpose and vision. Using a sport like skiing, tennis, golf, bowling, or even dance is a fast path to enlightenment. The skis go where you point them; the ball goes where you hit it—you are the controller of your destiny. If you don't change your direction you're liable to wind up where you're headed!

Thirty years ago when I started skiing I almost always felt uncomfortable, uncertain, and unsure of myself. I was constantly judging my body, my clothes, and how I skied. I didn't ski for the joy of skiing—I didn't know about that way of life yet—I skied to torture myself. I tortured myself mentally and emotionally a good deal of the time in those days. Fear of losing the man I wanted to want me was my limiting thought. I acted as if that thought were real. I felt a sense of the inevitability of loss and believed that all I could do was delay it. How could I have become a skilled skier when my mind, vision, and emotions were concentrating on something else? My fears were activated in the presence of others. I had no place to hide. Instead of cruising down a snow-covered hill feeling the thrill of the wind in my face, I endured amid my fear of love and danger.

So much of what we are doing isn't what we are up to at all. We appear to be doing one thing when we are playing another game. Some of our thoughts, attitudes, and beliefs sabotage our true desires; meanwhile we believe we are doing all we can to succeed.

That day on the slopes of Whistler, Canada, I noticed that I didn't ski downhill, I skied sideways. I'd go forward one moment, then pull myself back the next. I noticed that pattern in my life—I'd make a decision and then change it in the next moment if I didn't get the result I sought immediately. I had a pattern of starting and stopping, and my skiing showed it. I was ready to make some major commitments to my career, yet I feared both success and failure. It was time in my career to decide where I was going, commit to that direction, and go for it. It was time to bring my new attitude into physical action and ski for the sake of skiing.

I saw my old pattern of changing my mind often, depending on who I talked to and what they thought. That pattern showed up on the hill as I felt my indecision at the moment I was about to turn. I'd turn downhill and then turn uphill so as not to go too fast or hurt myself. The result was I was working twice as hard and having half the fun! What I did after I noticed that was to make my decisions when and where to turn before the run and carry through with those decisions. Once you become aware, make the mental, emotional, and physical connection, you can alter your experience.

The next day I tried to find an excuse not to ski. "Reuben," I said to my sweetheart, "I think I'd better write the book and not ski." Reuben, as he does so lovingly, said, "Why don't you ski just a couple of runs? It's such a sunny day, and the snow is ideal!" An old pattern of mine is to quit just before it gets good. Well, I did ski, and I ended up enjoying myself all day! And to top it off my skiing improved even more!

My skiing improved. Why? I corrected by remembering the basics I had been taught by some fine ski instructors and putting them into practice over and over. It is easier to not practice our new attitudes and beliefs, because it is uncomfortable and confronting. But what you get if you avoid the thing you really want is a sense of unfulfillment.

I had been my own worst enemy on the hill and in my life. No one sabotages us but ourselves, so guess who the savior is? Right! It's always ourselves. While skiing, one of my legs used to go one way while the other went another way. My balance was off, and I was going every which way at the same time. I was fighting myself. Unless I concentrate these tendencies recur. The most important thing I did that day was bring all the parts of my body into alignment as I focused all my energies in one direction. Amazing!

FOCUS YOUR ENERGIES

You can't achieve anything if you don't focus on and direct yourself toward a specific objective. That objective can be something as vague as learning how to enjoy yourself or as specific as writing a book, planting a garden, or having a loving relationship with your family members. Why do we resist focusing on what we say we really want? Counterpurposes and fear disempower us and cause us to work much harder to produce a result. These counterpurposes also keep us playing a game with ourselves. Our thoughts, creations, and beliefs must be aligned if we are to know and experience our potential. Once we are aligned with our purpose and objectives on each of our levels, it is time to take the physical steps. This chapter is about making the physical and behavioral changes that will make your life more satisfying and give you whatever you want from love and power.

There are many armchair skiers, just as there are countless spectators, judges, and critics in life who will tell you how to live. If you pay attention, you'll have to sit down next to them and be a critic and a spectator yourself. Life goes to the participators, those who experience themselves living.

What prevents people from being participators

is ignorance of who they are and the infinite power available to them. They fear others' judgments and attacks; they have negative beliefs from their past history. And they believe in scarcity; they erroneously assume that what they truly want is in short supply—at least too short a supply for *them* to actually have it. To free ourselves from limiting patterns that sabotage our participating with joy and ease in the adventures and activities we desire, we can use our life experiences as mirrors. When you notice an old pattern that's holding you back, change it to one you want, as I did with my skiing.

You can change your thoughts, which have a direct impact on your attitude, but until you act upon those thoughts, they remain just that, thoughts or good ideas. I started thinking positive, loving thoughts about my worth and value almost thirty years ago, and it's taken all this time for me to actually see the results. You don't have to take that long!

TRANSCENDING YOUR OWN HISTORY

It is easy to change our minds. The skill is in living our newly established beliefs and integrating them into every aspect of our lives. Transcending your personal history means being responsible for your past, learning the lessons, making the necessary corrections and changes, and making your present choices from love and limitlessness. Why be imprisoned by your past and stuck in the belief that some things are inevitable?

I thought about my past as a skier, and for a few moments I contemplated not skiing again. I considered being satisfied with my old pattern because, after all, "I'm getting older . . . why bother to change?" Realizing that my life is for living, I chose to commit myself to having a great time practicing the new habits I desired.

If your past history is full of pain—that was *then* and this is *now.* I didn't become an expert skier in one day or even in the moment after I decided to be, but I did improve by the end of the day, and I had great fun in the process. The next time I skied the best I ever had!

If you have been abused, ignored, or unappreciated—that was *then,* this is *now.* Your life is never over, and no incident is more important than another unless you make it so.

A woman came up to me at a talk I gave in Vancouver, British Columbia, and said, "Terry, the first time I learned about you was while I was serving a seven-year sentence in jail. I read your book *What You Think of Me Is None of My Business.* I was so inspired when I realized I could be miserable or make the most of my time, learn and grow." She did, and her life is blossoming right now.

Hope and hopelessness share the same bed. Both are based on "someone will save me." Of course there is hope. The hope is YOU—NOW! Take the time to answer the questions in the exercises at the end of this chapter. They will assist you in clarifying what is important to you. Let them help you realize what thoughts and beliefs you want to have to support you in taking the action to make those desires real.

I asked a sculptor once how she made a bust of a person out of a piece of rock, and she said, "I simply chip away what I don't need." To transcend your history and release yourself from ancient programming of fear, self-denial, and a belief in scarcity you peel away what you don't need (the fear, self-denial, and the idea of scarcity). What you have left is your true, brilliant, beautiful self. Affirm yourself and the power within, set your objectives, reprogram yourself, change your behavior, and be grateful. You are moving joyously out of the past into the present, creating your future.

Whatever you identify with you become. The greatest problem we can fall into by identifying with our limitations is believing that "disaster is inevitable."

We create boxes for ourselves like coffins and pound the nails in one at a time. We then wonder why we feel as if we are suffocating and trapped. Take out the nails, lift the lid, and get out!

At one point I felt trapped in an area of my work, and what kept coming to me was that an employee and I needed to move on from each other. Even though we worked well together in certain areas, we were limiting each other out of loyalty and fear. She had been wanting to move in with her lover who lives a few hours from our office. I'd been wanting a different energy that would stimulate my own creativity. We were not communicating with each other and it was stopping the flow of energy, which was reflected in diminishing enrollments for events. Things were getting worse. I had tried on numerous occasions to broach the subject and discuss what I felt were unspoken judgments on her part. All I'd ever get was, "I don't have any." Well, it could have been totally me, but the results weren't lying. We were declining. Something had to be done. Should I release her, or shouldn't I? It was like skiing downhill. Once you pick your point and objective, take the action and commit fully to where you are going. So I let her go and felt free, even though I still had some fears about how I would manage. I was "untrapped" and free again. I began to thrive!

SECURITY VERSUS DEPENDENCE

I love the feeling of the wind on my body and flowing through my hair. The exhilaration I feel means more to me than the "appearance of security." I say "appearance of security" because we usually base our security on something outside us. Real security comes as an inner experience of one's trust in life itself and one's ability to create whatever is needed.

The more I believe I have to have someone or something to survive, the more I fear the loss of that someone or something. Attachment is a condition of entanglement when there is no sense of your separate identity, just a commingling of self and something else. I feel that to merge with another in a healthy way one must have a separate sense of oneself and an experience of self-sufficiency. Dependence based on need is an unhealthy state of being that breeds fear, weakness, and pain. We all need each other and can be interdependent in a most wonderful way, but before one feels self-sufficient and independent, dependence is deadly.

We women are programmed and conditioned for mental, emotional, and physical dependence from before birth. That is one life, before you awaken to your own inner security system. After awakening is much more fun; it is the "afterlife" that goes on forever. It is the life we had only hoped for before but were unable to have because it was up to someone else to create it.

The myth about women that most of us have been living (there are exceptions) has been that our security comes from someone "out there." Men have been programmed similarly by myths and legends to be their own security and to provide security for others. We do create interdependent relationships that provide an agreed-upon reality in which we play roles and do a dance of love, nurturing, and passion, but it works best when both know how to take care of themselves and create separately. It is this dance of the goddesses and gods together that breeds the elixir of life called ecstasy and passion. Insecurity, by contrast, breeds fear, dependency, and a drive to live off of each other until both are drained, until there is nothing left.

The myths, stories, role models, and behavior modification that program us can also teach invaluable lessons, bringing ideals and celestial truths trickled down into our reality from higher ones. It is up to you to realize just which legends, stories, truths, and aspects of history open you up to who you are and which are simply ploys to manipulate, control, or destroy your female, "creator of the universe and mother of all life" identity. In the peeling-away process, I ask myself this question, "Does this empower me and give me greater life, love, joy, and freedom to be, do, and have, or does it deny me in any way?" With the philosophy of "find the good purpose in everything," it also allows me to always validate myself. Even in the worst situation we can find treasure. I don't mean you should keep tormenting yourself to find the treasures; that is the belief system "no pain, no gain." Relaxing in a hammock under the shade of an apple tree can create great gains as you surrender to pleasure.

Chipping away what you do not want begins with the thought of what you do want. It is your vision and imagination that sets the direction for your next adventure and the putting to rest of the old.

KNOW YOUR DESIRES, THEN ACT!

The peeling-away process begins with a desire. My own chipping-away process began when as a young wife and homemaker I grew tired of my pain. I got tired of hurting. I felt hurt most of the time. I felt the hurt of insecurity and of rejection by my husband. I felt the pain of conflict between my innermost dreams and the life I was living. I felt confusion about my role as a woman and the demonstrated inequality between men and women. Once I threw a glass of wine in the face of one of my husband's friends who had made a remark about female genitals. His friend had made my body something to be ridiculed, and my husband laughed! Having no money of my own and being considered a man's dependent brought the feeling of what it is like to be owned. I was taken care of, but I had to explain and account for every dime to the satisfaction of another person. I hated those feelings, yet there was a part of me that liked not having to be out in the mad, mad world earning a living and handling all the day-to-day stuff. I felt protected, yet I felt trapped.

Changing a reality can be a conscious choice, selected at will by the person, or it can be an unconscious choice based on an intended desire. It can also be an unconscious act of programming by something as simple as a friend telling you about something or a television commercial brainwashing you to buy a particular product. However we have been moved to action we have started the process.

Transcending your personal history means to own and love your past and learn from it but not to be imprisoned, controlled, or limited by it. How do you feel right now?

A woman I know says that she wants to be a chiropractor, but she doesn't have the money to go to school. I've known her for two years, and she's made no progress on her problem. It's an all-or-nothing proposition for her, so what she has is a condition called cope, manage, do without, and compromise. Her energy system is devoid of passion. There are no accidents. Her past history has her stuck in a safe, boring, nonrisk position. Passion is a direct result of a person's willingness to experience and feel any and all emotions, pain as well as ecstasy.

All she needs to do is sign up for one night course at a chiropractic school and she'll be in the movement of a new energy cycle for herself. All she needs to do is make a male friend and get into a relationship, even if it is as just a friend. Practice on the one you are with!

All I did was point my skis a little more downhill than before, and I opened myself to the next and more exciting and rewarding stage of skiing. I don't have to go straight down the hill. I'm not a downhill racer yet.

We learn by trial and error. We learn by doing. In the doing we create a new habit. Experts are those who risked and began something new and stayed with it until they naturally rose to the top of their area of interest.

How do you become comfortable in communicating your feelings? Practice! How do you eat an elephant? One bite at a time! What prevents you from saying what you feel and expressing yourself? Fear! How do you move past the fear? Communicate—even if you are afraid. Fear of rejection, fear of abandonment, fear of criticism, and the fear of success or failure can keep you from the joy of the freedom that comes with self-expression.

Overcoming your past history occurs the moment you want to think, believe, feel, or do something not in your past and to create a new present and future. The second part is to actually do the thing itself, one step at a time.

A dear friend of mine has told me that she is afraid to be rebirthed. My friend was born dead and was, of course, revived moments later. She is afraid to breathe deeply and rapidly for one hour. The reasons why she was born dead and the decisions she made at that time are bubbling beneath the surface, affecting every aspect of her life. I was talking to her recently about longevity, reversing the aging process, and activating her brain to 100 percent efficiency. She replied, "I'm not interested in any of that. I have good genes, and I'll take whatever comes." I've offered to rebirth her numerous times, and always the response is the same, "No. That's not for me!" How could breathing not be for someone? It's basic to life, unless there is a fear of the breath, a fear of life. The woman is in the medical profession, working specifically with dying patients. For her to change her beliefs from "Death is inevitable; aging is inevitable" to "I am ageless and timeless in my body" would require a 180-degree turn in her most heavily imprinted pattern of thinking, believing, and living. I tell people that "death and taxes are illusions and not fixed in truth." These are the most solid beliefs we have, so to challenge these and release death in exchange for life is a powerful process. Even if you don't take it to mean physical immortality but simply to concentrate on living, it is a tremendous gift to give yourself.

To transcend our past requires the desire, the action, and the risk taken to imprint a new thought or belief on all levels of our consciousness. The desire and appropriate action will bring to the surface through emotions and feelings any past history to release. Without the action there is philosophy, wishful thinking, hope, and "if onlys."

When Geraldine Ferraro entered the vice-presidential race, all her fears were activated and reflected back to her in the way she was treated by the press. Her beliefs became visible, and she let that stop her for a while. I hope she continues in public office. The more public I became, the more my beliefs were subject to scrutiny. Your history can make you bitter, or it can make you stronger. The key here is to realize it's your reality and your thoughts, beliefs, and fears that are created in your world. Change your mind, own your judgments of yourself, and get back up and go for your dream. Use some aspects of your life as I use skiing—find some mirrors to give you an accurate picture of where you are.

IT TAKES AS LONG AS IT TAKES

It took me four husbands and a number of boyfriends to learn about being myself and how to be in a loving relationship with a man without giving my power away. It took me creating a ministry debt when I was the minister to learn about finances. It took me years of blocked communication with my daughters and mother before we created blissful relationships. It took me years of facing and dealing with my body issues of food, exercise, and looking good to come to physical balance and a great sense of comfort, love, and respect for my body. I'm not saying that everything will take years. I'm saying it takes as long as it takes, but without action, it will never happen. The pain, upset, or terror you may face is simply a reflection of the degree to which you are dependent and attached.

The physical world is an amazing school. It teaches us, the creators, that we can create out of love if we desire and if we are willing to transcend our past, our fears, and our doubts. Her-story is in your hands. You are the creator, the sculptor, and the artist. You have a fresh piece of clay and a blank canvas on which to continue your neverending story. What will it be? It can be a repeat of yesterday—"Oh, well, it is inevitable and the way it is." Or it can be "Now I'm ready to experience it all!"

EXERCISES

First, take some time and a journal and list your desires, wants, objectives, and intentions in the following areas. Second, list at least one action item or correction for each desire and then—*do it* (even if you are nervous, uncomfortable, or afraid of failure). Set up a new pattern for yourself!

1. Five attitudes you desire to have about yourself as a person.

2. Five attitudes you desire to have about yourself as a woman.

3. Five thoughts you no longer want to have about yourself.

4. Five beliefs about women or men that you want to cast aside.

5. Five thoughts you desire to have about yourself and life.

6. Five beliefs you desire to create concerning women and men.

7. Five things you want to change.

8. The five most limiting thoughts and beliefs you have about yourself and the opposite sex.

9. Five undesirable parts of your life at present.

10. Five wonderful aspects of your life at present.

11. Five of the most unlimited, magnificent thoughts you could imagine having to do with you and what's possible for you.

12. Your ten biggest fears having to do with you having, being, and doing your heart's desire.

13. Ten benefits to yourself and others that will come from you fulfilling your dreams and greatest desires.

14. Five wishes.

15. Five desires for the world.

16. Ten awarenesses you have just gained for yourself by answering the questions.

Now write an affirmation for each item or correction; start with the most important. Speak these affirmations out loud as often as possible. Write them numerous times a day, and get the feeling that these statements are true about you. They *are* true, because *you* say so!

These questions can give you a clearer understanding of yourself and some of your beliefs. Transformation to me means a process of peeling away layers of conditioning, much like peeling an onion layer by layer. Sometimes the peeling is uncomfortable, even painful. The pain is the result of attachment. But the prize in the end is worth it all!

AFFIRMATIONS

1. Then was then. Now is *now*.

2. Who I am, I love forever.

3. What I, _____, have done has brought me to where I am.

4. I, _____, do not have to repeat any patterns I no longer desire.

5. I, _____, am willing to open myself to _____.

CHAPTER 4

You Are More Than Equal

EQUALITY MEANS SAMENESS, AND THE SAME WE ARE not! No one is the same as anyone else, yet we all share a common humanity.

Rather than thinking of ourselves as women or as one-half of a unit, I think it is important we think of ourselves as whole and not as one-half of anything. The word *gestalt* means whole. Gestalt therapy, as developed by the psychologist Fritz Perls, uses many parts of the self to illuminate the whole and the whole to understand the parts. To Perls everything was a hologram, just as one cell in your body can tell you all about itself as well as all about your body. He found that we can see ourselves in everything, and everything can find something of itself in us.

We can understand others by understanding and knowing ourselves. We can know the universe by knowing ourselves. We can know ourselves by knowing the universe. All of us together equal one, and each of us separately is the one in some aspect. A diamond is multifaceted, and each facet is unique. Together the facets make up one diamond.

We need to understand ourselves not as equals, for we each create ourselves as we are by what we imagine, think, and feel ourselves to be, but as facets and reflections of something much greater that we are expressing. There is a limitless supply of space, but the walls of your house define how much space you have in which to live. The one who defines the space is you; you put up or choose the walls. How much of anything you have, do, or feel is up to you. Your thoughts and beliefs about yourself define you, and what you are able to experience is that which is within your chosen identity.

Space is defined by the limits you and I set up as boundaries, form, and parameters for the games we choose to play. Limits are fine and natural and needed for any game. A body is your definition of self. Without the bone structure and the limit called skin you'd be everywhere and therefore nowhere.

You and I are separate by definition and distinct by choice. This separateness and distinction occurs within the whole. We are the parts, and the parts are each a whole in themselves. Every cell in your body is unique yet still a part of the body. Every cell has within it an entire universe.

DON'T LIMIT YOURSELF!

To use the term *equal* as a way to define woman is terribly limiting. "Equal" is a measurement used only by those who have defined another as greater, more, or better than themselves. *Those who believe themselves to be less, desire to be equal. Those who are whole desire only to be themselves.* The label is self-bestowed.

My anger hid the hurt I felt at believing I was incapable, unworthy, and not entitled to a whole existence. Being a woman meant I was one-half of another, and without that other I was a whole nothing. I do love being with my lover (that is a special and most delicious feeling and energy), so I am not denouncing relationships. But unknowingly, by my own definition, I was a nothing, a "zero," without something called a man, a "one."

As a woman I fought against being a nothing, but since men were the somethings, all I could hope for was to be the nothing of a something! I hated this but did my best. Underneath, none of this seemed right, but even my religion and the teachings of those who created Christianity supported the idea that women are possessions and must obey. "Shut up and speak when you are spoken to!" "When I want your opinion, I'll ask for it." "Know your place, woman, ten paces behind!" What was left was bitching, nagging, crying, screaming, and begging. I was constantly apologizing for my anger, rage, and jealousy, for crying and yelling. "I promise I won't do it again," but I eventually couldn't stop the flood of emotions.

I felt that I was to blame for each of my four divorces. I felt the most blame for the first, because, after all, this was the forever marriage with children to guarantee our future together. Down deep inside I blamed my husband for his failure to know and love me, but I still felt it was my fault for being unlovable.

YOU CREATE IT ALL

I still have some vestiges of those old beliefs and patterns in female-male relationships. When these beliefs appear, usually when I'm upset, I can take a breath, relax, and choose a different belief. Then I change the way I think, feel, and behave. The new attitude is then mine. There is part of me that loves an intimate relationship with a male, being with that special someone, someone to share a home with, to romance, to cuddle up close with at night. I still have the belief that to be loved like this I must give a man what he needs and wants. Today I realized that I feel a need, even a compulsion, to create for men, to give to men what they want. This is my pattern of giving and not receiving. This pattern is reflected in other areas of my life. Now I recognize it, so I can release it. Now I affirm, "I am worthy of receiving equal to what I give."

So many times I've felt that all too familiar cold shoulder from those husbands at a moment my life was taking off and I was starting to flourish. They'd act hurt—as if I had beaten them for no reason—when I'd feel the joy and excitement of a new venture, a new surge of life and opportunity. There would be put-downs, avoidance of physical contact, and ridicule. Was it just me? Did I create their reactions as a way to control myself, or was it their way to remain the center of my attention? I now believe that men want conscious, whole relationships, and this belief changes the reaction I receive.

An attractive, elderly woman, a ticket agent for an airline in San Francisco, said to me while I was getting my seat assignment, "Men are just little boys, not grown up." Is that so, and are we the Mother Creator who has created our men as our mirrors and children? How much we love them, how precious they are to us, yet how we have denied ourselves, our power, our genius, and our spirit to cater to them, to keep them happy, and to give them the toys and joys they say they want! We've allowed this for long enough. It is time for us to return to ourselves. It's time to define ourselves as whole and from that wholeness create our men as we desire them to be—whole. We've tried to be what we've believed they wanted. Now it is up to us to be what we want to be. Courage is the energy most needed when any woman decides to define herself by her own criteria and not that of another or of society.

You step outside the norm, but isn't that the role of a way-shower, an explorer, and role model?

Something inside me says, "Terry, you create it *all* the way it is, and all you need do is love yourself and live true to yourself and others will respond accordingly." We are reeducating ourselves, retraining ourselves thought by thought, feeling by feeling, and action by action. Patience is the key in redefining yourself, your relationship, your body, your career, and your relationship to the One. It takes a great deal for any woman to take full responsibility for her life and to love herself and know herself to be whole. Probably the number-one fear preventing wholeness is the thought, "I'll be alone, because if I were whole I wouldn't need anyone." But that is not true.

We are whole and we do need each other. We are part of each other. "I don't need you" doesn't mean "I don't want you." As a self-sufficient person you are also interdependent. The more whole I feel, the more I need and don't need at the same time.

We are both male and female just as light and dark exist at the same time within the whole. That's why sometimes we feel as if we know everything and in the next moment feel as if we know nothing.

I'm attached and unattached, which is again mathematics of something and nothing at the same time. This physical world is a world of opposites. Truth is both, which is called a paradox. The two opposites make a whole, so both are true at the same time.

There are three aspects of creation: start, continue, and stop. There is a beginning, a middle, and an end to everything except us—infinite, forever spirits. We as spirit are the gestalt, the womb and earth in which life is lived and experienced. The masculine is that aspect of ourselves that moves in a linear fashion from *A* to *B*. It all comes from the same nothing and everything that we call the One. So, the two aspects we call male and female are not opposites or even separate. They are distinctions that operate in unison. One cannot exist without the other, yet it appears that each has a *distinct* function. Not better, just distinct. When you merge these energies within yourself, harmony and balance are the results.

Yet there is a deep sense in me that the pervading energy of the universe is not male but female, a mother not a father. This has nothing to do with bodies but has everything to do with an intangible energy feeling, intuition, and extrasensory knowing. Those who "tune into" their feminine energy may be in a female body, but that isn't necessary. The pervading energy of the Creator is Mother, nonjudgmental and all-giving.

What happens in relationship is that we adore and worship our creations, our innermost opposites, so that we may discover and love ourselves in totality. To expect men to be like women or women to be like men is to set up constant conflict. Why bother to limit ourselves in any way? What works best for me is simply to drop all preconceived ideas about women and men and allow each person to be who he or she is. Each one of us, using the same electrical current, does different things with it, and it takes both the female and the male aspect of electricity to get a spark.

Harmony reigns when each person is valued for him- or herself and each performs his or her function in the whole, the gestalt of the created experience called life. Women, because we hold babies within us, find it easier to link up with this Mother-Earth feeling and the loving spirit of the Infinite.

It does seem as though men and women are different, though. I have many women friends who simply live with women so that they have a partner who is easy to understand and know. Many of my men friends live with and are in love with men. It's easier to find a mirror of yourself in the same sex. It's also a way for these people to love themselves and get a stronger reading of their own distinct energy. Sometimes it is because their fear is too great and the risks too demanding to get to know a member of the opposite sex intimately, and sometimes it's their highest expression of love.

I get a little crazy if I'm around too many men without some powerful women. I need to have women friends and men friends. Personally, I love being with men as lovers, playmates, and pals as my primary relationship, but without my women playmates, friends, and co-workers, I begin to think I'm losing my mind; I have no support for myself as the source and creator of my life.

Having close women friends lets us move deep within our feminine selves, bonding with each other. "Best friends" is a name given to a friendship that transcends exterior conditions and says, "I am there for you and with you under any and all circumstances. For whatever reason and no reason, I love you and who you are." Women of the past have gathered food together, beaded and sewed clothing, tended the children, healed the people, and watched over the domestic animals as well as acted as counselors, visionaries, and guides to Mother Earth and her elements. We have lost the power and gifts of female bonding at these spiritual and earthly levels because we no longer pursue these activities as before. Grandmothers were there for the children and taught them values, ideals, and wisdom. We have become a surface society in which looks are everything and women cannot trust anyone, even their women friends, if a man or advancement in their profession is the issue.

Love and friendship are more valuable than money, power, sex, or fame because the value of best women friends lets you handle and succeed in everything else out of that heartfelt bonding. Let yourself have your women friends. Become safe and let yourself be supported emotionally, mentally, and spiritually.

My favorite thing to do is to cuddle up with Reuben and enjoy our sweetness together. But when I want him to think and act like me, look out, major upset time is coming. For this type of reflection, I call my daughters, play with my granddaughters, or visit one of my enlightened women friends.

Women and men have been beating each other up for thousands of years. "Why Can't a Woman

Be More Like a Man?" is a song from *My Fair Lady*, a Broadway musical and movie. Why categorize? Yet there is a chemical difference between us simply because of our different biological functions. We are not the same, so we can't be equal, but we are each perfect. What we each must create for ourselves is our rights and the roles we choose to play in our movies, games, and adventures.

YOUR RIGHTS

Rights are something you give yourself, and they are only as inviolate as you decide they are. The only right any one of us is born with is the right to exist in each moment until we change our mind. Rights are rules to protect and empower people in support of their purpose, vision, ideals, and objectives, not to classify, negate, and separate.

Metaphysics, the study of that which is beyond the physical, attracted me above all other forms of religious thought because it said to me that I, Terry, had the right to be, do, and have what I wanted. Metaphysics made no overt statements about women being less than men. I didn't realize it at the time, but all the covert messages were there with the "He," "Him," "Father," "*King*dom," and sexist Bible teachings. Never mind that. What was important was the message that I was free, always had been free, and always would be free to be myself and live my dreams and realities as I choose.

Ministerial school brought me into a group of people in which the women outnumbered the men, but the men were favored and the women were quiet and "churchlike." I was rowdy, spoke out, clowned about, had fun, and never got an *A* on anything. I already knew what I wanted to do and was already doing it by teaching "Positive Thinking" classes at the YMCAs in La Cañada, San Marino, Van Nuys, and Whittier, California. I never followed the rules or stayed in the place others had provided for me. Later, when I had one of the largest churches and television congregations in the history of my church, "Religious Science," I was never publicly recognized or acknowledged by my church organization or my peer group of ministers. Given my rebellious attitude, I probably didn't want to be. It would have been too "establishment" for me. I still do love the teachings, though, and feel they are one of the best ways for people to rise above the fear-based religions into a philosophy of love and joy.

In class, professors would speak of the "men we need in the field." I agree now. We do need men in the fields—growing vegetables and restoring Mother Earth to ecological harmony. Of course, *they* meant, "We need men in the pulpits. We need men leading the people into Religious Science and up to God, through the teachings of Jesus and Ernest Holmes, the creator of Religious Science." No mention was made of the women, who were in the majority, but I knew what I was going to do, and then and there I realized that the only rights I have are the ones I give myself. So I gave myself the love I needed.

To me equality had meant our system of law as laid down by our founding fathers in the Constitution. Those rights as a citizen already pertain to me and to all people regardless of sex, color, religion, beliefs, or socioeconomic condition. Often those rights have to be written out, proclaimed, and enforced, if not by ourselves, by our system of government. But nothing and no one can give you what you haven't already given to yourself.

Often in my schooling for the ministry, people with supposed authority over us, like ministers and professors, would disregard the female half of our class. Forty to fifty percent of our class was women, but these women were never mentioned. "We need some good men in the field," a minister might say, despite the fact that half the people listening were women. I learned pretty quickly that no one, especially established, old, white, Christian men, was going to give me an inch. I knew then that if it was to be, it was up to me!

Recently, I visited my doctor, a dear friend, to have my yearly checkup. It was time for me to check up on him and see how he was doing. He was looking stronger, as he had taken my advice and gotten some rolfing, a form of deep-tissue postural integration for the body. I asked him about what was being done for women and menopause. Specifically, did he know anything about what I could do to keep producing whatever I needed for harmony, longevity, and agelessness in my body? He said,

"Terry, it's only been lately that medical research has taken women and their particular needs seriously. Before, women's problems were sloughed off as unimportant. Women are now demanding research for themselves."

Money talks in this world. The more we as women put our dollars into services and products that support us and our visions for ourselves, our children, and our precious Mother Earth, the more we'll be served and valued. The more women speak out and are elected to office, the more women support women, the more our needs and desires will be heard and fulfilled. When peace becomes more profitable than war, big business will create peace.

An agreed-upon set of values and ideals for all people is needed as a foundation of our ethics, but an intrinsic problem for any agreed-upon reality is that after a while it can be limiting and repressive to those who have transcended that particular level of expression. Rules, values, ideals, beliefs, and standards define the game board as well as the purposes, objectives, penalties, rewards, and payments of a game. When the game changes (which it does continuously), new agreements, purposes, and ideals must be created; otherwise, you are trying to play a new game with old rules. Conflict, frustration, and confusion are the inevitable result. The game is changing. The old context and rules don't apply and so to view what is happening now through the eyes of an archaic belief system does not and cannot work.

You and I are creators. So, what are the rights

we at this moment choose to give to ourselves and extend to others? Others have the choice to agree or not, but whatever they do, it doesn't affect you, because you are creating your own separate reality. Only your own beliefs affect you. The rights you give yourself are the most important, and it's up to you to see to it that your rights are recognized and honored. Equality may be an appropriate term to define rights. Whether or not someone exercises their rights is up to them. To exercise *your* rights, they must be ones *you* want and are in agreement with.

The right to happiness would make it a responsibility for people to be happy and therefore to not interfere in the happiness of others. Freedom is the right of all to live and be happy. Rights that exclude go against those who do the excluding. A lower class creates itself and an upper class, and an upper class creates itself and all classes below it. I don't agree to classes as necessary to society; what I agree to is that each person has the freedom to create his or her own life-style as long as it respects and honors the rights of others. We have the free will to live as we choose in harmony with all life forms.

Women's rights, to me, are no different from men's rights. Only those who believe they are less must fight the ones they believe are more. My second book, *How to Have More in a Have-Not World*, dealt with that issue. Having is a feeling of satisfaction and fulfillment. We live in a world of dissatisfaction, or "have not." To have is simply to bestow yourself with the feelings of satisfaction and wholeness and to give yourself what is important to you and yours.

Fear of losing what one already has is the motivation behind those who would exclude you from playing games you want to play. All games are exclusive to those who have agreed upon the purpose, rules, rewards, and penalties. Just because some people don't want you to play their game doesn't mean you can't play another game just like it if you want to. Remember, the way to win another's game is to break all of its rules. You break the rules simply by agreeing to another set of rules and then playing by those rules. The gatekeepers are those whose job it is to keep the rules of a game intact. Many games you want to play require you to get past the gatekeeper, and once you do that, you make the rules. Sometimes that looks like compromise, but actually it is a skill whereby another's rules are acknowledged and respected but do not limit you and what you are choosing to do. If I am not admitted to a game, why would I want to play? I would then go across the street, set up my own game, and create my own purposes, agreements, and rewards!

ROLES ARE OPPORTUNITIES

My first book, *What You Think of Me Is None of My Business,* carries the message, "My opinion of myself is more important to me than your opinion of me, and if we can respect that, then we can use our energies constructively instead of destructively."

"You are more than equal" means that you are greater than your rights. Your rights are what your greater whole self gives to itself as its gifts. You are also greater than the roles you play. Roles are opportunities to experience yourself.

Woman is a role. Man is a role. Child is the natural self, the real you in its pure, innocent, and joyous state. Children play dress-up. Children play roles and act out parts of themselves. We call the drama of theater a "play." Life is play, and we play a part, a role, so that we may know those special feelings, emotions, and qualities of being particular to that aspect of ourselves. Parts, roles, and separate identities give us the opportunity for limitlessness within an experience. You limit yourself when you have only a few identities and roles. Unlimit yourself with an abundance of identities.

Mother is a role, just as woman is. Daughter, wife, friend, lover, and genius are roles. A role is a distinct character whose attributes, job responsibilities, purpose, attitudes, and behavior are defined by the needs and function of the role itself. Roles are important in the game of life just as costumes are on the stage, but you have to remember that you are greater than any role.

I'm sure that in the beginning days of the human experience on earth we designed our bodies as functional space suits that could reproduce other space suits for other beings who desired to be human. Form follows function, as I see it, and as function changes our form changes: evolution. Survival drives and the deepest commitment to con-

tinue to live, express, and explore in a body create
the continuous process of our evolvement into the
next form. Dominant genes and characteristics prevail. I come from a long line of committed mothers,
mothers who loved and nourished their young without smothering. I learned from my mother, and I
deleted what I didn't want and added what I did
want. I don't have to be like anyone else. I am a
unique expression of life.

We learn about our roles from those to whom we
are closest. All roles are temporary, though some
last longer than others. Wife is a role we've played
for who knows how long, and what it means to each
of us has a great deal to do with our earliest programming in this lifetime and our lifetimes before
this one. (Women who are in intimate lover relationships with other women may believe they don't
play the role of wife, but they are playing the role
of mate.)

There are those who have criticized Ronald Rea-
gan for playing the role of president as an actor
would play a part. But we are *all* playing parts. We
dress ourselves in the appropriate garb, become the
character, assume the qualities, and, like a chame-
leon, change color to suit the situation.

We are so flexible and malleable that we can survive by becoming whatever is wanted and needed.
Down deep inside us there is always the feeling that
it is unreal, fake, all an act. Certainly it is—it's the
game. It's an act. What is real is you. What is not
real is the role.

When I was a child I loved to daydream just as

I was falling asleep and upon awakening. My favorite fantasy was one in which I was the overseer, giant, or spirit god of a large village. I'd watch my villagers go about their daily lives, and I'd pretend to be one of the villagers and have their experiences. If I wanted to buy things, I'd make tiny pieces of money and spend it all. If I wanted to experience sex, I'd be either man or woman of whatever age, physical condition, or class I wanted. If I wanted to do a particular thing, I would, and I always had the option of removing myself and becoming the supreme being when I grew tired of the game.

A master is one who can play any game and any role with ease and not lose him- or herself in the process. We are creatures of habit. We learn by observing and experiencing for ourselves through participation in our roles and games. Habits are improved through repetition of roles, characters, jobs, and parts we play. The danger in this is obvious. You lose yourself and become the role. We have so forgotten ourselves as the Mother energy creator and the Father energy reflection that we've reduced ourselves, stuffed ourselves into these tiny bodies. We lose our limitlessness in the smallness of our roles.

You can play the role of mother, but if you believe that mother is who you are, what do you do when your children don't want or need you as mother anymore? You can play daughter on stage with a mom and dad and run your life by resisting your parents, releasing your parents, or becoming your parents.

Define your roles and create a clear picture of your purpose and function and the rewards and other results you intend within any aspect of your life. Your life has many facets, and every facet has its own facets—into infinity. When I am myself at all times, I can play a role, enjoy it, get the job done effectively, then move out of it and into another role easily and joyfully.

It's all made up. "Let's pretend" is fun when we know that that is what it is. It isn't fun at all when taken seriously. Seriousness is heaviness, joylessness, density, and effort. Roles become heavy when they are reduced to duty and obligation and are forced into seemingly choiceless responsibilities. Roles are rewarding when consciously chosen, agreed upon, and played with passion, enthusiasm, sincerity, and commitment. When it looked as though men had all the power, I learned from them, but I didn't become a man. I learned from women, but I didn't need to be like them, either. I only had to be myself and bring to my roles the qualities needed to perform the task and play the part, beautifully and happily.

I can be 100 percent committed to something and responsible for it and at the same time know I don't have to do it. When I felt trapped, everything was forced, and there was no joy. All I could do was resist the role. I felt as if I were chained to a plow or to the heaviness of a downward energy spiral. Upward energy spirals are inspirational, uplifting, freeing, joyous, and fulfilling.

THE KEY IS CHOICE

Those who refuse responsibility never know the joy of commitment and achievement of the highest order. To be committed to your roles, objectives, purposes, and desires is to dive into yourself and discover what is available to you to be, do, and have. To be committed out of duty or obligation or as a condition with no choice is to never know the joy, elation, and ecstasy of freedom, play, and spontaneity. "Shoulds," "ought-tos," "have-tos," and "musts" don't bring forth the best from within us; they repress and limit.

Having children is a choice often made out of ignorance or simply as a result of not taking care of oneself. Young women who find themselves pregnant without a clear choice to do so can feel burdened, angry, and defeated. What we need is education that carries with it the cold, hard facts about having children and providing for them. Sex is one thing; love is another; and children need to be a choice.

The key is choice, wanting a particular experience or opportunity that a role, life-style, job, or other situation can provide you.

Loving whatever role you play brings the greatest value. If you feel a role not rewarding, don't play it. It is your choice. Your health is regulated by your attitudes and emotions. The way you do your job or the way you participate in your relationships is controlled by your innermost thoughts, beliefs, and feelings. And these are influenced by whether or not you are aware that it's *all choice*, not fate or destiny. Saviors are those who believe they are the ones chosen to save humanity in their way. Saviors are people with a mission. They believe the end justifies the means, yet the means is always the end. Simply offer your gifts and let people select what they want.

Mothering was a role I loved when I played it (and still do on occasion because it is so satisfying). Now I enjoy being a friend, and my children, whom I adore, I enjoy as women, pals, co-workers, and playmates. Being a mate is something that brings me marvelous and delicious rewards, lessons, and treasures. Being a wife offers me nothing. My sweetheart is a man/child and my most loving friend, co-worker, and mirror. I'm not his mother, wife, boss, caretaker, slave, or property in any way. Nor is he my husband, son, father, or meal ticket.

If you play wife and mother, both can be valuable if you define them in a way that brings you joy. I don't play the role of "woman" as defined by society, religion, and history because it would limit my rights and the scope of my games, activities, and adventures.

As a mother, my purpose was to create a loving, nurturing, and adventurous environment in which my children and I could play, learn, grow, discover, and create. Now as a grandmother, my role has changed; it is now to impart to my granddaughters all that I know without limiting them in any way. It is my choice to provide a space of wonder and acceptance. Why? Because the reward in each moment of our love and sharing is my treasure and blessing. My rewards are instant, for in the moment I feel the love, I feel the joy, I feel the excitement, and I am the treasure.

Equality is so limiting. Being yourself as one who has limitless playgrounds, adventures, learning experiences, and playmates offers you the greatest number of options. It's all mathematics! One goes into infinity an infinite number of times. You are infinite and divine forever.

EXERCISES

Answer these questions as honestly as you can. You may be surprised by your answers.

1. Are you playing roles that are not satisfying? Which, if any, roles do you believe aren't roles but have-tos, ought-tos, and shoulds?

2. List your five most important roles. For each of those, identify the purpose, objective, and rewards. Which, if any, of your roles have you identified as being your destiny, your predetermined responsibility?

3. Separate yourself and feel yourself distinct from each role. How much of your self-worth is entangled in the role? What would happen if you stopped playing the part, or at least stopped playing it so seriously? Who expects you to keep

playing the role? How do they keep you stuck or chained to the identity?

4. List the ten greatest fears that prevent you from changing or altering the script, the role, or the seriousness of the role.

5. Notice the roles that men, women, and children play. Notice which ones are limiting and which ones are satisfying and fulfilling.

6. List the rights and privileges you give yourself.

7. List the rights you extend to others.

8. Wait! Don't throw away your less satisfying roles yet. List the parts you like, and continue with them. List the parts that you don't like and discard them. Don't blame anyone else—or yourself. It has been a learning experience!

9. List the roles that are satisfying to you. What are the rights, purpose, function, and rewards you gain from those roles?

10. Are you allowing others to control you, keep you imprisoned, or deny you rights by the roles you expect yourself to play in order to please? If yes, what is your reward or payoff in being stuck in limitation?

11. What can you do to assist other people—women, men, and children—to have equal rights, fair treatment, love, respect, and opportunities to live magnificent lives?

12. List twenty-five identities that you can take on. (Example: I am a futurist. I am a being of love and light. I am a lover of life.)

13. List some roles you would like to play and aren't.

14. If you knew you were equal, able, and worthy in every way, list five ways in which your life would change.

15. If you stopped trying to prove your equality and value, what could you be, do, or have?

AFFIRMATIONS

1. I, _____, am greater than the roles I play.

2. I, _____, now accept myself as more than equal. I am whole.

3. I, _____, bestow upon myself all the rights and privileges I desire.

4. I, _____, proclaim myself to be whole, complete, and perfect, because I say so.

PART II

LIVE YOUR VISION!

CHAPTER 5

The Games of Life and How to Win

"ONE WAY TO WIN ANOTHER'S GAME IS TO BREAK ALL the rules." I've been a rule breaker and a nonconformist for a long time. I'm not a rule breaker in the sense of hurting or violating another or another's space, but I do break rules designed to control, deny, repress, or thwart my existence and my right to be fully who I am. Before I became a nonconformist, I was a people pleaser, a "goody-two-shoes, follow-the-crowd" girl. I discovered early on a set of spoken and unspoken rules that, when followed, allowed me to be accepted and, when broken resulted in my being cast out of the game. I didn't like the pain and hurt of rejection or ridicule. I wanted to be liked. I am glad I waited until I was older to rebel; however, whenever you do it is the right time for you.

It started when as a little girl I could tell that life on planet earth was and had been a man's game set up by men for men. Some of my earliest recollections were of my great-grandmother, Nanny, warning me not to speak to strangers, men in particular. She, in her desire to keep me safe and unviolated, made certain I knew I was in danger and to avoid certain situations at all costs. She would read me articles about little girls who had been molested and drove home the thought "Be careful." Her advice did save me from harm, but it also imprinted the thought that men could or would hurt me for their own sexual gratification.

Men also fascinated me, as did boys. Who were these people that they should be desired and feared at the same time? Somehow I knew I needed these people but I also had to protect myself. They seemed to have the freedom; they made the rules and had all the fun. The double message was, "You want them to love you, but be careful because they could hurt you."

I went along with the system of the late fifties and early sixties, and then I became very unhappy with the game. I got tired of the pretense and the conflict within myself, of the manipulative game playing. But I decided I wanted to win, too. The game was overwhelmingly stacked in their favor. As long as I acknowledged them as the source of the game and didn't jeopardize their position, I could coexist and gather some rewards for myself. The game most women were playing was the one in which women are rewarded by men for being "good girls." That reward was supposed to be enough for any lucky girl who didn't make waves. For the most part I used my charm, humor, beauty, talents, and abilities to maintain a place for myself in the men's world. But something wasn't right. Something didn't seem fair.

But how I longed to be all that I was capable of being and at the same time have a loving, intimate, romantic relationship with the man I loved! These two objectives didn't seem to go together, but deep down I knew that I could have it all and not sacrifice or compromise my most important desires and truths. It took awhile and with commitment, desire, and work on myself it did come about. I had to travel through swamps, mud, and fire. I had to climb over thorn bushes, scale tall mountains, and meet the dark side of my soul in the depths of despair before I claimed my prize.

I set out to have it all, and I do! Having, being, and doing it all took a tremendous amount of inner and outer work to release old thoughts, deeply ingrained beliefs, and negative, self-defeating games. Everyone plays games within games within games. Some games are fun and empowering. Some are painful. To have it all I had to clear away the complexity of these entangled games to find the common thread that would take me back to the original purpose of all games.

DEFINING THE WORD "GAME"

Let's take a closer, more specific look at the word *game!* The *Concise Oxford Dictionary* defines *game* as "a form of contest played according to rules and decided by skill or luck." A game must have an objective whereby you score points to decide who has won and who has lost. There must be some rules, which may include boundaries or a playing field. Penalties are levied when one breaks the rules—no cheating, unless, of course, no one catches you, right? Costumes or uniforms help you to distinguish games and team members. Don't forget, there must be a reward for the winner, especially if you want people to keep playing.

In some games the players play full out right in the center of the game board. In others people play spectator; they observe others playing and make judgments about their skill and intelligence. There can be injuries, time outs, foul plays, penalties, goals, heroes, winners, and losers. Every game has a beginning, middle, and end, even though some games seem to drag on. This occurs when the players have been playing for so long they've forgotten that it is a game and failed to notice that there are other games. Their game becomes so total as to limit their growth. I've noticed that people tend to wear their hair, dress, and decorate their homes in the style of the years when they had their best times—the forties, or fifties, or sixties, and so on. For me the best time is now!

THE PAYOFF FOR PLAYING

After much digging, looking, and soul-seeking, I came to realize that wisdom and/or certain emotions were the reward or payoff for me in playing games. Having it all meant feeling loving emotions and sensing my own creative energy. Having it all meant knowing, beyond a shadow of a doubt, who I am, loving who I am, and being true to myself under any and all circumstances. To feel and to experience the emotions, thoughts, and actions of being human was the main purpose behind all games, as far as I could tell.

The game of being human is one in which you discover the rules while you are playing. You are born and you're in the game. When you are tired of the games you are playing, aren't winning, and believe you can only keep losing, you put down the piece or card called your body and leave. Now you play dead until you desire to play here again or somewhere else in your imagination called the universe. The gameboard earth is the playground, the arena in which the action takes place. Earth is the stage, the garden, and we are both the players and the caretakers.

CHOOSE THE GAMES YOU PLAY

I choose to consciously trade self-sabotage games for self-love and self-support. For example, I discovered that I liked self-pity. I liked to feel "poor Terry." "Poor Terry" was a game I played so that I could feel better than others. I worked harder, did more, and did without. Looking back, which is an easier way to view oneself, for one has some distance and elevation, I realized I used self-pity. I used it to counteract my higher times when I felt powerful, beautiful, wealthy, and happy. I had a belief that said, "When you are powerful and successful others resent it and don't like you. They do their best to use you, drain you, and leech off you." To protect myself from being used I'd flip over into self-pity and "poor me," so I could complain, bitch, and brag about being overworked, used, and underappreciated. After enough of it, I'd stop and allow myself to generate my creativity once again. I'd use a little guilt to motivate myself to create more for everyone once again, feeling bad that I had dumped my anger on them. I'd make up for it. I'd ride high, and then when I'd see them beginning to flourish, I'd kick into the same game again. Catching yourself at games is a game. I discovered I was a controller, controlling through self-pity. Now I don't play self-pity; I play happy and satisfied.

Games can be simple or complex. The key for me is to find the emotion that is the payoff—reward or punishment—in the game. Why am I playing this game? Does it serve me or not? How do I use that emotion? What other emotion is similar to it, and what do I intend to gain or achieve from using these emotions, attitudes, and behaviors? The desire for an emotion creates a game and keeps it going.

When you are ready to stop, you must give up the desire for that feeling and want, instead, to be powerful and loving.

When I corrected by releasing the self-pity game, that simply meant I'd be more direct and straightforward. I decided to stop controlling relationships and open them and myself up to flourish. Self-supportive game playing is an act of being conscious, awake, and alert to what you are doing and what result or objective you have in mind. When you know this, you have the option to do it in a way that brings you the most love, peace, joy, and happiness.

CONCENTRATE ON YOUR OWN GAME

Much of our neurotic game playing results from the fact that our original intent, needs, and desires are lost or covered over by manipulation, hidden communication, covert battles, and tests. The game has become so complex you must be a genius at game playing (which is a game in itself) if you are to know what you and others actually intend. Whole cultures have games whose rules you don't know unless you were born into that culture. In parts of Asia, pointing to the bottom of your foot is a supreme insult that can lead to a fight!

One of the first ways I taught myself about games and how to know what was actually happening beneath the surface was to study both body language and transactional analysis. As a communicator what

I wanted to know is what is really going on between people. What am I *really* feeling and why? What are you *actually* thinking and why? But psychoanalysis is a game in which you can easily become lost in the labyrinth of your own mind. The process of figuring it all out, looking for the *real* reason for behavior can be endless. The more I tried to get to the bottom of things, the more confused, unhappy, and exhausted I became.

Eventually I decided to stop trying to analyze others and just be conscious, exact, and clear about my own intentions and desires. The direct method has simplified my life and allowed me to be consistently happy, enthusiastic, and creative. It is up to you to decide whether a particular game serves you and your highest purpose or not.

Changing oneself and one's games is a conscious choice motivated by the desire to feel good more of the time. My desire to achieve my inner and outer objectives in the most joyous, exciting, and satisfying way determines which I decide—to create or eliminate a game.

FAMILY GAMES

Games are habits, many of which have been passed down from generation to generation. The family is the "training ground" of insanity, on one side, and the heart, soul, and cradle of genius, love, and harmony on the other.

We learn from those closest to us, those who feed

us, change our diapers, and teach us language, values, and attitudes. And I feel we arrive on this planet with the wisdom accumulated from wherever and whoever we have been before. The cells of our bodies and our genetic code carry the collective body of knowledge, sense experience, emotion, and beliefs of our entire ancestry from the beginning of life on earth. Through my meditations, I have experienced levels of consciousness and awareness that I sense are consistent throughout all energy levels and systems. I feel the oneness of all life, spiritually, mentally, emotionally, and physically.

I have a feeling that games are common to many life forms. Games aren't good or bad, they simply are, and they exist for as many reasons as there are games. Play is a high state of consciousness; that's why it is usually found in children. When playing for fun stops, the joy of living is gone. If education were made into a fun and challenging game, children would keep learning literally forever. In counseling thousands of people I have found that those who had unhappy childhoods or childhoods in which they had to be "grown up" and serious don't know how to play and have fun. I give these people an assignment: find some children and copy them until you can bring play and joy into every part of your life.

Austin and Ahren Rose, my granddaughters, are my friends and playmates; with them I get into harmony with their sweet innocence and natural ability to have fun. What others think of my acting like a child at these or any other times used to be a great obstacle in my life—but no more! I am having fun, bringing joy into my life—and I'm staying young!

Recently one of my ex-husbands visited and made numerous references to my age. It was an old put-down game of his, but I refused to play. I let the comments pass right by. What occurred to me was that he was getting old and worrying about it! Growing old means believing you can't have fun. I, on the other hand, am getting more alive! Have fun and you'll stay young. I could have been drawn into the game "What does he think of me?" To play that game I'd have to let his opinion of himself determine my opinion of myself. What a win for me to have chosen not to play. Dumb game. No fun!

THE OPTIMUM

The optimum level of existence I have found so far, for myself, is to love myself and be centered in a peaceful, neutral position ready to choose my thoughts, feelings, actions, and reactions. I then decide how to play each moment. The question I ask myself is, "Is this what I want to be doing?" If no, I breathe deeply, exhale the old thoughts and feelings, and inhale the new thoughts and feelings I now choose. The point of power is in the moment. That is when you choose. Remember, you are never stuck in any game; simply change your mind. "You've made your bed, now lie in it" is a dreadful philosophy of life. I'd say, "You've made your bed;

if you don't like it, make it the way you like it or get a new bed or a new bed partner."

SABOTAGING YOUR OWN GAME

Sometimes we play the same game, over and over, simply because we know how to do it successfully. One of the biggest obstacles in anyone's life can be an unwillingness to do something new and different, fearing not to do it well. Success is a limitation if you use it to stop risking, growing, and evolving. The fear of the unknown, of looking like a fool, of making the wrong move, or of losing the point and not scoring keeps many players stuck in games they began lifetimes ago. "I might fail, be penalized, or die trying" is a thought that can stop many a creative genius from ever discovering just how magnificent she and life are as a team.

You can play a game with yourself and be your own teammate, opposition, referee, fan, and audience. I think we really play most games with ourselves, but within the illusion of playing with others. Self-sabotage is one in which you pretend that you are really on your own side, when you are actually your own worst enemy. When athletes are well matched, the one who loses is the one who makes the most errors. I was in London this year during the Wimbledon lawn tennis championships. Most of the players there were well matched, and, sure enough, the player who won was the one able to keep the best attitude and make the fewest errors.

Self-sabotage is an intricate game in which it always looks as if it is others who are victimizing and defeating you. Life for self-saboteurs is a bum ride, for they are always dumping themselves in the ditch just when they seemed to be getting somewhere. I've done my share of this. You are at cross-purposes and therefore go nowhere.

My self-pity game, which I mentioned before, was my main self-sabotage game. I'd achieve a certain level of prosperity, acknowledgment, or whatever I wanted, and then not feel worthy of it. I'd feel unable to handle all the "stuff" that went with getting what I wanted. I'd use "poor me" and find the littlest things to upset myself. Or I would get all excited about a direction but feel stopped by my team members, get upset, and quit (my skiing pattern all over again). I'd pull back within myself, want to run away, and be angry and blame others just so I could reach my comfort zone again (that place we're used to operating from, our personal status quo, whether it's "comfortable" or not). My comfort zone seemed to be a place where I had to overcome obstacles. In overcoming obstacles I found great lessons and growth. What I did to reprogram myself for a new game plan was to not play the old one when I noticed it kicking in. I'd allow myself to enjoy peace, harmony, and the beauty in my life and become comfortable with it. Little by little I extended my comfort zone and programmed myself to completely accept the value, abundance, and love I was creating. You can only have and keep what you give yourself.

Sabotage takes many forms. You're all ready for a special night on the town with someone wonderful, and you spill shoe polish all over your new, expensive outfit. You have an appointment for a job interview that would be perfect for you, and your alarm clock doesn't go off, your car is in an accident, or you have the wrong address and no phone number.

When I first started my television program I was married to a man I felt was verbally and emotionally abusive. He mirrored back to me the worst in a female-male relationship and pushed all my "I give my power away to men" buttons. It was an intense and valuable experience, and I never have to do that again! Whew!

The night before my taping of the program, he would provoke very upsetting arguments. I'd be drained of my life force but still get up the next morning and go on location. It took my good friend and program director, Jim Marino, to inspire me, pep me up, and get me going so that I could inspire others.

I felt this husband was a man who hated women and chose powerful women to destroy. I was a ripe candidate, for he came into my life as I was beginning to live my vision and flourish. The belief I had was, "If I am successful, wealthy, and powerful, men will leave me." This fear was bubbling away deep inside of me, and sure enough, I created a man who fulfilled the prophecy. I left him when I realized the future held only more of the same; I was finished with the game at that level. It took me a fourth husband who I felt was similar but in a much more charming, subtle way to finally dump the game. I stopped going for "hip, slick, and cool" men and decided to be with gentle, kind, loving, secure, and supportive men.

WINNING THE GAME

I don't know about you, but it's been only recently that I've come to fully support myself in winning—winning meaning to be victorious in a game. To know if you are winning or not you need to know what you mean by victory, the objective you are after.

I've defined winning for myself to be a constant feeling of love, peace, joy, and the freedom to be. Winning is being abundant and flourishing in my creativity. I like to win every moment no matter what's going on or who is on first base. I live my life from the attitude that "I've already won; I'm alive and I'm here." Before I knew this, I was always a loser even when I'd achieved what I was after. Winning at that time meant I'd feel wonderful only after the success. But after that, there was always a letdown, a feeling of failure. Now I feel wonderful, satisfied, and excited about myself just about every moment.

Self-sabotage is based on the thought "I'm not

worthy or I'm bad, and it's wrong for me to be, do, or have this or that." Self-sabotage as a game in itself can give you the payoff of self-pity, blame, resentment, depression, anger, and lots of self-judgment and hatred. It is a way of keeping you "spiritual," religious, and on your knees. It can also keep you humble and help you keep the friends you believe you'd lose if you achieved a particular goal. But you can be humble, spiritual, down-to-earth, fun, and loving and also achieve your objectives.

Recently I returned to San Diego and spoke at a Unity church at the invitation of their minister. It was like going home for me—a full house with "standing room only" for two services. I loved every minute of it and ate it up like a piece of rich fudge candy. Yum! Since that time a few people have come out of the woodwork wanting money or something from me, expecting me to be the same Terry I was when I left. I wanted to be loved and supported so much I would buy friendship at some level. It's been a win for me to realize that as people have come forward to get back in my game it is not the old me anymore, and no, the new me is not playing. Choosing new games is the best way to get out of old ones. Be patient with yourself, for the transition is dependent upon your desire to love yourself more than you want others' approval. Someone will always believe you are bad or wrong. Those are not the ones who appreciate you. You cheat all of the ones who want your gifts because those who don't want your gifts get your attention.

Take a moment and check out whether or not you

are your own worst enemy at times. What is that about? When and with whom do you sabotage your love, happiness, and success? What is your payoff in the game of self-sabotage?

This week I caught myself playing self-sabotage and with some help from Reuben I released the game. I'm also aware of the setup, and if I begin to move into the pattern again, I can switch myself onto the new track of my choice. The game was this: I'd begin to flourish; energy would be building toward my having everything I said I wanted, and then I'd turn in the opposite direction, talk down my project, decide no one wanted it anyway, and then kill it. The conflict was that I believed, "If I succeed at the level at which I am capable, then Reuben will feel insecure and unimportant and not want to be with me." Since I have directly experienced the truth of this thought so many times in my past relationships, it took my whole self to not believe it with some absolute truth in operation. Thoughts are creative, so I changed my thought. My new thought is this, "I can and do express my vision fully and my love relationship with Reuben flourishes."

We make it all up and then prove the truth of our thoughts and beliefs. Change your mind, and change your life. Change an attitude, and you open up a door to a new world of treasures.

This very belief in loss was implanted in us in about junior high school, when boys became important. I was watching an announcement for an upcoming television program as the announcer posed the question, "Why is it that girls score higher on tests and are more advanced in school in the first few years and then fall behind in high school, with few being at the top of the class from then on?" The answer was obvious to me, as I had deliberately suppressed my capabilities because I wanted to be attractive to boys (and later to men).

I was preoccupied with creating and keeping a boyfriend. Only music, theater, and some sports actually interested me as much as the game of relationships. Men and boys put their energies into other interests as a way to experience life. I experienced life through my male relationships and through my roles as wife, mother, and daughter.

It's only now that I am actually experiencing my senses, my body, emotions, talents, and dimensions for the purpose of my own pleasure and discovery. I feel in so many ways that my life has just begun as my true pleasures and thrills happen within "Terry" as a self-generating energy system.

Now I know there is no loss inherent in the idea *gain*—*gain* means the discovery and experience of a never-before-realized or explored aspect of myself, nature, or others. I have become fascinated with the most simple as well as the most complex. Life offers me all of it rather than a tiny speck.

What changed was the focus of the games I was playing. I was directing my energy as a magnet to attract and keep Mr. Right. Now I am my own source of love, attention, and pleasure. My energy is now used to play, love, create, and assist others.

THE PAYOFF IN BEING SICK

Some games are valuable because they take us somewhere. Some games drain, limit, and disempower. Sickness can be a game with serious consequences.

If you stop playing the game of illness to manipulate others, it can be a powerful tool to help you become aware of an inner imbalance, a part of yourself that needs some attention or correction and is expressing itself through your physical body. When I almost died while trekking above Katmandu in the Himalayas, it was my body telling me that I couldn't live the way I was existing. To survive I had to use every bit of my strength to will myself back to life. Sleep all but disappeared, and in my wide-awake state, hour after hour, day after day, I contemplated my life, values, and priorities. I even heard choirs and organ music for three days after I had been carried down the mountain piggyback by a barefooted sherpa (a guide who leads people through the Himalayas and carries all the equipment and supplies). I had to be with myself, will myself to be alive, and make decisions to change what wasn't working in my business and personal life. It was a game that gave me priceless rewards, but I can see that if I had bravely dealt with the issue I had been facing before the trek, I wouldn't have become ill. The sickness was a last-ditch attempt to wake me up, and it did.

THE MANY MONEY GAMES

Money is a well-known game. It is actually more than a game. Money is a part of many games: it can stand for energy, love, reward, survival, dreams, attention, power, value, control, or whatever else you want it to be. Having money, not having money, desiring money, giving money away, not wanting money, losing money, and hoarding money are all money games. Money is an illusion, but it's a very real symbol of energy in this world. It won't buy you love, happiness, peace, enlightenment, joy, self-worth, compassion, understanding, genius, or freedom. Money trades service for service. Some people have distorted the game of money and made it an ugly tool when it can be beautiful and life-giving.

Not having money can hold people back from living their dream. Never use "I don't have the money" to stop yourself. Take the steps, and you'll create the money (or the energy) you need. I've also observed people with a great deal of money who never live their dreams or discover the greatness within themselves because they are caught up in the show and glitz of money; money and power become the standard of personal value. But money is just money. Love is just love. Happiness is just happiness.

Television, which has an awesome potential to serve humanity, is simply a money machine in the hands of ego personalities pouring out shallow beliefs, thoughts, and realities. Television could awaken the people to our world, bring ecology into balance, educate our children, connect people, and support the arts and sciences. People in the television business believe people won't watch if it tried to do those things. Maybe they wouldn't at first, because withdrawal from a drug that puts one to sleep may be uncomfortable. But soon a whole civilization would awaken. The products sold on television are, for the most part, unnecessary pollutants of mind, body, and earth. The media are public relations tools spreading propaganda for their clients, who are in the business of creating realities in the minds of the public. If television is to change, peace, love, and joy will have to become more profitable than crime, pain, and perversion.

When money is a motivating force beyond the simple needs of food, shelter, and clothing, we then tend to make it an ego game. It's of the utmost importance for each of us to put money where it belongs: as a tool to elevate all people to precious, divine, and holy. The key here is self-sufficiency. When each of us as women can and do provide for ourselves, love ourselves, and commit ourselves to the values and ideals that bring enlightenment to us and to our world, we can move upward and forward into the Golden Age. We can then play magnificent games with money, spending it on education, health, parks, clean water and air, ecological balance, technology, space travel, art, and music.

RELATIONSHIP GAMES

Relationship games are our biggest source of entertainment, joy, and pain. Notice the games you play with your parents. Are they fun? Which ones require you to not be true to yourself? Which games have to do with money? How many games with your parents are about your sexuality and your freedom to feel the way you want to? Do you play child, parent, helpless victim, or big shot? Notice the games you play with your children. Are any the same as the ones your parents played with you? Are you direct, honest, and clear in communicating with your children, or are you vague, indecisive, and obscure, placing the responsibility on them to understand and respond as you have planned? Do you teach your little boys and girls to play the old games of inequality? Are you jealous of your children or threatened by their power and energy?

Games are what we play. The question is always, "Is this game healthy, happy, exciting, and energy building or not?" If not, change the game!

What games do you play with men? Do you play games at work? How do the games you play with men differ from those you play with women? How do your games change depending on who has the power or money or sex appeal?

One of the big games we play is "crisis and last-minute save the day," also known as brinkmanship. Just before we destroy our earth, our lives, and our relationships, we save ourselves, and "whew, that was a close call!" I used to do that; one small example was running to catch the airplane before it took off instead of being on time. My adrenaline would be high, I'd be breathing hard, and after I'd made the plane I'd feel as if I had accomplished something. We set up struggles to make life real and meaningful. But all our little games don't make anything more than it is. Life is life, and you make of it what you will. Life is the most wonderful game of all, for it allows us to fulfill our fantasies and our dreams and experience even self-defeating little games if that is what we want. The sun shines on all alike, and earth is our game board. Soon our game board will be outer space and other solar systems.

The ultimate game is the one you play within yourself, and it's the most complex, mysterious, and challenging game of all. We play hide-and-seek. We hide ourselves inside ourselves. Who would ever look there to find the answers to our questions? Who would ever look for purpose, meaning, and value right now, right here, within ourselves?

What games do you play with a higher power? Do you beg, promise, sacrifice, deal, pay homage, repent, fast, feast, say some words over and over a hundred times, dance up and down on one foot while eating an apple? By creating a God who is a macho-male, angry, vengeful, punishing, rewarding, and grace-giving tyrant, we can deny our own responsibility for ourselves. We can continue to pretend to not know who we are. We can convince ourselves that we're not in charge and we're not creating ourselves, our relationships, our world, and our universe. We create a devil to oppose a God and never take responsibility for ourselves and our choices. The greatest game of all is, "Let's pretend to not know who we are!" When you figure out what you are up to and the games you play with yourself, all others are easy.

EXERCISES

1. List the five most valuable and rewarding games that you play with yourself. List the five most valuable games you play with others.

2. List the five most limiting, self-defeating games you play with yourself. List the five most limiting, defeating games you play with others.

3. List the five happiest games you play with your family. List the five most unhappy and frustrating games you play with your family.

4. Observe the games that business, government, and religion play. Which game do you want and agree to play? Which games are you no longer going to support?

5. Observe and list the games you notice men playing with women and women playing with men.

6. What games do you desire to play?

7. List five rewards you now desire in the games you play.

8. Are you trapped by any part of your life or by any of the games you play? What has the game promised you? Are you getting it?

9. Whose approval, respect, and attention are you seeking? Are you getting it? Are you playing any self-defeating games to get this attention? How do you feel, playing those games? Do you want to continue? If not, choose other games to play.

10. From whom are you asking for permission in order to enter a game? What person or organization have you decided has the power to make you whole? Write out your deepest desires for yourself and how you want to feel and be. Now envision yourself feeling and being this way!

AFFIRMATIONS

1. I, _____, now allow myself to win in every game I play.

2. I, _____, enjoy playing games that bring more love and joy to myself.

3. It's okay for me, _____, to enjoy the fruits of my labors.

4. I, _____, call forth awareness of the self-defeating games I am playing.

5. I, _____, release myself from games I play with men that sabotage me or them.

6. I, _____, am safe at all times; therefore, I can relax and have fun.

CHAPTER 6

Your Challenges Make You Great!

CAPTAIN JAMES T. KIRK OF THE STARSHIP *Enterprise* in the old television series "Star Trek" remarked in one episode that humans need problems, for without them they become weak, and with them they become strong. What he said impressed me, because for so long I hated problems, felt controlled by them, and actually saw a problem as a flaw in my character. Now I know that problems *build* character. From this point on I'll call problems challenges, because problems are negative, while challenges call forth opportunity.

Whatever your challenge is at this moment, it is the issue to deal with. If you are faced with finding the right career or job, make the process itself one of self-exploration, self-inventory, and creation. If you desire to improve the quality of your intimate relationship, again you are opening a "Pandora's box" but one that must be opened if you are to find the treasures there. A challenge is something you deal with alone deep inside of you. No one can solve your problems but *you*, and you can and will.

YOU CREATE YOUR OWN CHALLENGES

I figure a challenge is something I am creating from some level of my awareness, conscious or not, that I know will bring me value. A problem is a puzzle to figure out, an indication of a desire to grow or flourish.

A number of myths always have the dark and light forces doing battle for some reward, usually the world. The hero or heroine has to face the evil of the dark side in order to be victorious and win the prize. It was fighting the evil power that made the person representing the light strong. Those who persisted in the attempt found the reward even more precious and meaningful. Many had failed before; the graveyards were full of those who had challenged the dark forces and failed. Life is a similar graveyard filled with those who have done battle and given up, believing they were defeated. We set up missions for ourselves to make us great, for without them we would never know our strength or our vast resources within.

The dark side, or the evil we have created, gives us a backboard off of which to bounce. Once you meet your dark side or the evil you believe is within you, love and embrace what you have judged and look for the gifts. They are there. Evil is no longer a thing but simply a concept you yourself have created and by which you define yourself, discover your strengths, and clarify your ideals, values, and beliefs. I've found that evil is in the eyes of the beholder, anyway. Instead of being afraid or threatened by the dark side or problem, I can recognize it as an opportunity and then decide what I will use it for.

Enemies, evil forces, and devils are demons we conjure up in the fertile soil of our imaginations. I use these energies as allegories of reflection that I may know myself more clearly. Evil is the creation I use to see if I believe in it or not. My guiding light is love, and love, for me, is real. If it isn't love, it is what I've created to not love. By fighting our devils and demons we keep them alive and flourishing. Mythological characters in legends and stories are depicting those parts of ourselves and the games we play for the purpose of self-discovery. Why battle an illusion? Dance with the illusion, and recognize it for what it is. You are playing games with yourself.

But remember, just because a legend, myth, or story is from the Bible or other ancient resource doesn't mean it is true. Someone made it up. Some of these myths were made up to control people into fear, submission, poverty, and weakness. If we find we are succumbing to that control rather than using the stories for the purposes of self-discovery, we need to discard those stories and create new ones.

THE ILLUSION: THE CONFLICT BETWEEN LIGHT AND DARK

The struggle between the light and dark as a way for the light to gain strength and know itself is ancient, but we need to steer clear of literal interpretations of old myths designed to perpetuate the power of men over women. We need a new game. I'm ready to keep whatever of the old is still valuable and finish with what isn't. "Cinderella" is the story of a woman who must dress up for the prince to recognize her, lose her, and find her again because of her dainty foot. Her stepmother and sisters are jealous. The women are at war over the love and attention of a man (the prince). It sets women up to fight each other over men. The sleeping beauty falls asleep and is awakened by a kiss from the prince. What if the prince doesn't come? Do you stay asleep? Why does the prince have so much power? "Beauty and the Beast" is about a beautiful woman who falls in love with an ugly monster who, when she kisses him, becomes a handsome man. Although the woman has power in this tale, she has it solely because of her beauty. Let's reverse it and have an ugly female monster. When the handsome man kisses her because he loves her, not for her body, she becomes beautiful to him. Better yet, as we learn to drop our judgments about beauty, we can write myths based on love as mutual energy and deep appreciation of each other.

Actually it is the feminine that when it awakens has the power to awaken the male. Our male energy is linear—the doer, the seed—and our feminine nature is the creator, the womb, and the earth that awakens the seed. The earth without the seed produces nothing, but the seed without the soil never starts—sleeps on.

Good and evil, problems, challenges, and obstacles have been glamorized and are the basis of every plot in our books and movies. Good faces evil, evil almost wins, and in the end good triumphs. I'm bored with that scenario. There is a limitless number of games to play, but the needle is stuck on conflict as the way to grow: man versus woman, the poor against the rich, health fighting sickness. Of course, the challenge is an opportunity to grow, to call forth our strength. But why can't we leave conflict behind and learn to grow without it?

The programming is deep, and we have given our monsters too much power over our lives. The problem is the belief that disaster, loss, pain, and rejection are inevitable. *We* create our monsters, so *we* can bring forth our latent energies to transcend the illusions.

This theme is what many myths are reflecting back to men, at least. Don't let your challenge get you down, but be victorious over the illusion of the dark. But we as women don't have as many legends that convey our powers as men do. What there is survives in Sumerian, Celtic, or Greek mythology, as much of our Goddess mythology and history has been obliterated by the male-created religions of the more recent past. When the patriarchal powers ascended, the matriarchal powers descended. If, as a woman, you are looking into the recent past to gain strength and wisdom for your present, you probably won't find much to validate your divinity or your earthly powers.

Women of today, however, are creating new legends, myths, stories, and archetypes by their courage and willingness to create themselves as they desire to be, without external validation. Soap opera characters and movie heroines become our new archetypes if we allow it. It is so easy to stereotype ourselves and then live out our self-fulfilling prophecy.

"Survival of the fittest," Darwin's theory of evolution, weeds out the weak and helpless. To survive you must be strong enough to overcome any threat to your existence. To survive, some of us are cute and smile a lot, others of us battle it out, and the winner is the one left standing. Certain diseases, viruses, and germs may weaken and kill us, yet if we mutate, that same killer strain can make us stronger. Problems can develop us into stronger beings, yet too many can defeat us. I feel the secret of meeting challenges lies in each of us connecting with and staying connected with our higher self.

DEALING WITH THE ROCKS ON THE ROAD

A challenge is an obstacle on your way to somewhere. It is a test that you must pass before you've earned the right to get there. The first time I got married, my husband and I moved to San Francisco and rented a one-room apartment near Market Street. The first meal I cooked in a frying pan was a poor version of Spanish rice. Today I am a marvelous cook when I choose to cook, because I kept on cooking and didn't stop after my dismal beginning. I felt depressed at the time but that didn't stop me, even though I've burned my share of meals in the process. The challenge was to be able to cook food that was as good as or better than I could eat in a restaurant at a fraction of the cost. I rarely use a recipe; I simply make up what I want to taste and eat. Our connection with our inner spirit allows us to explore, experiment, fail, and succeed—and it's all in a day's work.

In facing any obstacle or setting out on any journey, frustration, confusion, hopelessness, fear, and other emotions are bound to surface. "This too shall pass" is a Bible quote I like because it illustrates what I have discovered. There are rocks on the road, and those rocks are there to teach me. Nothing stops me for long, for it will change or move or I'll get bored with it and go around it. Some problems seem to hang around a little longer than others, but that is because there are others in the game who have their own challenges.

There is an old psychology test that asks the client to answer the question, "If you were walking on a path through the woods and you came to a big wall, what would you do? Would you stop, go around it, wait for help, jump over it, or blow it up?" Your answer to this question will give you a more objective view of how you deal with the events in your life. How do you deal with your "walls," your challenges? To be defeated is to pretend you didn't create the challenge. When you own it, the challenge can be fun and exciting!

COMFORT ZONES

Comfort zone is a term for the boundaries inside which one feels at ease. Some people are actually comfortable with pain. For them, happiness is an uncomfortable experience. What is comfortable is what we are used to, feel worthy of, or think we deserve. Comfort zones are the boxes we live in that contain the least amount of challenge, upset, or growth.

Mastery requires that one have a high tolerance for being uncomfortable, for risk taking and venturing into the unknown. The line of least resistance can be valuable at times, but it can also be limiting. Taking the easy way can be the most difficult in the long run, because instead of building character and strength, it simply reinforces fears and shrinks the arena in which a person can play and express. A woman who desires to awaken herself must have the courage to step outside of her comfort zones and explore new territory.

Playing the game of life as freely as you desire will push your buttons as well as the buttons of others. Your comfort zones and your patterns of breathing, relating, and living will be altered. Patterns are anchored within all aspects of ourselves: our bodies, our brains, our psyches. Creating new patterns in breathing, moving, speaking, thinking, and feeling creates insecurity, at least temporarily. Mutation is occurring moment to moment as we are evolving. Our thoughts, emotions, patterns, habits, and bodies are in a constant state of change. All life becomes more in each moment as the old makes way for the new. This is the process that makes life, life.

If you are looking for peace and quiet, find it within yourself. Bring that peaceful state of being into your activities, and remember that being the light, unafraid of the dark, is a game, a test, a challenge. Fear makes us hide or strike out to protect ourselves (though sometimes those fears are justified, and it is time to run or lie low for a while). Take some quiet time to contemplate your situation. At some level, I know I'm creating this drama. Whatever the drama is, I give myself some time to meditate and sort the gold from the sand.

Wisdom is a by-product of discovering what doesn't work and choosing what does. It's a wise woman who runs the other way when a hip, slick, or cool woman-hater comes along. It's a wise woman who looks to herself for her own advice and takes it. I know of no other way to become wise than by participating in life and learning from our challenges. A very wise woman is one who knows the beliefs and thoughts that cause pain and gives them up for the beliefs and thoughts that bring the warm, cuddly, and loving feelings of pleasure and happiness. Each challenge is a lesson and an opportunity to own more of ourselves. There are no rules! I always go back to this so that I can dissociate myself from beliefs or patterns that cause me harmful, limiting, or destructive patterns. I choose to go it alone and to love humanity. Breaking old alliances, patterns, beliefs, and agreements that are no longer valuable can be tough, yet necessary if you want the ultimate freedom to be as you choose and not a clone of the past.

If you know that you create your own discomfort you can do virtually anything you want outside your comfort zone and feel comfortable doing it. Any challenge, going to the gym and working out with weights will hurt because you haven't been using those muscles. Go easy; breathe into those parts; enjoy your body coming alive; and then relax in a nice hot bath or jacuzzi and release the toxin build-up so you are not sore tomorrow. Discomfort can be a signal to avoid someone or something; at other times it signals the awakening of part of yourself that has been dormant. It is up to you to know the difference.

Challenges are self-generated. Find ways to take care of yourself as you expand your comfort zone.

Drop whatever simply keeps you stuck in the past and enjoy new ways, for they do bring enormous gifts. You want to find material, emotional, physical, and spiritual blessings. The only way I know to do that is to jump into the game. You have a problem, a challenge, a test before you. What do you do?

BEING VICTORIOUS: A CHECKLIST

Here's a checklist of possibilities to explore to help you be victorious.

• Write down the problem, challenge, or test in as much detail as possible. If you don't want to write it, clearly think it out or tell it to someone and ask that person to just listen without judging or giving advice (unless, of course, you want that).

• Write down in detail what it is you really desire. Forget about all your excuses, justifications, fears, conditions, or reasons for not having your ideal.

Write out or tell someone the obstacles you'll have to face. An obstacle may simply be something that needs to be taken care of, paid attention to, or somehow handled.

Write out any inner blockages, attitudes, or feelings that are obstacles. Figure out how to dissolve the blockage and create the feelings and attitudes you want.

Know that you can "uncreate" what you don't

want and make it disappear. It may take some time, however.

• Now imagine yourself being, doing, or having whatever it is you desire. Feel the way you would if that was yours now. Feel gratitude that you have a solution or the new reality now. The more you can visualize how you'll feel when you have achieved your desire, the more energy is generated for moving in that direction.

• Do the easiest things first. After you've done the small stuff and gotten it out of the way, take further action toward your destination. Here it isn't so much what you do but *that* you do *something*. You are getting your "get up and go" flowing. Through action your energy will build and get you where you are going faster.

• Remember to use your powers of creation. It's simple: want it, own it, and accept it as yours. The way you have created for your men and children, create for yourself. If you don't really want it, you'll stop it, so make your intentions clear.

• Work your wonders! Get into the fun of creation, having little miracles, and giving blessings at every turn.

• Do what you need to do to improve the quality of what you do, and if you love what you are up to, your interest and active participation will make you magnificent!

• Keep your mind open and ask for specifically what you want to know, identify, discover, realize. Trust your answers, and trust your intuition.

• Persist. Don't give up until you get or become it in your being.

• Pay attention to what others are doing that's working; they may give you some ideas or insights.

• Communicate what you are up to so that others know what you want them to know.

• Remember, if you have the desire, the fulfillment for it must exist. Create out of the void, out of emptiness and nothing. You must and will transcend any obstacle, for all obstacles lie within your mind and body. Itself, the desire to go beyond this obstacle implies dissolving this obstacle, this limited belief, and the reward of a new treasure chest filled with goodies on every dimension.

• Be happy this moment! Don't wait for the problem to be gone before you are happy. Feeling creates circumstances. Circumstances just give you the opportunity to feel again whatever it is you like to feel. Happiness sets up happy circumstances for more happiness. Be happy, be grateful, be alive, and be in this moment in peace and love.

CHALLENGING YOURSELF

The strongest people I know are those who, no matter what, bounce back and keep moving on. Fear disappears when you face it. Fear lives in the dark corners of our imagination; we are the ones who create it and we can make it go away.

Maybe you are a working mother, want to be with your children and still have a satisfying occupation that earns you the money and opportunities you desire. This is the problem—actually the test or challenge—for you to solve. Maybe you are working in a field that is dominated by men or in which you can't achieve what you desire without someone else's permission or good graces. This is your test!

You need more money to make ends meet, but you have a fixed income and no one is hiring at this time. What to do? You've chosen this situation to challenge yourself. Move out of your comfort zone and find more within yourself.

You or a friend has a serious illness, and things look dismal. Yes, you are in the middle of a dark forest, and all around you are animals, so you must be careful as you find your way through quicksand and through swamps and out into the safety of dry, open land and a new day. To the one who makes it out safely will be given the keys to the queendom and any treasure she desires.

The real treasures are the feelings, lessons, wisdom, and realizations that build your character and your self into the goddess you have always wanted to be. If you define yourself using a measuring stick of success or failure in single incidents, you'll cheat yourself. Little by little you will whittle away to nothing your enthusiasm, your excitement, your childlike wonder and playfulness. If you let people's opinions, beliefs, feelings, and thoughts direct you,

you'll become their creation, and many of their creations are tired and dying because they are. To be who you are, that special you, you must follow your own lead and no one else's, even that of some so-called spiritual master. Make each event an opportunity, and don't give it any more power than that.

Think of your life as ongoing successive moments of now. Each moment moves into the next moment as one event and one day dissolve into events and days, events and days. What comes forth are cycles and tendencies that create you as an awesome goddess becoming whatever you want to be.

HOW TO MAKE THINGS YOU NO LONGER DESIRE DISAPPEAR

The key to overcoming any challenge is to know that you can uncreate what you no longer desire. Our attention is the fuel that feeds the monster. Without our attention our creations can't live. Problems and obstacles that continue to persist hang on because we hate them, think about them, feel them, talk about them, and allow them to consume us. Helplessness, hopelessness, and depression are the result of feeling drained, repressed, and controlled by someone or some situation. Your light, your aura, is vast and extends far out into space from your body. A problem, even a comfort zone, becomes a box that contains and limits your light. In the process your light is diminished and you feel contracted, controlled, and powerless. The only thing left is to cry, bitch, moan, eat, drink, whine, and indulge in self-pity.

When the doors of the Terry Cole-Whittaker Ministries were closed in February and March of 1985, everything was a colossal mess. When you change your mind, your house and past creations are still there. You can fall in love with yourself in this moment, but the bruise on your leg from where you bumped yourself is still there. The bruise will go away—just don't keep hating and judging yourself for the bruise, or you'll bruise yourself again.

I knew that physical things take time to clean up and clear out. I faced the mess, and piece of paper by piece of paper I cleaned out the clutter with the help of some wonderful friends and staff. I had created the ministry out of my inner self and now, when its usefulness was complete and the job had been done, I set out to uncreate it. Now, four years later, the job is finished, the slate is clean, and I'm creating my next adventure.

I learned how to "disappear" old creations when I got out of a destructive marriage. My husband was angry, foul-mouthed, hateful, and destructive, which was what I needed to bring my unworthiness and poor self-image to the surface to heal. When I moved out, I never spoke to him again except for one brief encounter. I stopped talking about him (even criticizing him) and thinking about him; I refrained from attempting to get even. I also got help from friends who were therapists to express and release my pain and anger and change my low self-image. I did some past life work and found a couple of past life relationships with this man in which we had made intensely strong commitments to be together through pain and torment. I released the energy charge, broke the agreements and commitments, and released myself completely.

If I had entertained him in my mind, thought about him, fought with him, blamed him, defended myself, or played with that creation in any way, he would have been in my life and tormenting me.

If you play with it, it's there. We keep old creations around because they give us an identity. Who would you be without your problems, complaints, and battles? What you resist persists, because your resistance in and of itself acknowledges the reality of the problem and gives it power over you. Those who fight the system create the system. Those who fight city hall make city hall the enemy and keep it frozen in its state of affairs.

To "disappear" something, give your attention to what you want and not to what you don't want. When you create out of reaction or opposition to, what you are affirming is the enemy. The enemy exists because you believe it is greater than you and believe that it can control or limit you in some way.

I, ALONE, DETERMINE THE QUALITY OF MY LIFE

I learned a long time ago that because I am responsible for myself and my creations, I and I alone determine the quality of my life. I used to always believe that another person or thing was stopping me from living my dream. This was really my excuse for not doing, being, or having what I wanted. Now when someone or something appears to be limiting me or holding me back, I know it's me and not "them."

My relationship with men was what I created it to be, even if it was dismal at times. Even so, I never fought men, in the sense of seeing them as my enemy or the reason I wasn't free to live my life as I chose. For me to blame men and fight against a male-dominated system was only to reinforce the belief that they were in charge. Why fight an enemy and make that enemy responsible for my life when I have the power right now to do as I will? Fighting an enemy creates an impasse, a standoff, for what you give out always comes back to you.

I used to judge and criticize, mentally and verbally, other ministers, religions, and political views. All of this came back on me, and I, in turn, was judged and attacked. What I do now is allow others to be as they are and simply put out the message of love that I feel is important. Any form of attack stems from a judgment of oneself and a belief in limitation and scarcity.

A problem is a temporary opportunity to strengthen yourself. To attack and create an enemy makes a slight challenge into a nuclear war. Most of us find our identity by classifying ourselves as different from or similar to others. When I create myself as I desire to be, I'm not defining myself by others' values, bodies, standards, creations, or life-style. I am who I am because that's how I like to be, doing and having what satisfies, nurtures, and fulfills me.

Jealousy, envy, and unhealthy forms of competition are signals about something you want but won't allow yourself to have. The ego trip called judgment can paralyze you, for you decide that what brings you joy, excitement, and fun isn't okay. Whatever you determine isn't okay for you to do stops your dream machine.

Let others live their dreams, realizing that no one can stop you from living yours except *you.* When you are complete, unhappy, or ready to move on, begin to shift your attention to your new project. Finish up what needs to be handled from the old creation and let go of it as you move in the direction of the new.

Move right through the temptation to go back there and stir up the muck again. Let it die of starvation. Drain it of your light by using your energy, attention, love, and light for what suits your new self-image. Why bother to get even with men or women who are not supportive of you? All you do is decrease your own light and energy. It's not worth what it does to you!

BEING RESPONSIBLE

Taking responsibility for your life in every aspect is the most difficult and powerful thing you can do. What do you want now? Exactly how do you want to feel? If that person, problem, or challenge wasn't there, what would that mean to you? If your problem was solved, what would you be doing? Answer these questions and put your energy on your forward motion as you move toward your objective.

If you knew you couldn't fail, what would you do? This question puts your desires, visions, and dreams out of the realm of the fear of failure as an excuse. An obstacle is just an obstacle, a rock in the road—not a mountain, an end, or a verdict.

Nothing is inevitable except what you unceasingly commit to. Peace and love is inevitable in my world. Paradise is inevitable, for it's the natural manifestation of people who are whole living in harmony with Mother Nature. This will take time, as the physical world exists in time. But paradise, love, and ecstasy first must exist within and as me. The next step is my relationships, home, business, and the extensions of that into the world. I've taken some detours, experienced setbacks, and had numerous learning experiences since I decided on these objectives. The challenges have not deterred me; they have only helped me in my creation of bliss, ecstasy, love, and paradise.

You may experience frustration. Press through it. Rejections, nos, and discouragement may take place. These are simply old ideas and values appearing to challenge you. Keep on.

Right now it appears as if the women's movement is going backward and we're putting ourselves back in girdles and high heels. Many women are, for oftentimes right before an enormous change things look worse. Fear of change, the unknown, rejection, and failure make people retreat to a past time or a so-called safe haven.

I tried that a few times when it seemed too difficult to communicate or to change my ways in a relationship. I'd go back to an old pattern. Eventually, I'd realize it was too painful to not be myself and I'd choose life and freedom. I'm an impatient person and I want things to happen now. What I have done to deal with that is feel the way I want to feel and be what I want to be in the future *now*. I can be patient knowing that now is the time and I don't have to wait for anything to happen later. I don't have to wait to love myself until others love me. I love myself and others and I stay in a constant state of bliss and joy. Little by little others who are tired of the old games of pain, sacrifice, suffering, and conflict will desire and manifest peace, and it will come.

If we knew we couldn't fail, what would we intend for humanity, our earth, and the quality of our existence? We have been too easily defeated, too easily hurt and frustrated. Never take no for an answer if your desire is important to you. See, sense, and feel your victory and the inevitability of your desire and objective. Erase your past creations. Keep the value and lessons, commit to your intended results, and know you can't fail. Don't make the little problems big problems—petty problems can sink your ship. With the attitude "you're already there and the outcome is certain," you can hold onto the big picture that will carry you through any problem.

I've let minor irritations become big wounds. I've

let simple mistakes become enormous failures and defeated myself numerous times. Now I live each day with as much joy as I can, allowing the little irritations and problems to be just pebbles in the road, not boulders.

As women, we have challenges that we have created and games that we play for various reasons. The relationship you have with yourself transcends all the games and all the challenges. The battles are won within the self, the prize being whatever is important to you. Each of us sets up the challenge, the game, the obstacle with our own growth in mind. We do this at unconscious levels until we are conscious about our intentions.

Balance and equality become a certainty first within oneself and only then a certainty outside of self. When peace and love are a certainty within you, it is just a matter of time for people to notice that it is available to them too. Paradise is first inside our heart and soul and then it is carried out into the far corners of the earth. Whatever your intention, objective, or dream, know that the outcome is certain. Begin your journey and enjoy the ride.

EXERCISES

1. Write out the names of some of your favorite myths, legends, fairy tales, and stories. Notice if these legends have had an impact on your values, ideals, and belief system. Create your own myth with yourself as the heroine.

2. List your ten most important challenges at this time. List five ways in which you can handle each.

3. List five frustrations or roadblocks you are experiencing at this time. For each write out a description of the "big" picture.

4. What are ten things you want to "disappear" or uncreate? For each describe what you want to create.

AFFIRMATIONS

1. I, _____, have within me all I need now to overcome this challenge.

2. I, _____, am one with all that is now and forever.

3. I, _____, draw the intelligence, genius, and creativity into me now for whatever I want.

4. I, _____, can, I will, I am.

5. The creator lives within me, _____, and comes forth as my desires and dreams.

6. I, _____, call forth all that is needed and wanted to be victorious over my

challenge and fulfill my plan for a beautiful and
wonderful life.

7. I, _____, take this challenge as
my opportunity to prove my skills in creation
and manifestation.

8. I, _____, always have what I want
and I now open myself to the treasures and gems
of this challenge.

CHAPTER 7

Springing Forward from a Setback

"DON'T TAKE YOUR LIFE PERSONALLY!" I READ THIS on a card once and it has stuck with me. The more I can detach myself from my life but still be loving and caring, the greater my flexibility and the easier I am on myself and others. Being both attached—involved, committed—and unattached—less critical, less sensitive to negatives—to what goes on in your life helps you to have your boat in the water but not the water in your boat. Why sink the ship when, to play the game of life, you have to stay afloat?

Discouragement is an emotional state of being without courage. Something or someone has convinced you that you are valueless, unworthy, and unable to continue whatever it is that is important to you. Something you've done or not done you have labeled wrong. The label "wrong" causes you to punish yourself in some way.

If these judgments are actually others' ideas about you that you have internalized and taken for your own, you need to recognize them for what they are—other people's problems, not yours. Dismiss them, be at peace with yourself, and continue in your own direction.

If these negative value judgments of yourself are your own, you still need to rid yourself of them, for they serve no useful purpose. In fact, they harm when they cause you to place unrealistic expectations on yourself, and unrealistic expectations are the number-one reason people have setbacks. Value judgments of yourself or an incident cause you to get involved in feelings of low self-worth and doubt, and those feelings keep you from making what are simple corrections—nothing more, nothing less—in what is not working in your life.

When a number of things collapse at once you can have a major setback. It's important to try and not have all your changes at one time unless you really want to. You may place more expectations on yourself if you are growing in many areas at once. The more arenas in which you are playing at the same time creates more opportunities for growth—and also for upset. The key here is to be easy on yourself. Why burn with the intensity of a fire? Just get nice and warm.

Women and men who are growing rapidly and

learning quickly are vulnerable to a constant barrage of awarenesses about themselves. Awarenesses are revelations and have to do with the way you are living your life and the beliefs and thoughts that motivate your behavior. The more judgments you make about yourself having to do with appropriate or inappropriate behavior, the more you'll be disappointed in yourself. If you are willing to be aware, be even *more* willing to be gentle on yourself. Dealing with and relating with people will surely bring you face to face with whatever has been hidden or protected within you. If it comes as their judgments about you, remember you are actually creating them from within. As these come forth, release the thoughts and accept new and more loving thoughts.

FINDING THE ONE "RIGHT" WAY TO BE

I used to be on a mission to find the truth and the right way to be. Knowing and doing the right thing was important. I'd give my power to whatever I felt was the right thing, for I wanted to be right. Unknowingly at an early age, about ten or eleven, I decided I wasn't "right." My folks didn't have enough money. My hair wasn't "right." My face and body weren't "right." I wasn't smart enough by the teachers' standards and therefore not "right." Certainly my clothes weren't "right." These decisions about myself led me on a wild goose chase to find "right" and become that. It seemed the boys liked a certain "right," the teachers another, parents and grandparents another, and my girlfriends still another, yet I foolishly believed in an absolute "right" even though I didn't know what it was. Surely it was there and I'd find it and become it.

"Right" girls weren't boy crazy. "Right" girls liked boys. "Right" girls studied hard and got good grades. "Right" girls lived in pretty houses and their fathers were presidents of companies. "Right" meant survival, it meant friends, it meant good grades, it meant parental approval, it meant men would be attracted to me. "Right" was the magic word. The rich are "right"; the famous are "right"; the obscure are "right"; the joyful are "right"; the serious are "right." There was "socially" right and "culturally" right or "intellectually" right. After that, "right" turned into the word "spiritual" and there was "spiritually right." I grew up with all these conflicting judgments bubbling around inside of me. Imagine the conflict of trying to be right in all the games!

Expectations I put on myself had to do with what I thought was right. It was right to be happy and wrong to be sad. It was wrong to be happy and right to be serious and worried. It was right to be egoless and wrong to be ego-centered. The list is endless. Every person and every group has its rights and wrongs. And if you are right with one group, you are wrong with another. You will most probably be wrong with *someone* until we all stop judging and simply love ourselves.

Some major "rights" affected me the most. It was "right" to be a good little wife and stay in a marriage forever, no matter what. A divorce was a setback because I believed I had failed. I felt embarrassed, humiliated, and apologetic because I had done wrong. Never mind that neither my husband nor I got along or were happy together. I'd hear, "Can't you get it right and stay in a relationship?" After much agony and many disappointments I've discovered that right doesn't exist as a constant. (If you need to convey a necessity or a standard the word *appropriate* is better, but it still should not be a final judgment as to the merit or value of a person.)

We all know killing another is wrong, but why is it okay if it is a national enemy and you kill for your country? Then it is wrong not to kill. You are then a draft dodger and coward. It is wrong to steal, but if you are a spy and steal foreign secrets, it's okay and you are a hero. It is wrong to have money and be successful and happy when so many people are starving and miserable, but it is right to pay taxes and be a responsible citizen. It is also wrong to live on the street and beg for money—you should get a job, be a taxpayer, and become a yuppie so that we can judge you in a new way. It is wrong to be fat and not care about how you look, but it is wrong to be assertive and love yourself. Be successful but not too successful. Men will be frightened of you and you'll be alone. Be dependent so you'll be taken care of but stand up for yourself and be independent.

My experience tells me that each time I have had a setback it was because I had an expectation about how I was supposed to be and what I was supposed to do. I wasn't too kind to myself. I was actually much more allowing and forgiving of others. I made my mistakes more important than what I was doing that was working well. Setbacks also occurred because there were things I was unwilling or afraid to face and be responsible for. Those setbacks occurred because of ignorance and lack of knowledge and experience. I could have gone to an expert for help or simply forged ahead in the game called "Being Human." "Being Human" is not a course with tests you can pass or fail and your grades are recorded for all time; it's about opportunities and growth. Be gentle with yourself when you play!

The revelation that is the clearest to me is that the love of yourself under any and all circumstances is the most important gift you can ever give yourself or another. We're so easily disappointed in ourselves and one another. We're so quick on the attack. It can be too easy to nitpick, to find small things to make enormous, and forget the beauty, love, and value.

When I was a minister I asked for donations to run the church and pay for the television program. We were always two to three months behind in paying the bills. I was judged and made wrong for not having the finances handled and I was made wrong for asking for donations. I couldn't win, because either way I was wrong. A friend of mine wrote me a nasty letter attacking me for asking for money and not having my finances handled. How did he think a ministry handled finances other than to ask people to give to what they believe in? Giving money away is a powerful healer in people's lives. Keeping your money and receiving from others is equally as powerful. When I quit the ministry, I never heard from him. When you are in the public eye you are never right; someone will decide you are not enough or too much.

Being disappointed in oneself is a devastating experience. Gossip is about who is right and who isn't. We are brainwashed with conflicting messages. This experience feels like driving a car with a foot on the gas and a foot on the brake. Stop, start, stop, start, and so on.

The more you define yourself by another's standards for success and failure, the more difficult it is to know and love yourself. Who you are can't be defined, only experienced. It is in knowing yourself and all of the special aspects and nuances of your particular energy system that the fun begins. When "right" is removed as a measuring device of personal value or worth you can enjoy yourself and the games you play. Some setbacks are simply the result of buying into others' judgments about you. You felt good about yourself and then you changed your mind.

When we are hard on ourselves we are not too forgiving of others. There seems to be a large part of ourselves that actually likes to hear of another having difficulty, especially if that person, organization, or country has been considered very powerful and successful. It makes us feel a little more right and a little less wrong. We seem to favor the underdog until it becomes top dog and then we shift our loyalties to the new underdog. "Top dog/underdog" can also be played with oneself. I found this to be one of my patterns. I'd work to reach a certain plateau, then judge myself wrong, and swing to a low. I was afraid of too much power and also of not enough. I'd swing fanatically in one direction and then in the other. Now as these opportunities come forth I can stand back, breathe, relax, and stay centered.

No one is beyond the judgment of others. A person can be on top one day, a guest at all of the social, political, and business events of the season and the next moment on the list of the unwelcome. What happened to all those close friends? They now pretend they never even knew the person. Shunning, ostracizing, ignoring, imprisoning, institutionalizing, humiliating, and abandoning are some of the ways we deal with people we have judged as wrong, different, or failures in some way. Shunning is an ancient method of controlling people in order to keep the tribe, religion, or belief system intact. Shunning meant abandonment where the one was cast into the wilderness to make it on their own without the "safety" of the group. Conformity, the need to be wanted, to be accepted is so basic that it starts at birth. Leaving or being left has been and remains our most powerful control device other than physical violence and confinement.

FAILING CAN BE THE BEGINNING OF GROWING

Failure in your own eyes is devastating to your being. It's called sin or missing the mark. A sin is an offense, a mistake, an error. But I know of nothing that can be learned or done without making mistakes or errors. We learn by trial and *error*. We forgive some things but others are unforgivable. Why? I would say because of an outdated belief system. If we simply stay within the confines of yesterday's beliefs, values, and discoveries, the learning process is hampered. Much from yesterday is valid for today, but life is an ongoing upward spiral of new awareness, technology, discoveries, and knowledge.

I remember questioning my first marriage. My marriage was fairly normal compared to that of other married couples I knew. The men were "bad little boys." Drinking, telling dirty jokes, coming home late, not calling, having extramarital affairs, swearing at the wives, and laughing at women was "real man" stuff. The woman stayed at home, cleaning, cooking, scolding, nagging, begging, and pleading for love. There was very little if any real communication, mainly out of fear and ignorance. I wanted more—I hated being a second-class citizen relegated to the house waiting for someone who rarely showed up when he said he would and when he did was critical. I'm sure I was not a lot of fun either. He probably felt unappreciated and unfulfilled too. When I questioned the state of our relationship, it was the beginning of the end of the marriage and the beginning of my training in relationships—starting with the one I wasn't in with myself.

By many people's standards I failed to hold a marriage together. Today I know that dissatisfaction or failure can be the beginning of growth. A bottom-out experience may force you to seek therapy, read a book, or ask the spirit within for help. We do whatever it takes to give us whatever it is we are seeking. Whatever it is time for us to learn and realize, we do in a variety of ways. Life is this infinite reservoir of opportunities. There is no goal, no final destination, and no "right" way to be.

The point is this: to label anything as a failure is to negate the experience and invalidate yourself and the others. There is a vast array of gifts and treasures available to you, if you look. Labeling something a failure or loss can defeat you and drain your life force. So much more is going on than meets the eye at first glance in even the simplest situation. The key here is to not let others' opinions defeat you or cause you extra pain.

It's taken me four full years to assimilate my experiences in the fast-growing, stressful, and high-impact world of television ministry. No one can know what I went through to build the ministry to reach millions of people with what I feel is a very important message and no one can know what I went through to say good-bye and deal with what I had to, to alter my life when I knew it was time to move on. No one but you lives in your body and no one but you knows what is right for you.

RECOVERING BY LOVING YOURSELF

Recovering from what we call setbacks and restoring ourselves after what we call failures, disappointments, and illness requires a profound love, appreciation, respect, and acknowledgment of yourself. The first step in successfully rebounding from a setback is to give yourself permission to feel love and appreciation for yourself once again. No one may understand or appreciate you but *you.* Start with this love of yourself and build from there.

FIND THE GOOD PURPOSE

The second step is to find the good purpose in the experience. Whatever setback you face has the key to your victory within it. There is a good purpose, there is a treasure, a gift hidden within the situation. What is it? A major gift may be learning to call forth as much love as you can for yourself as you stop living for the attention, respect, and acknowledgment of others. Sometimes you are an imagined threat to others and no one will let you win. Then it is time to transcend the smallness of others and be all you can be.

If you call an experience devastating or a failure,

it is. If you call it a learning experience then you will learn and gain wisdom from the experience. The question "Did I do that 'right'?" leads you to invalidate your past, what you did, and who you were. Watch for invalidation and learn to deal with it not as an enemy but as a companion. Every moment there is an opportunity to blame yourself or another for the "error" or "mistake." Invalidation is painful to one's being and generates blame, anger, resentment, and guilt. Unhook the "blame game" and refuse to play.

No one knows what is in your heart but you and no one but you knows your values, ideals, standards, beliefs, and purposes you find important to the evolution of your soul. You are an ever-evolving creature, alone within yourself. You are also in relationship with other ever-evolving souls who are thinking, feeling, believing, judging, and growing.

The world's standards for personal development are so shallow that very little of what we use as a yardstick for success and failure goes any deeper than the level of appearances or the projections of the one judging. The lack of depth and breadth leaves only a surface crust of value. If we have a sin, it is in being shallow, appearance-seeking people, rather than explorers of the depths of our souls and unconscious and the heights of our spirit.

How you perceive yourself and what you hold as the purpose and meaning of your life will determine how you deal with your challenges and how you label your experiences. You, in the aloneness of your being, are your very best friend. Tune into that essence within that is always there for you and become the best of friends. You know it because it only speaks highly of you and everyone else.

Personally I choose to now call everything valuable. My purpose is greater than a single event or series of events. What I perceive are trends, cycles, and learning experiences instead of simply life-and-death moments of all or nothing. No single event will stop me in my ongoing upward-spiraling adventure, purpose, and plan. If you call everything valuable, you will never lose because you always find a treasure. In fact then, everything helps to further your purpose and objectives.

A master charts her own course and sets sail for the next port. The journey may include storms or fair weather and anything you meet on the expanse of water, but what's important is what you become in the journey and whether you wind up where you intended. I know that if I don't wind up where I intended, it will be somewhere even better than I expected! If you almost capsize and then hate yourself for the rest of the journey, you have defeated yourself and ruined your joy and happiness. Remember it's a game to be played, not a sentence to be endured.

What I've found is that there is very little enlightened living happening, so don't really expect anyone else to have your depth of understanding. You'll have to create your own attitude about how wonderful you are, then believe, act, and feel it. The world is still giving awards to the victims and victimizers, whose roles can switch at a moment's notice, when the underdog becomes top dog or when top dog becomes underdog.

If you are not looking for recognition, understanding, or even acceptance from anyone, then I feel you can set sail for anywhere for any experience and always be victorious. If the recognition comes, that is nice. But if it doesn't, so what? *You* are living fully.

There is no more devastating experience than to invalidate and cancel yourself. It removes the desire to live, for you have judged yourself as not worthy of life and life as too painful. What I'm also saying is that no person or thing can make you feel anything you don't want to feel. You and I determine for ourselves how we choose to feel. What a relief! Feeling devastated, hopeless, or dejected can be games you play when you feel powerless. We women have blamed and not been trained to provide for ourselves for so long that when we have to do so, we may feel powerless over our lives and what happens to us.

Find the value and get the lessons. As you discover what you've learned, apply those priceless lessons to your life and the projects and relationships that present themselves now and in the future.

BE WITH THOSE WITH WHOM YOU FEEL ALIVE

Step three is to get away from people who drain

your energy and repress you. You can love everyone at some level yet not be empowered and inspired by being around them. When you are around draining people you may have mood swings and roller coaster emotions. The test to use to gauge others' effect on you is to evaluate how you feel when you are not around them. It could be an electrochemical reaction between you, you may have withheld communications, or you may be judging each other. I'd say there is a lot going on within that isn't expressed, which generates a drain. Sometimes all it takes is to remove yourself from them and you feel a weight lifted, joy returned and your purpose for living is reactivated. You can feel possessed and controlled by another that you feel you "need."

Angry people who aren't willing to express and release that anger will drain you. If you are angry at yourself you will attract those who are angry at you.

Sometimes a setback or a feeling of being down comes about because of your companions. Be with those with whom you feel alive. Nothing is more precious to you than your aliveness. You can be depressed and think it is you. Sometimes you can simply correct a problem with another by communicating and sharing. Other times it is hard to define. You can spend years trying to "figure it out." Get away. Be with yourself for a while. Then return and see how you feel. You may need to move on from that person. Our lives always become more bountiful and results improve when the drain is gone.

What can keep you down is giving more of your attention to someone or something else than you are giving to yourself. Some people demand all of your attention and to keep them in your life you have to give up yourself. These people are charming, adorable, and quite wonderful. What is most amazing is that we'll do anything just to be with them. It is a case of giving everything but not getting back that which is at least equal to what you give. Everything that you have is then gone and you feel like you are falling apart because what you had for you you gave away to keep a person like this in your life. These people need to be the center of attention and for sure the center of your attention. When you need their attention for your creations, there isn't any or very little left for you.

Sometimes this can be corrected and better balance achieved. If the other person is willing to come into balance with you and create an even relationship, then you will begin to flourish once again. If the person puts you down and continually turns the conversation back to him- or herself and their interests, the scales are too far in their direction and all of your light is going to them.

At one time, I had all my light in my own direction and I really wasn't interested in anyone who wasn't interested in me and my vision. If people wanted to be with me, they had to be involved in my life. I know now how sad and draining it was for them at that point in my career. I had become interesting and not interested. That is the danger in fame or in believing that whatever you believe in is more important than what others believe in. Attention is an addiction and it can make someone a corrupt tyrant if that person is living off the light, love, and attention of others.

Change is devastating to one who lives for the attention of others. A classic example is the "beautiful" woman who gets old, is cast away (in her mind), and lives in her past. Another example would be a child who gets all the attention and doesn't give any to others. The child becomes lazy, unproductive, and demanding. Men like this make lousy mates. Since Mama gave him her life, he will expect his mate to do the same.

The lesson here is that this doesn't create balance in relationships. A correction is needed. What we call a setback may be just a learning experience of compassion and understanding and it took that particular circumstance to teach you that. The beautiful woman who felt she lost her beauty may be learning to love herself and not just her body and face. The child who becomes spoiled will have to learn what happens when he is disrespectful of others and that learning may be a painful experience.

A setback would be the name you'd give a period of time in which you rest, review your life, and make the appropriate moves to compensate. Since everything seems different than before, you think that you had a setback when you actually are preparing for a great leap forward.

The physical universe is made up of opposites

and for every action there is an equal and opposite reaction. If your pendulum swings to one extreme, it must swing back to the other.

The Goddess Mother energy at one time ruled this planet as it is a female planet. The male energy took over and the pendulum swung all the way in that direction. Some would call that period of time a setback for women. I call it the natural swing of the pendulum. Now we are coming to balance and in balance we will be awesome in our love and power. Whatever occurred in our history that caused sexual abuse, inequality, persecution, and the slavery of women had to be allowed by women to have ever occurred. To deny this understanding is to deny our power and continue the illusion of "I'm not the cause of my experience." This is not placing blame on anyone. It is a statement of our ability and power to alter our lives in this moment and for ever more.

I have found it to never fail that people who are fanatics about something, whether it be religion, food, exercise, sex, or money, will reach the height of their fanaticism and will then believe in that which is now completely opposite of where they were before. If these fanatics allow themselves to realize it, they can learn a vast amount of wisdom in a short period of time. Balance will then come to them as they realize that they can relate to others and their experience in ways that other people can't because the fanatic has lived so many lives.

Each experience has a wealth of treasures, so why concentrate on only one treasure? Find the good purpose in everything. Transcend the present, view the past and future, realize the trend, the pattern, the flow and the direction. It is at this point that everything works in your favor, unless you judge yourself and your setbacks as devastating instead of a natural tendency of the human experience. We're here for the lessons and the experience.

People who don't know this are most assuredly stuck in their need for attention or their need to give attention. Another name is giving and receiving. If you have to have all the attention you are in a "baby need" mode and if you have to give all the attention you are stuck in a "parent need" mode. Either one of these stuck positions will feel as if something is wrong. If not enough receiving energy is experienced, you will feel overworked, frustrated, and impoverished. If you are not experiencing enough giving energy, you will be dependent on others' giving and never feel able to create what you want on your own.

Your "get up and go" is dependent upon your ability to give and receive equally. When you do, miracles occur and your enthusiasm, energy, and self-esteem increase. Now you are happening and life is good.

TAKE ACTION

Step four is to return to the basics of creation and carry through with the appropriate action. The more you think about something, analyze it, mull it over, and worry about it, the more entrapped you become. You get stuck in confusion. Decide what you want, clear your space of negative energy, set your purpose, goals and methods, and do it.

A wonderful process to help you in having the feeling and consciousness of ableness is to notice physical things and say, "I can have that. I can have that. That is something I can have." Havingness equals beingness. It doesn't matter if you want any of the material stuff you are looking at. What does matter is that you get outside of yourself and your mind and get in touch with your ability to do and have what you want.

Another game to play is to notice if anyone else is doing or having what you want. Then say, "If they can do it, so can I." Realize that they are as human as you are and they have no more power than you do. You are an amazing Goddess/Creatress of the Universe.

TIE YOUR CAMEL

Step five, tie your camel and trust the Goddess energy. Once you have set your course, fuel your dream with your attention, desire, and enthusiasm. Do whatever you feel and know is important and needed. When you know you can't do any more, then trust the Goddess Mother, the Higher guidance system of the creative light to handle everything else in a way far better than you could ever imagine.

An ancient story illustrates this point. A woman who had a camel that was quite valuable to her rode into a new town and needed to leave the camel for the night. Another woman came by and they talked for a while. After a bit the woman with the camel said good night and started to walk away from the animal. The other woman said, "You'd better tie your camel so that she doesn't wander away or get stolen." The woman replied, "Oh, I don't worry. Goddess will protect my camel," and she left. In the morning she came out and the camel was gone. The moral of the story is, "Trust in the Goddess *and* tie your camel."

I've known countless numbers of people who simply hope and pray and nothing happens. I've also known lots who work and struggle and never get anywhere. It takes both. Without spirit as your partner, you are not inspired, nor do you have the benefit of a link with the celestial realms. Without your effort, you don't know the experience of being a co-creator in the Divine Experiment called life.

All life is creative. The One sent itself in all directions at once to create and to offer whatever it created back to the One. What we get is infinite and everlasting creation. Sometimes what is wanted is brought here intact from another part of creation and allowed to evolve. Both creation and evolution are true. Nothing unreal exists and it is all true. It is all unreal and doesn't exist at the same time. There is also the higher truth that allows all other truths to exist.

Setbacks, challenges, and upsets are not what

they appear on the surface. When the experience has reached its zenith, the gift is complete and you are presented with the wisdom of that experience. You are working in partnership, so what you have to contribute is essential. Collective consciousness is what creates worldwide happenings. The earth has awareness, the sun has awareness, everything is aware and made of consciousness and energy. If we take this approach into the inner planes, all animals, plants, insects, reptiles, and birds as well have their awareness. All of it is creative. This action is occurring constantly, instantaneously, and you have free will to act in harmony with the will of the One. It is also changeable, now.

So what do you want? Does what you want feel good within you and your body? If you have the validation of joy, love, and a burst of upwardly spiraling energy, then go for it. Do what you want and need to do and trust in the divine Mother/Father/Creator.

FEELING THANKFUL

Step six is to stay in a mental and emotional state of gratitude and appreciation for yourself, those you love, what you've learned, where you are, and what you have now! To move from the belief system of "not enough" into "enough and more," we need to appreciate, acknowledge, and care for what we have. Cursing things in your life simply creates a setback into scarcity. For example, if a check comes to you for $9.50, do you feel thankful or do you toss it aside and think, "Is this all?" Your energy is directed through thought into the emotional and physical worlds. The world of physical manifestations is created from your thoughts, notions, concepts, and ideas. The physical can only be what has come through from the celestial and ethereal planes and the physical contains that total consciousness. The physical and spiritual work together in upward or downward spirals. The physical creates the spiritual and the spiritual creates the physical. It is all part of the Divine Experiment. Take care of and nurture what you've received and ask for more when you want it.

Stop the downward flow of action by appreciating and taking care of what you have. If your relationship is deteriorating and you really love yourself but feel confused about how to be happy again, stop criticizing, stop arguing, stop the sarcastic comments, and stop wanting the other person to change. All of this negativity validates the "not enough" belief and what you get is *not enough*. To reverse a downward cycle and to flourish again, start appreciating and feeling truly grateful for yourself, the other person, and your relationship. Start accepting yourself and him or her as you are. Later you can work out the challenges, together.

Take care of the business you have to. Handle the mail that has come in. Fulfill the requests you have promptly and with appreciation and quality. The more you wallow in your self-pity, the further down you will go into the depths of despair and wondering, "Why me?"

Take action for what is needed in the moment with an attitude of gratitude. Gratitude is an energy of blessing. Anything you bless is blessed by the universe. If you negate it, it ceases to exist for you. Bless the "hell" out of it and what is left is "heaven."

KEEPING YOUR AGREEMENTS

Step seven is to keep your agreements—*and* to not make agreements you can't keep. Never let others make agreements for you and when you do make your own, make sure you know the full ramifications of what you are committing to. And making agreements, signing contracts, saying yes, or committing yourself for the wrong reasons—you feel you have to help someone out, you feel pressured, or you don't want to be unpopular—can cause a major setback and throw you into a downward tailspin.

Some agreements you will be held accountable for no matter what, for example, those with the government, banks, and agencies. Some agreements can be revised by communicating with those involved. Start at this moment and think before you agree to anything. Look forward and see if you are willing to follow it through; if you are, make the agreement. After you have committed yourself, then follow through even if it takes extra effort. This will get your energy into the upward spiraling direction and you will feel capable and proud and have a heightened sense of well-being.

HELP IS EVERYWHERE

Step eight is ASK FOR HELP! We forget we have an infinite wellspring of overflowing supply of guidance, wisdom, and truth available to us from our higher levels of consciousness as well as from experts and those whose job it is to assist people. Help is everywhere, waiting for you to ask. Be willing to receive and act on what feels right for you.

What always astounds me is how long it takes me to ask my higher self for guidance and how quickly the assistance comes. The quality of the guidance is awesome. The Mother Goddess energy is there for the asking. You don't have to do anything to qualify for the right to ask. Ask specifically for exactly what you want and then act on the guidance you receive.

The miracles start to occur when you move in the direction of where you desire to go. If you are true to yourself and move in the direction of your bliss, you will manifest what you love.

Ask for guidance. Ask to have clarity about what is troubling you. Ask to be cleansed of negative energy. Ask to be flooded with love and light. Whatever you want, ask for it. Know you get exactly what you ask for and allow the gift to come in a package even more wonderful than you expected.

Your answers will probably come when you are doing something fun or relaxing. I ask and then I walk in my woods, dance to a good song, play, or exercise. It comes in a flash and I write it down so I remember. Sometimes I get a direct flow of information as if I am being taught by some teacher in some far-off galaxy. Sometimes I have a feeling or sometimes things just clear up, love is restored, and I never get a conscious answer.

I find it a waste of time to talk about my problems with those who can do nothing about them. They start giving me advice that doesn't pertain to me and I start feeling drained or angry. The more you talk about a problem the more confused you will become and the more the problem will increase in size.

My least favorite thing to do is listen to people who don't want to take responsibility for creating a problem of theirs and really don't want a solution. One of my favorite pastimes is to work with people who are excited about themselves and who want to benefit from their challenges.

I don't ask miserable people for advice. That doesn't mean that those people don't have gifts to offer in other areas. Everyone is a divine genius with unlimited gifts to give. However, if you share your problems with people who are depressed, angry, bitter and fearful, they may give you more negative energy and it may be more difficult to get out of your rut. Keep your own counsel or seek professional help that can help you clear away the cobwebs and let in the light.

I have come to cherish the instant light and practical guidance that comes to me from my higher levels of awareness. We all have this connection within the quietness of our own being. Ask and let it give you your wisdom.

BE ENTHUSIASTIC

Step nine is to get excited and enthusiastic about yourself, your life, and your purpose. Excitement and enthusiasm combined with desire will propel you to great heights of achievement. Your attitude is everything, for without excitement and enthusiasm nothing really happens. You may have to keep asking for guidance as to your purpose, gifts, and services. When your desire to live fully is greater than your desire to hide and protect yourself, you will get excited. A setback can occur if you judge yourself or have succumbed to the judgments of others. If you have lost your enthusiasm, feel despondent, and lack motivation, it may be because you feel invalidated, unappreciated, or wrong. Shake off the judgment, make the appropriate corrections, and get connected with people who empower you.

Self-esteem, self-love, and self-worth are essential, for love is what you are. You are the frequency of love, so the more you feel the feelings of love directed inward, the more you have to direct outward. For every action, there is an equal and opposite reaction. So if love is what you are directing toward yourself, it will also extend out from you.

Your attitude is an essence, a delicate energy that will propel you and your dreams to fruition. Your attitude of expectancy, joy, love, and enthusiasm creates an aura of magic and inspires others to work and play with you in the fulfillment of your objectives. Your enthusiasm is contagious and uplifts everyone around you. Some will try to rob your energy only because they don't know they have some of their own to use. Love them in your heart, wish them well, and don't stop to deal with them. Some are persistent, but the less you play their nasty little games, the less effect they have on you. You can't satisfy, please, or make them happy. Don't try. Focus on your light where it will do some good.

One evening I was watering my front lawn by hand and noticed how much water I was giving to the spots of bare dirt. There wasn't even any grass seed in those spots, but I wanted the whole yard green, so I watered the brown spots more than the green areas. I realized I was focusing on what was nonproductive and giving less attention to the productive areas. I decided to water what was already growing, sprinkle the brown spots, and later plant grass seeds.

People have the tendency to give love and energy

to what isn't working, hoping that it will flourish, and neglect what is already flourishing. The outcome is predictable. Something that receives no energy (the part that seems to work) wilts and dies. The part that is not working (but is receiving the energy) limps along never growing and never ending.

Don't be a teacher who neglects all the bright young stars to handle the few troublemakers. Give the light to the light. Love the dark and if it wants the light, it will come to it. Reinforce loving behavior and loving behavior will flourish.

Life is an adventure and the only way to get to play is by being involved. Jump in and go for the ride.

EXERCISES

1. List five to ten setbacks that you've allowed to affect you and from one to five ways in which you've punished or penalized yourself. What lesson did you learn from each? Write ten ways in which you can now and will in the future reward yourself for the experience.

2. List five beliefs, feelings, or attitudes you have about each of the following subjects. Write as honestly as you can. This is not a test. It is an opportunity to clear up any cross-purposes or conflicting values and beliefs.

Love	Your body	Sex
Money	Power	Happiness
Wrong	Right	Clothes
Possessions	Men	Women
Parents	Brothers	Sisters
Ego trips	Good	Bad
Success	Failure	

3. I deny myself love and abundance because
_____.

4. List five main points of the chapter in your opinion and how you will apply them to your life.

5. List five steps you will take to empower yourself to achieve each of your desires and objectives.

AFFIRMATIONS

1. I, _____, no longer have to be "right" or "wrong."

2. It is okay for me, _____, to do what I do and be as I am.

3. I, _____, love and honor myself for my courage to be myself.

4. I, _____, am not here to live up to others' expectations, not even my own.

5. I, _____, release myself from punishment and set myself free.

6. I, _____, have a vision and dream for myself and the world that is as valuable as anyone else's.

CHAPTER 8

Your Attitude Is Everything

AN OPTIMIST SAYS THE GLASS IS HALF FULL AND A PES-simist says the glass is half empty. What's the difference? Attitude! How you label something determines the value of a person, place, thing, situation, or experience for you. It's a good thing or a bad thing! It's a blessing or a curse! Broad labels limit tremendously the gifts one can receive. I discovered a long time ago that any person who found some value or gift in everything could not be beaten! That individual would always rise again and be better off because of whatever occurred. Nietzsche, the philosopher, wrote, "What doesn't destroy you will make you stronger."

I've listened to people lump a whole day, a whole

month, an entire relationship, and even life into one category, either bad or good. "I had a bad day." What does that mean? "It was a bad relationship." "I had a miserable vacation." "I have the worst luck with men." "It was a failure." "It was a success." "What an ugly person." "What a beautiful woman." "What a tragedy!" Our vocabularies are filled with statements that limit our experience and put a rich shining treasure into a minuscule container on a tiny shelf somewhere in a dark and dusty closet.

"It's a man's world." "Women are helpless whiners!" "Men are egomaniacs!" These labels, generalities, and blanket statements represent concepts, beliefs, and ideas that you believe and accept. When we simply open our mouths and let words come out without realizing what we are doing, we reinforce these beliefs and perpetuate the limitation.

If you are going to label something, find a label that opens up instead of closes down. The half-full glass is an attitude of abundance. The half-empty glass produces a feeling of lack and scarcity and an attitude of "not enough." The attitude itself creates more of the attitude and a life to match. Your attitude sets the stage for the play that is your life.

"Opportunity knocks only once." "This is the chance of a lifetime." "Time is running out." "With your first breath you begin to die." "This is your last chance." "Your luck is running out." "You'll be ruined forever." "This is the best thing that will ever happen to me." These are more statements that produce attitudes and reinforce beliefs that limit your choices and the quality of your existence.

People have themes and slogans by which they direct their lives. I love to read bumper stickers and statements on people's T-shirts because it tells much about those lives. Pessimism is popular, chic, and deadly. Often pessimists are labeled realistic and their beliefs about life are considered the intelligent ones. Optimists are considered flighty, unrealistic, uneducated, or airheads.

Recently while traveling on an airplane, I saw a precious movie called "Harry and the Hendersons." A family literally ran into a bigfoot while driving through the Pacific Northwest. Harry (the bigfoot) became a dear friend of the family. It was a touching story, full of love. It taught an attitude of understanding and how love can transform people's lives. It gave me a wonderful opportunity to feel love, compassion, and understanding. Stories like this are often called fluff—irrelevant and unrealistic. Stories of violence, pain, crime, frustration, and anger are called real, honest, and true. Attitude is everything. Your attitude determines the quality of your existence.

Do you see the glass of life as full or empty? The full context is one in which you experience yourself as whole, sufficient, satisfied, and with a full measure of freedom for unlimited self-expression. Being whole and free implies that one can experience whatever one desires. An open attitude offers you a full range of experiences. A closed one offers you very little.

EVERYTHING CAN CHANGE

Nothing is static. Everything is changing, moving, and flowing each and every moment. When you view your life as living art, one moment flows into the next and whatever you are experiencing is for the moment. You are not stuck in any position. Labeling sends you off in one direction and it is then very difficult to change course because of the momentum.

When I have labeled an incident or given it a sense of permanence, I have produced an obstacle, a hurdle, a blockage. To overcome my obstacle, I need to create courage and enough energy to blast through it so that I can flow into new release and freedom. My attitude created my blockage.

To evaluate a situation as solid, inevitable, real, impossible, or certain is to create it being that way. Many people are creating AIDS that way, just as has been done with cancer and the common cold. I know of two people who have healed themselves of AIDS and I read about two more on the cover of the *USA Today* newspaper. An "in"curable disease means that it is curable from "in"side or within. The moment you accept any verdict as final, it *is* final. Creativity stops and disintegration follows. Death, sickness, aging, loss of love, and decreased ability to manifest are all thoughts that people have made real.

Attitudes about life, death, time, space, and what is real affect the fabric of our hearts and souls. Time and space aren't solid, fixed, or unchanging and neither are we. A fixed opinion is called a fact, something we can prove is so. But even facts are a matter of interpretation.

WELCOME THE OPPORTUNITIES

Your attitude sets the stage for the gifts you will experience. What I've discovered is that we can create our lives as being far greater than we could ever imagine. Our preconceived expectations and labels simply limit us and keep us from what could be ours. Time and space are arenas not sentences. Open up to your possibilities.

It's raining here in Maui. Reuben and I arrived yesterday from our farm in Washington State. Someone else might say, "Oh, isn't that sad it's raining! I want the sunshine. It is our vacation. What bad luck!" Reuben and I happen to love the rain, just as we love the sun. I don't want sunshine all the time—I need and want the sacred waters to flow. In finding the value and good purpose, we look for it and claim it. I feel my body absorbing the moisture and the precious gifts of the tropical climate. When we arrived yesterday we were welcomed by the nature spirits with a double rainbow across the valley between us and the ocean. A white owl greeted us last night as we acknowledged this magical and mystical island paradise.

What if it rained your entire vacation? Would you label it a waste, a disaster, or would you welcome the opportunities you were given to live in a way other than what you expected? Playing in the rain is one of my favorite things to do. Go on a picnic in the rain, find cover under a giant tree and see what an adventure it can be!

I was fired as an assistant minister once and at the time I felt embarrassed and hurt. Yet I knew deep inside of me that I no longer wanted to be in that job. I knew it was time to move on, but it was still a big challenge to face. I had the push I needed to move on from a completed part of my life, but new fears and new experiences still lay ahead. I could have used the firing as a way to dump resentment and anger on the male minister who fired me and used the situation to validate a belief system of prejudice and unfair treatment. I decided to use my energy to move forward and not fight my past. I knew I created the firing as a way to be a full-time minister, not an assistant any longer. If we don't move graciously, life has a way of assisting us out of our nest.

Pessimists believe in the inevitability of disaster and the realness of bad luck. They take the stand that things won't get better and most probably will become worse. An optimist says, "What's the value from this situation? What is the desired outcome and what needs to happen here?" One's underlying attitude creates more of the same attitude. You are what you feel.

There is always space for the pessimistic aspect that says these are the reasons it won't happen or won't work. They have some good points to consider. Stop and consider what they are saying. If it has value, do what is necessary and continue on with the project. A pessimistic attitude defeats you before you've started. An optimistic attitude and positive thinking without the careful consideration of what needs to be handled and dealt with goes nowhere but up in smoke. Dreams that become real in this world begin first with an optimistic attitude and to complete the dream, many obstacles and challenges will need to be faced and overcome. Don't quit until you reach your destination.

Some pessimists are simply suppressive, destructive personalities who, because of some unhappy experiences in their own lives, put the stop to others and their good feelings. The fear of failure keeps them from even attempting to achieve their objectives.

Then there are "pretend" pessimists. They've developed a game they play with themselves and others to throw others off what's really going on. They actually have accomplished quite a bit but downplay everything and pretend they are surprised that everything turned out so well. They pretend to not care or to not believe things have a chance of working out so well. This is so that if things don't work out, they won't be disappointed.

And I've known "pretend" optimists, those who only *seem* optimistic. Deep down inside they have shattered dreams and don't really believe that good can happen. They have a billion ideas, plans, and projects and seem to have a great attitude, but nothing ever works for them. Their games are games of self-sabotage—they are much more comfortable with disappointment and loss than with joy, happiness, and achievement.

Confidence determines your attitude and just how high you'll fly. Notice your slogans, your witty sayings, and fast comebacks that will give you a clue as to how you really feel. Do you put yourself down or are you affirming yourself in life? Any attitude can change. We can transform ourselves and re-create every aspect of ourselves if we want. Reversing a trend takes commitment and a loving attitude toward oneself and others.

THE ATTITUDE OF A PRACTICAL OPTIMIST

I've always been an optimist. At one time, I wouldn't listen to the pessimists, the ones who I believed were throwing wet towels on my fire. Now I'm a practical optimist. A practical optimist is one who knows she can be, do, and have whatever she desires, but also knows it may take time, a lasting commitment, and a great deal of work to achieve it.

I knew a man who at first seemed jovial, optimistic, and able. Shortly after I met him, I felt suppressed, depressed, unhappy, and invalidated. In spite of his apparent optimism, he was really sending out a constant barrage of criticism, judgments, and attacks on everyone we knew. In many instances he was right about these people and situations, but his negative, destructive attitude was so intense any gifts he had to give cost too much for me to receive. The cost was my life, my joy, and my natural optimistic attitude and I refused to pay it.

Sometimes my attitude is lousy and I feel as if life is a ridiculous game. Then I feel hopeless for a while, irritable and cranky. Something has occurred and what it is has stopped my joy in the moment and my forward motion. Here's an example to illustrate my point.

When I recently returned to San Diego to speak for two church services, it was a thrill for me to return to a town that had been my home and to be reunited with friends and members of my old congregation. I held a press conference after the second service. The conference was exciting. I loved sharing with the press how I felt and what was happening in my work. Their reports contained typical responses. Some were aligned with me and some were a little angry; some were aloof and one was cynical. Yesterday I read part of one of the articles, which is contrary to my standard policy. It angered me and "bummed" me out. I lost my great attitude. I became a little depressed and started to take it out on Reuben. I felt a threat to my relationship with him and started acting as if he and I were separating. I lost my desire for a new television show when I realized that I would be playing with the press and the public again. I gave my whole life over in a minute. I lost my will, my joy, my passion. More than anything else, I stopped loving myself and invalidated my own most precious purpose. I wanted to quit and felt disaster was inevitable.

This morning I thought, Why am I so fragile? Why do I care? Why do I allow some unhappy person to rain on my parade? Why do I doubt myself even for a moment? This event and my reaction let me know how I can lose self-confidence by letting someone else determine my attitude. First, last, and always love and attention only come from within ourselves.

I ran away from the press and the public so that I could take care of the little girl inside of me. Now I'm public again in my work and assisting others in believing in themselves, raising their self-confidence, and fulfilling their destiny. It's my choice. Both women and men need to know there are choices, alternatives, and opportunities open to them. Getting back into the public eye meant having to deal with the same issues I left behind. My attitude is now one of choice, not "have to," "should" or duty.

Our attitude and feelings are so fragile and precious. Imagine how fragile a hummingbird egg is. Well, our most gentle, vulnerable self is more tender and delicate than that. We need our shields up and surrounding us in order to provide our most precious self with warmth, love, and joy.

DEALING WITH SHARKS

I believe that everyone, at some level, is loving, honest, and trustworthy. I do this because I want to be treated that way by others. Most of the time, people respond the way they are treated, but sometimes, usually when I least expect it, someone makes a quick turn and takes a swipe. My guard is down and I'm vulnerable as they move in for the kill. People who do that may have soul memory from past lives having to do with the best attack being a sneak attack—warrior strategy. Our past controls every moment in our present unless we consciously choose love in this moment. Fear and paranoia motivate these people and most people who have moved beyond warrior tactics simply aren't prepared for the onslaught.

The Bible says, "Be as gentle as a lamb, and as wise as a serpent." If you are dealing with sharks, snakes, and alligators, you'd better know it and raise your shields to take care of your heart and spirit. Otherwise you may end up wondering what happened and feeling like a victim. You forgot to protect yourself and make sure you were receiving what *you* needed.

An old saying goes, "Don't share your visions, wants, or objectives with others or you'll dissipate your power." That is true if you are sharing with people who are doubters, skeptics, or pessimists. If you open a vulnerable part of yourself to these people, they can crush an idea, snuff out a light, or trash a dream, if you are not aware of what is happening. Protect your optimism and protect your dreams!

WHAT YOU CREATE EXTENDS OUT FROM YOU

If you give and give and give and receive only negative feedback, it is because you don't believe you are worth much. What you are worth is what you believe and know yourself to be worth. You may be one who gives because you believe in giving your all. Make sure you give to yourself first and then to others out of your overflow. We need balance and balance comes from taking care of our own needs.

Women have perennially given their all to men, hoping they would love them and give them what they needed, what they had given away. What happened that made men so important, more important than our own lives, our children's lives and well-being, and the well-being of our earth and all its inhabitants?

The male energy and the female energy are two aspects of creation. Each is co-creating as an ongoing event. These energies took on bodies and these bodies took on functions of reproduction. Women loved themselves and their male counterparts and all was beautiful until woman began to look to her male reflection for love. He became the source of her beauty, love, and light and at that point he became the tyrant and she the slave. Disharmony and imbalance was introduced and the female began to fear her own power. We women have turned our attention to pleasing men when it was originally a mutual job to bring ourselves joy and pleasure.

Separation and disharmony continue. We reduce ourselves to parts. There are men and women who know themselves only as genitals, stomachs, intellects, or hands. Who we are is spirit and what we have are bodies, jobs, relationships, and so on. We are fully able, whole beings and when we are stuck in one mode, we repeat ourselves over and over. We see our lives only in relation to some prior loss. "I don't want that again so I'll do this next time." We try to avoid the failure, but it happens again anyway. Why? What you resist persists.

If we are to have hope for your lives, our families, and our world, we need to regain balance. This means the clearing of our outdated beliefs and past programming and realizing where those ideas take us. If you point yourself in a certain direction, you will end up where you are headed.

The main purpose of my first book, *What You Think of Me Is None of My Business,* was to assist people in being strong in their love of themselves regardless of other people's attitudes and beliefs. But certainty of oneself does not necessarily come quickly; it is something that we build. The shields we feel we need to support ourselves are not armor or brick walls. They are invisible light shields of color, fragrance, and sound. They do not isolate you from what is going on or allow you to live in another reality. They do not keep you from feeling or caring. Quite simply, what you create extends out from you. It is an atmosphere that is all around you in which no harm can come to you. Before I go out into the world I know to create and call forth my light shield of pure love. I send it before me and make my path clear. I leave it behind me and leave love wherever I have been.

Your attitude is a sacred state of mind, body, and emotions. It is personal and it is your force field. If there is a chink or opening in the force field you can be hurt. Center yourself before a phone call, a meeting, or any event and call forth your love shield and your radiance. As you go about your activities stay centered within the shield by remembering to love yourself. Remain loyal to your chosen qualities of being and steadfast to your purpose. Let other people's garbage bounce off you; recycle it as love.

Life is an energy game, an amazing opportunity to become crystal clear within yourself about who and what you choose to be. So many people are cynical, jaded, angry, hostile, and attacking; they live off of conflict. Don't take on their ways. Don't judge them, but I've had those feelings and it is a miserable way to live. Life is a confidence game. You need confidence in yourself, your product, your service, your relationship, and everything that is part of your life.

In many ways you and I are babies. We are newborns, just as vulnerable as a tiny seed that is beginning to sprout. A large oak tree was once a tiny sprout. You and I are creating attitudes, creating feelings, creating values, ideals, and beliefs that perhaps have never been planted before. We don't have a history of love, peace, and joy to back up our attitude. We are out in a giant oak forest planting new seeds that must be cared for, fertilized, and watered, so that they can become strong on their own.

Humanity has become entrenched in fear and its defense called attack for a long time. You have worked hard for your new attitudes and your new emotions of joy, happiness, peace, and bliss. The key is never allow another to dig up your "bliss" seed.

It only takes a moment to lose what you've been nurturing and it only takes a moment to plant the seed again. Ask yourself, "What is the outcome I desire?" It does take time for this new attitude and feeling to become strong and firmly established. We have old, worn-out attitudes about ourselves as women, about the roles we play and about our opportunities. What gets me into trouble is attempting to program others for attitudes, feelings, and beliefs I want for myself. The more attached I am to the feelings of others, the more in danger I am of losing my own good feelings. I can be sensitive to you, your feelings, and your needs and I can also protect my own.

When I started to write this book I thought, "I should put a lot of male/female, God/Goddess historical material in it. I should write about women's struggle and really get into the pain and shame of it all." These thoughts kept me stuck for a while, because that is not me. That is not my special gift. I decided to be myself and express my point of view and forget about trying to win a Pulitzer prize. I decided to be true to myself. The more attached anyone is to other people's opinions, the less authenticity, the less joy, and the less spontaneity she will feel. I also thought, "Terry, some of your awarenesses are too far out. Quiet down!" My integrity tells me to tell it as it is.

GUIDELINES FOR A HEALTHY ATTITUDE

Here are some guidelines I have found helpful in creating and maintaining my attitude.

Don't bother to:

Ask someone for permission to be, do, or have anything if it pertains to you and your feelings, beliefs, and dreams.

Make anyone else's opinion of you more important than your opinion of yourself.

Get people's approval and attention by giving up your dreams, desires, attitude, or state of mind.

Think anyone else knows more than you do about you.

Give others all your money because you want to give 100 percent.

Believe that another is special or more tuned into universal wisdom than you are.

Beg anyone to stay with you or love you.

Put your dreams aside to help others live theirs.

Succumb to a negative, fear-ridden belief system because its proponents have the "right" credentials or you believe they are more successful or smarter than you.

Make men more able and therefore better than you.

Hate and judge yourself because you are alone.

Evaluate people by the amount of money, the type of career, life-style, education, or body type they have.

Blame yourself if another is miserable.

Change your happy attitude because of another's reaction.

Spend time and energy trying to get even or seek revenge.

Worry about how other people can prevent you from living as you desire.

To follow another's path or emulate him or her.

Live up to others' expectations of you.

Think of all the reasons why you might not achieve what you want.

Plan a dismal future.

Use your precious time constructively in a way that serves you and humankind in the most loving way. If it's truly a blessing to you and you are uplifted in love, it is good for all.

One of the best ways I've found for keeping my attitude joyful and at the same time being a constant winner is to find the value and the gift in everything. A winner is one who can't be beaten. You can't lose if you seek and find the treasures among the trash.

Whatever you curse curses you in the same way. Whatever you bless blesses you. You curse or bless yourself every moment depending on your attitudes.

A woman traveled to Africa as a shoe salesperson. After arriving, she was so discouraged that she called her boss and said, "I can't sell these people shoes. They aren't wearing any!" She left Africa and went home. Another woman was sent to replace her. This woman, upon arriving, was so excited that she immediately called her boss and said, "Thank you for sending me here. This place is a gold mine! No one is wearing shoes, so I can sell a pair to everyone!"

Take a moment and contemplate how an attitude can defeat you or encourage you. Finding the good in every situation will set you up for finding gems everywhere, not just where you expect them.

Nothing is all bad. Nothing is all good. It just is. You are either in an ascending spiral or a descending spiral. You are either awakening from the dream or becoming more unconscious and asleep. To awaken even more as a conscious person find the lessons and gifts in every experience.

One day I decided I really was through putting anyone else down. I don't believe that I need that kind of thing to make me feel better about myself. Sure enough, the next day I was talking on the phone to a writer from a women's magazine, giving her my thoughts and opinions about a certain person, some of which were negative. After I hung up I remembered my decision. Instead of cursing myself for forgetting, I acknowledged myself for remembering when I did, even though it was after the fact. I released the need to put down anyone to build myself. The next time this person came up in conversation, I felt no need to put the person down. Find a way to always acknowledge yourself and release the old patterns of feeling and thinking as quickly as possible.

It takes time and work before new habits, a whole new way of being, is integrated into your energy system. The creation of any new habit starts now. Time is the illusion. Now is real.

Finding the value and staying in a constant state of acknowledgment becomes a habit that will give you great rewards within yourself, your relationships, and your outer world.

Take a few moments to find the value and good purpose in some situations that you may have judged wrong, destructive, or defeating. Remember, you are the judge who passes sentence and you are also the judged who must then live out the sentence. "Not guilty on all counts" can open you and the quality of your life to an infinite number of new gifts, experiences, and opportunities. After "not guilty," create a code of ethics that you can follow to bring yourself and all life into harmony, love, and oneness. "Do unto others as you would have them do unto you" is an ancient wisdom that serves us today.

Be patient and loving toward yourself as you are a tender, precious seed of exquisite proportion, design, and pattern. You can't be too good to yourself, for the more you support yourself with your own love, respect, and acceptance the more you will automatically have love, compassion, and support for others.

SUGGESTIONS TO HELP CREATE A SHIFT IN ATTITUDE

The following are suggestions for improving your attitude in every aspect of your life.

Be willing to:

Feel the way you are feeling and not fight it, even if you are depressed. Simply let yourself be the way you are. This too shall pass.

Know that everything works out for your highest good and the highest good for all.

Be aware of your infinite and immortal life. Nothing dies in the universe; energy simply changes form.

Get exercise by dancing, walking, jumping on a trampoline, or whatever you enjoy.

Love yourself, your personality, your past, your body, and everything about you.

Do the things that are fun and play at things that bring you great pleasure and satisfaction.

Have flowers and beauty around you. Create a sanctuary within your home that reflects back to you the beauty, harmony, and perfection of yourself and the universe.

Know you are one with the All. You are the All and the Everything and within every cell of your body is the blueprint of life.

Ask for what you want from both your higher self and from those around you.

Be responsible for creating every aspect of your life and find the value and good purpose in everything. Always win! Winning means to always be good to you. You are the gift and you are the treasure.

Acknowledge yourself, as well as others, just for being. Instead of being aware only of mistakes, notice in yourself and others every little tiny wonderful thing and praise, praise, praise.

Do what pleases you and what brings you excitement and fulfillment.

Be outrageously yourself under any and all circumstances.

Start over each moment by releasing the past and beginning again, as you desire to be in this moment.

Bring humor into your life.

Live in this moment! Be here now!

These guidelines will give you something to work with to perceive the happenings in your life as gifts, treasures, blessings, and lessons you can use immediately to effect the changes you desire.

AN ADDITIONAL KEY

Here is an added key to the Golden Age of actualized and realized Goddesses and Gods. Watch for the signs and validations by allowing your mirror, your reflection to expand to include all of life. Birds, insects, wind, rain, clouds, animals, other people, phone calls, bells ringing, chills in your body, feelings, voices, and events are all parts of the whole. Pay attention to the obvious.

Life is you experiencing yourself as one song, one cosmic orgasm after another into forever. It is happening now and you are right in the middle of it. Enjoy!

EXERCISES

Attitude is everything—it becomes the carpet upon which you walk, the fragrance you breathe, the music you hear, and the body in which you travel. Take a few minutes and contemplate these questions.

1. Who is it that can push your buttons and control your attitudes?

2. What person or situation makes you forget to love yourself?

3. Take out your journal or a piece of paper and jot down what first comes to you as you read

these statements. How do you feel, what do you say, and how do you react when you hear them?

"Well, you're a woman! What do you expect?"

"My, you've gained weight!"

"Look at that beautiful, hard body!"

"She is so young and beautiful!"

"You'd better exercise or look out!"

"So, you're having another birthday! Getting older, huh!?"

"He left her for a younger woman."

"You and your happy face make me ill."

"You have to have more money. You just don't have enough!"

"Why don't you get a real job and quit playing around?"

"You don't create your life. What about people who are starving and bums on the street?"

"I'm disappointed in you."

"Are you going to let them treat you that way?"

"You can't do that. It will never work!"

"Who do you think you are anyway!?"

"You're crazy! Shut up! I'm sick of your talking!"

"It's all your fault! You didn't give enough."

This is not meant to upset you. It is to assist you in realizing that each of these statements may challenge what you say you truly believe. New beliefs are fragile, but old, fear-ridden beliefs have become solid through reinforcement. But nothing is inevitable or has to continue. We are freed in a moment simply by investigating a feeling, body sensation, need, or desire and reframing that aspect of our life.

4. List five to ten events that you have labeled bad, wrong, devastating, unfair, traumatic, or miserable. For each event list at least five lessons and gifts that have come to you as a result of that experience. If applicable, discover the connection between the event and a belief or attitude. Has the event proven or disproven your belief or expectation?

5. Have you allowed any man or woman to convince you that you were not sensual, feminine, or passionate? If you have, who was it? Why did you make that person greater than yourself? Who actually wasn't sensual and passionate? Who is in charge of your body and your emotions?

6. What is the number-one issue keeping you from being completely happy and feeling glorious about yourself and your life? Train yourself to imagine yourself without this problem or any similar problem.

7. Train yourself moment by moment to feel happy, peaceful, and relaxed for no reason at all.

Feelings create circumstances, just as do some hidden fears. Make everything okay, and feel the feelings of joy, bliss, ecstasy, and love. Get in the habit of being happy for no particular reason at all.

8. Feelings create situations; they produce a magnetic field of energy that attracts to you circumstances that produce more of the same feelings. What feelings do you want to feel? Recall a time when you felt them, remember how you felt then, and feel that again. Increase the feeling and have the thought that corresponds and you have an attitude. Practice feeling the way you like without a reason. The more you feel these feelings the more you effect a change in your nervous system.

AFFIRMATIONS

1. I, _____, am creating my life now to be far more beautiful, loving, and glorious than I could ever imagine.

2. Everything works for me to bring me into more awareness, love, ecstasy, and unlimitedness.

3. I, _____, am happy with my life and all things.

4. My attitude is uplifting to myself and others around me.

5. I, _____, live in this moment, now.

6. I, _____, am one with all there is.

CHAPTER 9

Let Yourself Prosper and Be Wealthy

IMAGINE WHAT YOU WOULD DO WITH A LIMITLESS SUP-
ply of money flowing in to use in any way you
choose! Have some fun and write down how you
would spend it on yourself, others, the environment, animals, nature, and so on. Don't think about
how you would make the money, just have the joy
of jotting down whatever comes to your mind. List
what you want in the areas of business, health, relationships, finance, life-style, and quality of existence. Brainstorming, fantasizing, imagining, and
"blue sky" thinking allows you to expand and begin
to entertain new possibilities.

Money and all else will come to us women quickly
because we are slightly closer to our creative selves.

What is needed is the action, the follow-through that allows us to ground our vision in the world. Action is what you will need to master to bring balance. There are three problems and each is solvable. A "problem" in this instance is defined as the result of cross-purposes, at least two opposing ideas or beliefs that keep you stuck on hold. The first problem is that you believe being wealthy is not possible for you. The second is that money is in limited supply. The third problem is that it is somehow wrong to have what you want.

My personal desire is that all people have a limitless supply of wealth flowing into their lives by doing what they love as a service or product for others. Something for nothing does not exist. There is always a trade of some kind. Sometimes it is the simple joy of sharing and sometimes the challenge of receiving.

Wealth is an attitude of profound trust in oneself and the Goddess. It is a way of framing one's life from an unobstructed and limitless point of view. It opens your mind up to the vastness of space, space being unlimited potential.

A wealthy person always experiences the feeling of having enough no matter what material possessions he or she owns. A wealthy woman can be "broke" but never poor. Wealth is a feeling one has when one is connected to the vastness of life. "Not enough" is a belief in scarcity. "Not enough" is an extension of a person's belief that *she* is not enough. Impoverished people believe they are limited and this blocks their self-expression. Poor people think money and material possessions will solve their problems. The rich know that money won't solve anything except a money problem. "Enough" is a statement of satisfaction and fullness in each moment. With love and wealth as your foundation, you are virtually limitless in your potential to be all that you can be. You are limitless in your ability to express your innermost desires, gifts, and talents. Without love and a profound sense of the infinite, your natural resources within you will struggle to survive. It is time to put survival behind and step into creation. Creation is a constant state of birth and death.

Our earth is a classroom for advanced souls to discover and actualize their innate ability to create. Our earth is also a garden in which we as spiritual and celestial beings can enjoy and discover ourselves in the emotional and physical realms.

As a female, you are pure emotion. You are the Creatress in all her glory. You are the feeling, love, desire, and compassion of life itself. Your male self is your ideas, doingness, action, and intellect. One without the other is like a ship without a destination or like a destination but no way to get there.

I now feel prosperity is absolutely essential to anyone who desires to revel in and master this life and make a positive loving difference in this world. I've created an eleven-step prosperity plan that includes all that I now know on the subject, yet these steps may change in the future as my thoughts evolve. Nothing is static. I used to believe that there was a destination or a final outcome. Now I feel that all is ongoing.

In my earlier teachings on prosperity as one aspect of a person's life, I had neglected to serve the earth. Just as so many others, I had forgotten the Mother. We live on Mother Earth. She cares for us. Our bodies are made of her, but we have forgotten her and thus ourselves. Without a healthy environment we cannot exist and play our games. We tend to take Mother Earth for granted and fail to recognize her love and generosity. She gives us a stage, a playground, and a garden in which to live our dreams. All of life is a partnership.

Even if we've acquired that automobile, that great apartment for the perfect amount of money, and the closest parking space, we have forgotten the obvious. Without a healthy ecology it won't matter how much we acquire. Everything else has no importance!

I've loved nature ever since I can remember. I have always thought it was terrible that we were polluting our environment, our minds, and our bodies but really didn't feel there was much I could do. So I worried, blamed "others," and ignored it. Maybe the problem would take care of itself.

When I left my television ministry, I ran back to nature to be healed. I had been almost completely immersed in the urban world and it was time to return to nature. I needed to remember my roots in the earth and live once again in simplicity and balance. A mountain stream, the smell of the sticky pitch on a pine tree, and the sound of the wind through the leaves had been part of my childhood and had given me comfort, peace, vitality, and a sense of deep, inner fulfillment. I longed for nature once again and so we first moved to the tropical island of Maui. Many people say that Maui is what is left of the ancient land of Lemuria.

Maui, the heart chakra or energy center of our earth, warm, lush, green, and delicious, bathed me in her waters, lulled me to sleep at night, and breathed love and acceptance into my being and my body. From Maui we moved to the deep woods of the Pacific Northwest, into the silence of the Mother and nature.

Now is the time for us to awaken to both our bodies and the earth as ourselves and no longer pollute these most valuable aspects of ourselves. We are co-creators with the Creator of the universe, each other, and nature and it is time for us to awaken to who we are and to what is possible for all of us if we work in harmony.

Money and power have been used to fulfill ego needs. The only problem with using money, power, and things to fulfill oneself is that they never do. Unfortunately, we destroy ourselves, others, and nature in the process. Greed has become a disease and the starving people and the battered children are what it leaves behind. Ego needs to me are the feelings of lack, pain, loss, fear, and separation that we believe others cause, that we feel powerless over. We've tried to get rid of those "yuck" feelings by being smarter, richer, prettier, stronger, and more powerful than others. We've raped the land, stockpiled useless weapons, and abused our bodies; we've raged, criticized, judged, imprisoned, shunned, killed, starved, and violated all to rid ourselves of our fears. All it has done is perpetuate them. We've tried to "have" in order to "be." Simply "be." Have what you want, do what you want, and be what you want. Each is separate. Money, sex, power, and physical things do not fulfill emotional needs or determine my self-worth or self-esteem.

"I am not enough," "I am not good enough," and "I don't have enough" are the beliefs that keep us stuck in "scare-city" and out of the land of ENOUGH. Plenty-land is the place where we can all live, share, play, and love each other.

Fear-based beliefs keep us tied to greed, anger, resentment, guilt and all sorts of miserable feelings, thoughts, actions, and conditions. Women, in giving their power away to others, have reinforced their beliefs in scarcity and powerlessness. Powerless people can only complain, nag, cry, manipulate, and feel hopeless, depressed, and angry. Women have been taught that all good and bad comes from "him." When life isn't wonderful, women feel hurt and angry. "She" is immobilized because, "if she is powerful, she will be alone." "He" is afraid that "she" will wake up, remember who "she" is and he will lose his power. It is time for these games to be over and new ones to begin.

As women we've created a double bind. "If I am powerful, rich, intelligent, and capable, I'll be alone. What man would want to be with me?" We've created the belief that being powerful, capable, and wealthy will take away from us what we really want—love, touching, tenderness, and intimacy. We've believed that love and power don't go together and we have to choose one or the other. Actually they are two sides of the same coin. You can't have one without the other. Loving yourself and being immersed fully in your own power is an awesome twosome.

STEP ONE: KNOW THAT THE SUPPLY IS LIMITLESS AND INFINITE

Supply is directly associated with love. What does love have to do with wealth? Everything! Love is the fabric, the vibration, the frequency that we call life. All of life is love and love is who and what we are. When you know that you are love and that you are worth loving, you will know that you deserve to be, do, and have whatever you desire. There is no scarcity of love. There is no scarcity of supply of whatever you need.

There is no scarcity of energy, yet forms of energy may be temporarily depleted if we don't recreate them. Love is something that disappears only when you stop feeling it. Energy is something that stops when you stop expressing and using it. It doesn't really disappear. It only seems that way because you've chosen not to feel it. Love is wealth and wealth is love. Wealth is a word used to describe what is available to you for your use. Everything is first that which is without form. It is energy before it becomes a physical object or circumstance that we measure and call reality. The energy realms we'll call ethereal, celestial, imagination, vision, dreams, desires, revelations, inspirations, ideas, thoughts, and knowing. There is no shortage of ideas. You can test this by asking people what they think about something in particular. The amazing thing is they will each tell you something different. There is no shortage of opinions!

Loving yourself, loving life, and being excited by your ideas and dreams is a wonder-filled way to live. Sometimes without knowing it, we let people rob us of our dreams, visions, and self-love. The subtle realms of dreams, thought, feelings, and visions are your connection with your higher levels of self and the All. This is where you are fed, guided, and directed as to your function and purpose. When you let others kill your ideas and dreams, you die a slow death. There is physical violence and abuse to oneself, nature, and others. There is also a greater violence—the invalidation of oneself, one's truth, and one's visions.

I used to believe that people wanted to stop me and, more importantly, that they could actually prevent me from being, doing, and having what I desired. I learned to hide my dreams and I learned to negate myself and my wisdom. I did such a good job of hiding that I lost myself and couldn't find my true desires, intentions, and dreams.

Last night I sat down at my piano to sing. As I sang, my dream of being a singer came back to me.

I was angry at others for what I imagined they had done to me. What I had done was give others the power to make my dreams come true or not come true and the power to make me worth loving or not. Of course, that can't work.

I was embarrassed by what I wanted and I felt that others would laugh at me. I was afraid they would think, "Who do you think you are?" or "You are too old," or "You aren't good enough," or "You are a woman. Forget it!" I believed that entertainers weren't noble enough, so to be noble, sophisticated, and worthy of respect, I stopped singing.

There isn't a thing wrong with people having any opinion of you they want to have. Their thoughts have nothing to do with you or with your life. Only your thoughts affect you. Rediscovering the love that you are is the key to reawakening to the dreams that you have hidden within yourself and making them realities, here and now.

Learn to think, feel, talk, and act from a limitless supply of whatever you want or need and the manifestations of love. Feel yourself immersed in ecstasy and the colors, fragrances, sounds, and feelings of love. "Whatever the question, love is the answer." I've found this to be true in my life. If we could love ourselves enough, we would feel ourselves as one with all that is now and forever.

Love is worthiness. Love is happiness. Love is ideas. Love is self-trust. Love is deserving. Love is gratitude. Love is enough. Love is all there is and more and you are love. You are all that is, was, or shall ever be. Think, speak, feel, be, act, and know this NOW!

Meditate by sitting quietly, alone, with your eyes closed. Breathe deeply and rhythmically as you pay attention to your breath and how your body feels when you breathe. Get a sense of yourself as being the breath flowing in and flowing out. Feel your body and your essence as the One that is all of life. The vastness of space and life is the essence of you and this is what you are drawing from for whatever you need, just as you draw in a breath when you need air. Just as with breathing, there is a gentle rhythm to life.

If you sit back and wait nothing happens. If you force, push, and shove, nothing happens. Balance is having your feminine and masculine energy flowing together in harmony and oneness with the All. This is spiritual networking operating at its most efficient. "I am one with the Infinite Wonder of it all." "I am guided by the loving essence of the Divine One that I am." "We are moved and directed by the loving will of the Creator." These are some beautiful attitudes you can assume.

You are creating it and it is creating you. Co-creating is creation in a circle with no beginning and no end. It is ever-evolving.

There is nothing more wonderful than the feeling of being swept up in the loving arms of life and having nothing to worry about ever again. Last night after my sweetheart and I climbed into bed, we held each other and I allowed myself to feel all the bliss of love that I could. Because of our fear of being left, we deny ourselves the full feeling of the love, passion, joy, and happiness. I will no longer deny myself any part of myself and what is available, because I might lose. I've lost if I am not feeling and doing what is valuable to me. The sharing of this is what will bring every cell alive. I finally realized that full feeling was my gift to myself and by not feeling totally I was denying myself what I wanted. Know that what you desire, you already are.

STEP TWO: FOCUS YOUR ENERGY THROUGH DESIRE AND ACTION

Remember the nursery rhyme about wishing on a star? That was the first prayer that really worked for me. I'd go out at night to catch the first star. I may have been wishing on the planet Venus or perhaps even a spacecraft. Who knows? Whatever it was, I'd look up at that faint, twinkling light and with a dream in my heart ask for what I wanted. I always got it! Most of the time I asked that my folks not find out about something. Now that I look back the things I wanted to keep hidden were no big deal, but I sure thought they were at the time. I was such a people pleaser, I didn't want them to be angry or upset at me.

That first star was more real to me than what I was told in church. I wished on my star until I forgot how good it was to me and I went on to other things, such as praying to a specific Deity. Of course I did that so this Deity would find favor in me and keep me out of hell. The first time I had sex in the front seat of a Chevy, I had the thought before I took the plunge, "What if I go to hell?" My answer was, "So, I go to hell." I wanted to experience this before I die and I could die tomorrow.

Recently I bought a colorful child's book with the words of the Walt Disney song "When You Wish Upon a Star," written by Ned Washington, and recaptured the joy of my childhood star! I realized again that each of us decides just what it is that we want to experience. It is our choice! "If your heart is in your dreams, no request is too extreme." The key is to have your heart in your dreams. Your heart contains your fondest visions, ideals, and desires. You can actually feel your inner physical being become excited when you think about, plan for, and share your fondest visions and dreams with those who understand and accept you.

What gets you going? What fires up your motor? What gets your adrenaline going and your creativity and imagination pumping? What makes life worth living? The answer to all these is the joy that comes from loving oneself and all of life. You are joyful when you are playing the game full out.

What can prevent you from knowing what you want to create is your inability to believe that you can be, do, or have it or that it is even possible for anyone. You may also believe what you can imagine or want is wrong or bad. I've dealt with these issues before in another chapter. Use those processes and teachings to get beyond the limiting factor. Get yourself up with the eagles and out with the angels. "Angels fly because they take themselves lightly."

Now is the time to brainstorm. Come out of hiding and reinstate any forgotten dreams, ideals, or visions. In what ways could your dream of what you want to do serve, enrich, and empower others? Wealth is what comes to us in return for our contribution to others. Money flows to you in exchange for your goods and services that are of value to others.

Knowing what you want, where you want to go, what you want to do, and what you want to have focuses your limitless supply. When we give space a form we can define it as something. Everything is all made of energy and thin air. What else is there? This planet is hanging in thin air. Space is the medium in which we live, move, and have. Knowing what you want is a continual, ongoing, flowing experience. What you have is what you wanted. What you have is what you believe. Being responsible for turning your dreams into realities is a process of focusing and of taking the steps to do it. Simply create your plan and know precisely the results you want. Ask the Goddess for assistance and to know exactly what you want. Be committed to that and do it. Know that you and the entire universe are creating together.

The moment you ask for help, help is there. Learn to ask specifically for what you desire. Each moment everything is moving, evolving, and changing. What worked yesterday may not be working today. Go with the flow and feel your divine connection with the loving Creator of the light. Miracles, surprises, gifts, and blessings flow to you from the infinite oneness of our love.

Divine guidance comes when you ask for help. Ask for what it is you are to do as your destiny. The answer is always obvious. It is whatever feels right, whatever brings you excitement, joy, happiness, and passion.

Last night I spent my first night alone in our log house in the middle of the woods. No one was around but the animals and the sounds of absolute darkness. When I felt little fear thoughts bubble to the surface, I'd choose to release them and stay in peace, trust, and joy. I had the powerful realization that I am alone and yet I am never alone. I have always been alone with the universe. I am always taken care of, always safe, always loved even if I am alone in the middle of the wilderness. At first I was a little frightened at the realization, "If it is to be, it is up to me." Then I was overcome with a profound sense of love, safety, and bliss. I am never alone and will never be alone. It is up to me and the Goddess. What a team!

My whole life is in front of me simply awaiting my command, my will, my commitment, my love, my energy, my persistence, and my action. You can sit and hope and wait all you want for someone to discover you and make your dreams come true, or you can get up and get going with the trust that you will be supported by the full energy of creation. Focus your energy by creating your want list. Make a treasure map. Use your manifestation basket or fill out the form at the end of the chapter. Set achievement dates and do what it takes to get there. There are no secrets. You can find a way to do anything you want.

STEP THREE: DO WHAT YOU LOVE WITH EXCELLENCE AND MONEY WILL FOLLOW

If you settle for doing what you hate just to have a job or other people's approval, that is all you will end up with. When you step into the river of life, hang on for the ride because it is awesome.

This third point in my prosperity plan is so simple, yet it is the most difficult to practice. We've received very little support even as children for doing what we love. We've been told to get a "good" job. We've been counseled by experts who tell us the future of business and how we should fit ourselves into the job market. Rarely have we been told to simply do what we love to do and *that* is our career. If you keep your energy focused on doing your business and serving others, the money will be there.

Insanity is a process of self-invalidation whereby we have succumbed to the thoughts and beliefs of others that there is something wrong with us. To avoid being hurt by them, we go deeper within our own fantasy world and lose touch with others. You can also give so much of yourself and your power to people and things "out there" that you lose your identity. Sanity is a balance of the two. Sanity is one's gift to oneself of self-trust and self-validation. By following your bliss, you step into the "right" career out of self-trust and self-validation.

There are many ways to generate money. Why do something that isn't a joy for you to do? I had my share of jobs where I was bored and unchallenged. The best thing about that experience was that I discovered it was a waste to be unchallenged. As you write down some ideas that come to you about what you love to do, also look to see how it will fill a need others and society have.

Who you are is so awesome that you can only begin to tap into yourself and the resources available to you by putting yourself fully into your creative experience. We all have the potential to be geniuses if we go for our dream with all the gusto we can muster. In the process we won't have time to be fearful and warlike.

We've been told, "You can't make a living doing that!" We've all heard or said, "You can't do that. Why don't you get a real job?" Children are naturally curious and experimental in their approach to life, qualities that would continue if they were not discouraged. The child in us is what loves to create, design, play, express, dance, and sing. This childlike ability tunes us into the genius channel and the frequency band of divine inspiration. The stops, the "shoulds," "ought-to's," and "have-to's" repress that most important part of our lives. Now that I've found the singer in me, I am producing my own music tape. Terry Cole-Whittaker sings her favorite love songs for you! I don't have to wait to be discovered and neither do you. With modern technology, you can sometimes inexpensively live your dreams and serve others through your work.

Growing up for me meant looking forward to the roles and professions normally reserved for women—wife, mother, secretary, teacher, nurse, and so on. Although women contribute much in these roles and I've loved being a mother and a teacher, I just didn't like the few choices offered me as a woman. I felt I had just as much right as any male to live my life as I choose. This thought made waves, upset apple carts, and has presented a great many people with "opportunities for growth." But it isn't just women who have had difficulty in claiming their power. Men had little slots to fill also. The truth is none of us fits into a box because we are limitless in spirit and therefore in a continual state of movement, exploration, testing, evaluating, expanding, and contracting. Instead of asking children, "What do you want to be when you grow up?" ask them, "What do you want to do?"

We have become addicted to security, attention, approval, status, money, clothes, makeup, and bodies instead of remembering who we are and what it is we want to do, accomplish, and be.

It is like the child who does everything for attention and approval. Nothing is done purely as an extension of who the child is but for a response from others. Money, attention, praise, and "perks" are the future substitutes for Mommy and Daddy's attention. Less and less is done for the pure joy of doing it. Put your attention on the career that interests you. Make it up! It is what you came here to do! When you pinpoint your objectives, you focus an energy that is incredibly powerful.

Because you love what you do, do it with excellence. Serve your customers or clients at the highest level at which you are capable. Take some time and evaluate the way you do business or the way in which you present your talents, products, or services. Is what you offer the best or is it sloppy, uncaring, irresponsible, shoddy, or cheap? You don't have to circulate a lot of money to upgrade the quality of your work or waste our natural resources in ridiculous packaging. You do need to present quality if you are to flourish. Why fill the world with junk? Quality is satisfaction.

Whatever you do, do it because you want to. Forget about success and failure. They are both abstracts or evaluations based on results. Quality and excellence build good feelings inside of you. They are nothing more than that. The most difficult and wonderful thing I can imagine would be for all of us to drop our motives for doing anything and simply do or not do it because that is what we want! Sharing yourself is absolutely necessary.

Money can be a great indicator of whether or not you are doing what you love and whether you are willing to flourish. If you don't have enough money it is because you don't want it. You are not doing what you love. You are giving more than you are receiving. You desire to receive more than you give.

You feel guilty for having. You are angry and resentful or you are not networking with people who are committed to your projects. Money and sex gives you instant feedback on where you are and where you are not. I am not judging more money as being intrinsically better or more sex as being better than less sex. I am just saying it is an exact mirror. Money follows after you when you leave a trail of personal integrity, of being true to yourself, and of offering your gifts on a silver platter.

STEP FOUR: COMMIT TO YOUR PROJECTS AND DREAMS

Commitment is the step you take into your life and it is the door you close to an alternative plan for escape. Before you commit there is hesitancy, confusion, and vacillation. What you do is hope, wait, fear, doubt, avoid and do everything else but commit. But it is the *doing* that gets it done. It is true we don't have to do anything but you do need to *do* something. Without doing, life is boring and all you'd need to be is a brain, not a body. Doing is the fun! When you are committed to what you do, you are absorbed by your passion.

You can be committed because it is a key to success and you want to "succeed," or you can be committed because that is what you are. Commitment means to me a process whereby you focus your energy without any leaks or opposing forces. All your energy becomes directed as you become an energy vortex. Support then comes from all directions.

Commitment requires that you take a step into a reality of "go for it, do it, be it, and have it." This reality has no signs of certainty before you take the step. By committing you have said, "Yes, this is what I want and this is where I am going. I ask that the universe get behind me and together we create this happening beautifully."

I've noticed that right before I am ready to take a step from the world of "I'll wait and see what happens or if . . ." into the world of "Yes, I'm going in the game 100 percent, so let's go!" there are petty, fear-filled thoughts. Without commitment there is a tremendous waste or leakage of energy because you are in opposition to yourself. You want to go anywhere you are headed but you are afraid that you will lose, be hurt, or do something wrong. Questions such as, "How will it happen? Where will I get the money? What will people think? If I do, will I lose this or that?" may plague you.

The fear of being stuck in a relationship or in your creation can keep you from fulfilling your deepest desires. The truth is that nothing truly wonderful can happen for you unless you are fully open to it, ready for it, and willing for it to happen. Keep stepping into the love light and leave fear behind.

When I started to write this book, I decided that I didn't want any help in writing except from my wonderful publishers, Harper & Row. I wanted to write every word and to let what I really felt spring forth onto the paper. For a while I fluctuated. "Will the book be good enough? Do I have anything to say? Will my publisher like it? Will I sound dogmatic, fanatic . . . ?" Who knows? I made a commitment to do my very best and go for it 100 percent. Imagine how excited I was when my editor at Harper & Row wrote me a letter upon receiving the first draft saying that she was happy with what I was writing. She gave me great encouragement. That, along with my unrelenting commitment to keep writing through all sorts of interruptions, pushed me through into the flow of creativity.

Writing can be lonely work, but I've found a way to write that keeps me in the center of what is happening. I write in the loft of our log house. It is like a crow's nest or an ivory tower from which I can have an overview of our land, be involved with what is happening in the house, and still be writing the book. I've found a way to live that and fulfill my needs.

The difference between those who just dream and those who make their dreams come true is just that. You make a cake by first deciding to make a cake. If you doubt you can do it or are indecisive about it, you don't bake it. You have to decide, commit, and then do it. You first gather the ingredients and combine them. Next you put it in the oven, bake it, take it out, frost it, and EAT it. That is the cycle of action. First there is the thought or vision. Second is the decision to do it or not. Look ahead and decide, "Is this something I would enjoy, learn from, get value from, and would it make a wonderful difference in people's lives and the harmony and balance of nature?" If yes, even if you have no idea of how, then commit. "Will I fail? Will I be thought a fool? Will others judge me? Will my parents be upset? Will I make any money? Will I be hurt?" are all thoughts that can spring forth from your mind. "Peace to you or to heaven with you!"

In your commitment there will be issues to address on your path of mastery. Don't be afraid of them. Welcome them with open arms, as they are gifts in disguise. Treat them as beautiful opportunities and treasures. Keep going even if you need some time out or a few rest periods. Time out is important for meditation, contemplation, strategizing, and reevaluation. Time is a concept whose proof of existence is only in the material realm.

Earth is a place of demonstration where we can put into practice our beliefs, thoughts, and concepts in a physical experiential framework. I feel that earth is a training ground for creators, for those who are ready to remember and know who they are. It is a place to demonstrate knowledge, wisdom, and a connection to the Divine Mother, the creator of life, and the Divine Father, her consort. Life on earth is where you realize that, "If it is to be, it is up to me!"

I'd say that just about all of my illusions have fallen away or are disintegrating right now. Everything and everyone that I ever believed was responsible for my life in any way I now realize were not even involved. It has been me and the universe as one co-creative partnership all along. You can realize this and it usually comes upon you in the dark of the night as you lie down to go to sleep. It can feel terrifying or freeing.

The terror comes from, "Poor me, I'm helpless. Someone help me. I can't do it and I am powerless over my life." The freedom and excitement come from, "Well, I've gotten this far on my own. I must be a remarkable creature. My future is wide open. I think I'll go for it."

Whatever you are committed to is what you will generate and produce. You don't have a choice about life as I see it. You are alive and will always be so. Your choice is everything else. Take a little time and look at what you desire and your planet. Make your commitment and go for it! The moment you give your full commitment, Providence moves in your direction and miracles and magic become your partners.

STEP FIVE: RELEASE THE HURT OF SHATTERED DREAMS

I don't feel that there is anyone who hasn't been hurt by money or the lack of it. Money and its symbols can be a nightmare. Prisons are filled with people who have committed crimes for money. Women are in prison mostly for love, for they loved men who were committing crimes. The men committed crimes for money; they thought money, sex, drugs, or violence would free them from their pain. Money, jewels, metals, cars, and clothes are just stuff and nothing more. They mean what we say they mean. We need to change the meanings if we are to set ourselves free.

Love and money are neither equal nor inter-changeable. You cannot get one with the other. It is easy to have money and no love, or love but no money. You can respect yourself whether you have money or not. You know you can be happy and poor and be happy and rich. Feelings like happiness and respect have no direct relationship to material things.

I was angry at my father for not being rich be-cause I thought that would have made me more popular, more worthy and valuable. It took me a long time to realize how ridiculous that thought was. My father was a wonderful father. He was probably a lousy husband, but he was a loving fa-ther who was there in my life consistently after I turned seven.

We have shattered dreams that we believe were caused by our not having enough money or by our family and loved ones not providing for us as we wanted to be provided for. "Old money" is a belief system that invalidates anyone whose ancestors didn't leave them money. They are the American royalty. "New money" people are looked down upon and "no money" people are considered to be of little value.

Dreams have been shattered because of too much money also. If you and I can get really clear about money and what it is and what it isn't, then life be-comes our playground once again, not a sentence to be endured. Survival is not a purpose for living. Thriving and flourishing is.

Take some time to contemplate your life and see if you have any heartbreak, shattered dreams, hurt, or pain having to do with money and things. Did anyone ever cry because you had more? Have you put yourself down because others had more money than you? Have you blended self-worth and money? Was there ever a time when your asking for money hurt someone? Who yelled at you because of money? Were people fighting over money in your life? Did anyone tell you that they couldn't afford to keep you? Have you ever been used for money and things? Have you stolen or been stolen from?

These events have affected every decision we have ever made. These thoughts are just a few examples of potential heartache because of money.

The main blocks to having what you want are ideas like the following:

I'm not worthy and deserving of what I want.
I'm not good enough.
It is wrong for me to be rich, happy, loved, healthy, and free.
If I'm rich, my mother and father will be upset.
I can't have what I want. If I have what I want, I'll lose the love of others.
No one will love me for myself.
If I am powerful, men won't want me and I will be alone.
There isn't enough money for everyone.

No matter what I do, I can't get ahead or do enough.

There's not enough time, love, money, ideas, energy, or life.

If I am rich, men and women will use me to get my money.

Men are supposed to take care of me because I can't. If I do, they won't feel needed and I'll end up alone.

These thoughts, if believed, cause you to set up your life and your relationships to prove you are right. "Well, I am right again!" "Poor me, it will always be this way. It would be best if I ignored it, found a new partner, and pretended that it will be different next time." Hopelessness then follows hope and the trail of shattered dreams continues.

Blockages, countercreation, and self-sabotage are those negative thoughts that we believe to be true that get proven over and over in our lives. They may feel as if they are inevitable and as solid as laws. No. They are just habits that continue to get reinforced. Let yourself feel your grief and then change the meaning. None of it meant anything. You are the meaning. You are the value. If others can't see that, it is because they also have shattered dreams.

You simply have to like the feeling of wealth, love, and power more than feeling poor, wretched, unloved, and weak. We don't give our power away without cause. We never have. We have traded it for love. We believe we have to, that we will not be loved any other way. This belief is then proven by the conditions and events of our lives. Just stop and see what happens—you'll never know if you are loved for yourself alone until you only offer yourself and nothing more.

Give yourself permission to feel and have all that is dear to you without compromise. Scary? We know the games we play.

Ultimately, you have to make it okay to be rich or poor, beautiful or ugly, powerful or weak, loving or not, or whatever else you desire to be. It doesn't mean anything; it just is. Feel it. Be it in every cell of your body and every aspect of your personality. *Be* the feeling of self-worth and value. When you feel it, act as if you already are that. You can't use money to heal you or money to prevent hurt. Learn to use money for what it was created for—a system of exchange of service for service. It is the energy to do what you love, your work. Use your money to create a life-style you desire; plant and grow your garden.

Feel how you would want to use your money and then use it that way. Use it to take care of your business, invest in your future, and take care of your physical needs. Money can be wonder-filled in the hands of those who have released the nightmare and are living the dream. Be wealthy always. Do it not to avoid the nightmare, but to create what you desire.

We create our dreams by feeling and doing. Having looks like the objective, but feeling and doing are the fun and true objectives. Having is the result.

Ever notice that once you have attained your goal, you want something else? We can also enjoy the having because the having reflects back to us the journey and what we became in the process. Feel as if you already have it and you will never be without.

STEP SIX: SUPPORT YOURSELF ON ALL LEVELS

This book is about support. Whatever you have chosen to become or whatever you want to do and have is up to you and your relationship with the universe as a co-creative support system. Wealth is definitely an attitude, a habit. Change your habits and you change your life. Don't try to "get rid of" old habits. Simply create new ones by each thought you think, each word you speak, and each action you take. Create a loving support system of people, lifestyles, thoughts, beliefs, attitudes, and actions.

Visualize yourself as you desire to be. Visualize yourself living as you desire. See, taste, feel, and smell your co-creations. Asking opens the door and you step into the next adventure. You access the computer of the universe through request and it responds exactly as you've asked. (When I make a request of the universe, I always add, "for the highest and most loving, gentle good for all.") See the end result in detail. Then ask, "What do I need to do to have this happen in harmony with the divine will of love?" Write whatever comes to you and then do it.

Create a support team of others who are sharing of their talents and abilities with love and integrity, commitment and excellence. Everyone is equally as powerful as we are, and synergy and networking are much more powerful than competition and disparity.

Find ways to take care of yourself and your precious, Goddess body. Deep massage is a wonderful way to release old patterns, emotions, and experiences that are recorded in your body. If your body has pain, it is emotional pain you've stored. There are wonderful body tools that help you massage yourself wherever you go. The result is allowing yourself to have as much pleasure as you desire by getting deep into every cell of your body and releasing the stored up energy of past hurts, genetic programming, and soul memory. You are a whole, living organism, so everything affects everything else. Reprogram your body for comfort, pleasure, and health as you reprogram your thoughts, feelings, visions, and actions. Some of our conflict has deep roots. Uproot the old in your body, emotions, and beliefs by recognizing it, breathing it out and breathing in the new.

We must reprogram the way we live and every aspect of our lives if we are to survive and have a planet that is fit to inhabit. Little by little, we programmed ourselves into toxic waste dumps. Now, little by little, we must program ourselves into being loving, caring, healthy, happy, wealthy, and responsible divine beings, co-creating paradise, beauty, and heaven.

STEP SEVEN: LEARNING THE WIN/WIN PRINCIPLE

Life is contribution. Whatever you want to share give to yourself. Then you can give it away to others. Contribution is the act of sharing and only those who have can share. That is why those who have seem to have more, and those who don't have, have less. Those who desire love hold onto the love they have, fearing that they'll have no more. They shut themselves off from the flow. The flow moves through you, and if you believe in scarcity, you are choking the natural flow of the universe by holding on too tightly. You are either giving away too much or not enough. Giving away too much comes from the belief that it is not okay for you to have. Not sharing comes from the belief that what you have is in scarce supply and running out quickly.

Win/win is the same principle expressed in business. Participate with others who are committed to your winning as much as their own. Win/lose has been the way the world has worked. If someone wins, then someone else must lose. This is no longer acceptable because each of us is a precious being of love. Negotiations no longer need to be about who can get the best of whom. They can now be based on fairness and the level at which each person is contributing to the project, event, or relationship. No one needs to be cheated, nor do any need to deny themselves the fruit of their labor. Capitalism and socialism have taken polar opposite views. Neither works in its pure form. The clever outmaneuver the humble in a capitalistic society and the lazy drain production in a socialistic society. Money has become the ultimate, when in truth it is you and I and our evolution that is the purpose of life. Money is just energy in motion, serving us in our creations. Let's share our food. Let's share ourselves.

Prosperity is an attitude of plenty. Prosperity is a feeling of oneness with the ongoing flow of life. Open yourself to the flow by giving what you desire and by setting yourself up to receive. You receive by giving to yourself whatever you want. If it is respect, respect yourself, your wishes and dreams. If it is appreciation, then appreciate yourself and your creations.

When you negotiate in your business relationships, let each share what they want and find ways to meld each other's needs. In this new time, we cannot afford to pretend that it is not up to us to take care of ourselves.

It has been difficult for me to break the habit of being Mama, the big breast that feeds the world. To continue this is not satisfying and it is disempowering for everyone. Yes, I can nurture, and no, I don't need to create for others in order to keep them in my life. Men play big Daddy and women play big Mama to a mess of "helpless" kids, and the kids stay helpless. When one Mama and Daddy get tired of playing, another set of "parents" comes along and the "beat goes on." For the kids to gain their power and own the responsibility of creating their lives, they will have to stand on their own two feet. By taking care of others we delay maturity and promote weakness.

You need to treat money with love and respect for what it is: a vehicle that keeps the ball rolling. Money is not the purpose. It is a supportive energy. Money doesn't mean you are successful or not, just as your body size, shape, or gender does not add to or subtract value from you. Who you are as a person is your gift.

This one may take some time to practice. It is not about you or others being paid what you are "worth." You cannot equate self-worth and money. You are worth more than money. Money is paid for the value of what you do. If many people have the same skills that you have to offer, then your pay is less. If you have unique skills that are essential to what is happening, then you will be paid more. What appears to me to be happening is that the major portion of the money goes to those who take the greatest risks and are willing to hold their success or failure as their creation. Friendship and business are separate but can be found together. You are not paid nor do you need to pay for friendship; you are paid for a product or a service.

Giving and receiving represent inflow and outflow, the breath in and the breath out. As you exhale, the universe is inhaling. As you inhale, it is exhaling. Life works as a pump system just as your body pumps air in and out.

STEP EIGHT: MONEY KEEPS YOU AC-COUNTABLE

The eighth step can be the most difficult because it involves actually dealing with the medium of exchange itself: keeping records, paying bills and taxes, buying things, saving, investing, and so on. Below is a list of some of money's rules.

Money is an energy exchange. Without an energy exchange there is no money.

Money is an illusion. It is simply paper or metal backed by a promise (and sometimes hard assets) in which we must have confidence. Money won't buy you happiness. Knowing that you can always have what you want will.

Decide on how much money you need to have what you want.

Decide on a plan to produce income.

Record all inflow of money.

Direct all outflow of money. Use your money to make money.

Put 10 percent aside as savings and don't spend it unless it is a planned purchase of something that will generate more money for you. Keep the savings as a cushion upon which you never fall.

Contribute a tithe to something you support in this world, such as saving the whales, helping preschool education centers, cleaning up toxic waste sites, or your spiritual center.

Set limits on purchases and plan for what you need.

Spend less than you earn.

Be happy with what you have and where you are.

Make yourself, others, love, and nature more important than money. Use money. Don't let it use you.

Practice win/win business.

I'm sure your list can grow. Pay attention to your money and your records just so you know where you are. Then turn your attention to what you want to generate in regard to your career and the product or service you will contribute to the good of the all.

Be very clear about what money is and what it isn't. Learn to live in the worlds that have no money: worlds such as bliss, joy, fun, intuition, nature, love, peace, and the celestial and ethereal planes of existence. Don't let money interfere with these worlds. Don't intermix them. They are separate and should be enjoyed for their own intrinsic value. Put your attention on the value you are offering.

STEP NINE: CORRECT WHEN IN ERROR AND PERSIST!

We tend to give up too quickly. It is no big deal to make a mistake. In fact, if you are not making them, you are too comfortable! We don't like to feel uncomfortable. We've been programmed to fear both failure and success and so find ourselves stuck in neutral and fighting it. We think we will be punished if we get ahead and punished if we fall behind, and we are frustrated when we stay stuck. The key to the resolution of this conflict is to transcend any and all previous input that teaches us to be uncomfortable with other people's reactions to who we are, what we do, and what we have. I empowered myself to live my dream and be prosperous by doing everything I wanted regardless of others' reactions.

It is natural to make "mistakes." "Mistakes" are essential to discovery and learning of any kind. We have to be free to experiment, explore, discover, and invent. We've been taught to memorize and parrot the beliefs and values of others to the degree we have lost our own adventuresome spirit. Too much pressure to conform and we quit, lay low, and hide.

The cover of *Newsweek* this week has a picture of the space shuttle *Discovery* with the words "To Dare Again!" in bold letters. "Yes," I said to myself, "yes!" We must dare again or die. The gutters are filled with gentle, sensitive people who couldn't handle the apparent rejection. They took it personally when in actuality it had nothing to do with them. It had everything to do with the conditioning of the people who were doing the criticizing. No one is to blame, and if we are to flourish and come into our own as the geniuses we are, we need to move on. Learn the lessons and continue.

What I used to do when I made a mistake was to stop everything, feel terrible, be embarrassed, apologize profusely, and punish myself. This created the "stop and go" jerk effect I mentioned earlier with reference to my skiing technique. Full speed ahead until the slightest problem came up. Then I would turn 180 degrees and run away with my tail between my legs. I must have brought this programming with me into this lifetime because I don't recall my family or even teachers being hard on me, unless the unspoken rules of the family's games did the programming very subtly and deeply.

I wanted approval so much that the slightest disapproval sent me into guilt, embarrassment, hiding, and self-judgment. When I was on my weekly television show I would receive letters of appreciation, which were wonderful. The critical letters really got to me though. I felt I could never do it right—which was true if I was there to please everyone, indeed anyone else, but me.

Self-defeat is the only defeat! Yes, some of our "mistakes" have bigger consequences than others, but that is how we needed to learn those particular lessons in our evolution and journey of discovery.

Persistence is your continued movement toward your objective. Correction is what you do when you discover that your action or inaction did not achieve your desired goal. It is up to you to decide what your desired goal is to be. If you have decided to experience yourself as love that is consistent and without limits and you are not feeling consistent, unlimited love, you are off course somewhere. Don't hate yourself. Instead, acknowledge yourself for participating and for catching yourself (or creating someone else to catch you) as being off your chosen path. Get back on track as soon as possible without any self-condemnation. This does not mean to be careless or uncaring. It means to focus on what you want, love yourself for being human, and persist.

This point has been a major challenge for me because I have judged myself so harshly, comparing myself with others and never being quite good enough or sometimes being too much. Being "just right" was something that eluded me. But I now know the secret of being just right—it is when we patiently, patiently let ourselves and others be exactly as we are and at the same time stay committed to excellence, quality, and the best that we can be, do, and have. The best means being able to share our talents, abilities, and self in such a way as to experience our creativity as total and free from suppression.

All we can do is shrug our shoulders, shake off the judgment that mistakes are "bad," and move on to the next step. Dare again to hold your head high, be proud of yourself, and step into your vision. If you have money problems, get back to basics. Make your correction in your priorities and continue walking toward your vision.

STEP TEN: TAKE CARE OF WHAT YOU HAVE AND LIVE IN A STATE OF GRATITUDE

We have lived in a throwaway society that doesn't appreciate itself, what we have, who we are, or even life. Life has become a struggle, something to bear rather than a gift and a wonder. What you don't appreciate disappears. What you hate can only give back hate. What you love blesses you. Being a caretaker means taking care of ourselves, our bodies, our natural resources, our animals, plants, our possessions, our relationships, and our talents.

The belief of "I'm not enough" causes us to be unsatisfied with everything. It keeps us negating what we do, trashing what we have and going for more, better, and different in all the wrong ways. We're never satisfied with where we are. "It" (be it greener pastures or more money) is always over *there*, never *here*. Living in a constant state of gratitude and appreciation transforms our daily existence into an adventure full of treasures and surprises. Count your blessings and let your heart and soul be full of the richness of your being alive. Wealth is everywhere in your life.

Take care of your clothes, your car, your home, and all of your material things. Make do with what you have unless it can't be fixed or repaired. We've been trained to throw everything away. When the thing didn't fill the void, the longing inside that we had hoped it would fill, we try to find something else that might.

Go out into the woods and camp. Pitch a tent on the beach. Have the experience of getting by with what you have so you will know the feeling of satisfaction and joy regardless of who is with you, what you are wearing, how much money you have, or how much attention you are receiving.

Be grateful for the clients you have. Be grateful for the customers you serve. Be grateful for being alive. Start each day with a feeling of appreciation for the day, the people in your life, yourself, and the gifts you are about to receive. Let's take care of our natural resources. Recycle and find ways to conserve our precious resources. Adjust from being the consumer into being a caretaker. There is no better time than now. Praise, caretaking, gratitude, and thanksgiving as an attitude, a way of life increases the blessings that come your way.

STEP ELEVEN: COMMUNICATE

Promote who you are and what you have to offer. Build a myth around your product or service. A myth is your legend. Your legend is your inheritance. Generate a myth that suits who you are and your highest aspirations. Let others know about your product or service. Share yourself and what you have to offer. The more people who know of your service, the greater the chance of your potential customers learning of what you have to offer.

Communication is two-sided. One side is the sender and one side is the receiver. It is a co-created process in which both are involved. I recently realized that I have a tendency to be condescending. Someone I work with used that word in referring to someone else and I realized that I have been condescending toward others. I believed that only I could do the job right and was therefore smug, supposedly tolerating other people's reality all the while knowing that *mine* was really right. The flip side of that is the belief that "I can't do anything right, I'm a loser and others are really superior."

Great! I have the awareness. Now what?! It is time for me to listen and at the same time be true to myself. I don't want to be condescending any longer or feel less than others. It isn't productive and it is a lonely place to be. What moved me out of this was to set up my business on a results-oriented basis. Then love is taken for granted and we can get on with what we came here to do.

Life is full of lessons and treasures that come to us as we give our gifts and participate in life. Prosperity comes to those who are in communication, in touch with their product or service, their customers, the public and especially their partners and co-workers.

If you want to know what is going on, ask someone. Then listen to what they have to say, tell the truth, and share of yourself. Sometimes you may not like what you hear. If it applies to you then use it. "Don't worry. Be happy!"

Create a demand for your service or product. Let the right people know of the value they could receive from what you offer. Build the legend and then back the promise with results. Stay open to feedback and do surveys to find out what people want. Seek evaluations of your products or service. Communication is the key.

Make your life about service. Service with a commitment to excellence is the unspoken vow of any true professional. Be clear as to what your service is and offer that to others. Ask yourself, "How can I serve others?" "What can I do to improve the quality of what I offer?" "How can I do my best in this situation?" "What is needed here and how can I fill that need?" Be generous with your service and the rewards will be great!

I like to share and I like to be with people who share. Generous people have big hearts and know how to share of themselves with love.

Money, sex, and power can either take us for a nasty ride or we can enjoy them and use them as aspects of love. Let's lift ourselves above the "I'm not enough" belief system and live from "I am enough and there is always plenty." Be a happy woman creating and generating love, beauty, joy, and value wherever you go and in whatever you do. The world will then be restored to a balance of its energies. Let yourself receive the blessing of the Goddess and ask her love and guidance to bring miracles and magic.

EXERCISES

1. List five blockages to having more wealth and money in your life.

2. Finish the sentence: If I had more money I would _____.

3. List five problems you no longer desire to have that have to do with money or the lack of it.

4. List five ways in which you could bring about ecological balance by living your vision and having more money.

5. List five dreams you have for the world.

6. Write down the desires that you have longed for in your heart and never achieved.

7. List the desires of your heart that you have achieved (little and big ones).

8. What are your religious beliefs about money and wealth?

9. What are your parents' beliefs about money and wealth?

10. Who would be upset if you were rich, loving, and powerful?

11. List your thoughts about you and money.

12. Complete each sentence:

People who are rich are _____.
The problem with having money is _____.
My biggest fear in having lots of money is
_____.
The rich people I know are _____.
If everyone was wealthy, the world would be
_____.
I can't be trusted with money because
_____.
Men will _____ when I am rich.
Women will _____ when I am rich.
My Mother and Father will _____
when I have money, love, and power.
To be rich, I will have to lose
_____.
If I have, others won't have _____.
The things that are wrong with having money
are _____.

13. Write out the five most negative
thoughts about money and yourself.

14. Write out your five most positive thoughts
about money.

15. My payoffs in struggling are _____.

16. What are you proving by denying yourself your most cherished desires?

17. Who are you making wrong by denying yourself your most cherished desires?

18. List the good you can do with your abundant wealth for:

    The environment: _____.
    People: _____.
    Animals: _____.
    Plant life: _____.
    Children: _____.
    Your life-style: _____.

19. List five failures with money and having what you want.

20. List your five most challenging aspects of wealth and money.

AFFIRMATIONS

1. I, _____, am the abundance I seek.

2. I, _____, am enough.

3. There is always enough for me and everyone.

4. I, _____, am powerful and loving at the same time.

5. My income always exceeds my expectations.

6. I, _____, am a rich woman and I deserve it!

7. It is okay for me, _____, to be a wealthy woman.

8. I don't betray others by flourishing in my projects.

9. I, _____, use my money wisely and in harmony with nature.

10. I, _____, am a money magnet. Money loves me.

11. I, _____, enjoy money and I direct it for good purposes.

12. Money is energy and I, _____, use my energy to create health, love, peace, and harmony.

13. I, _____, do not have to lose love to be powerful.

14. I, _____, do not have to take care of anyone in order for me to be loved.

15. I, _____, am capable, able, and intelligent.

16. Money blesses me.

17. I, _____, am an excellent money manager. Everything I touch turns into prosperity.

18. I, _____, manage my money as I choose.

19. My perfect livelihood is now apparent to me.

20. I, _____, love life and all it has to offer.

PROJECT CHART

(Use this chart with the second step of the prosperity plan.)

I. Purpose of the project:

II. Goals and objectives:
  1.
  2.
  3.
  4.
  5.
  A. Methods to achieve my purpose and objectives:
    1.
    2.
    3.
    4.
    5.
    a. To-do list (short-term objectives):
      1.
      2.
      3.
      4.
      5.

III. Personal and global rewards:
  1.
  2.
  3.
  4.
  5.

PART III

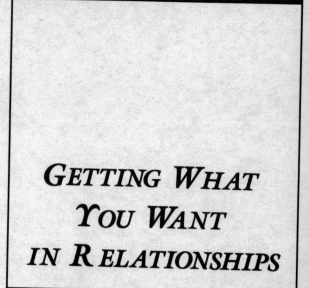

GETTING WHAT YOU WANT IN RELATIONSHIPS

CHAPTER 10

Relating to Your Body as Your Temple

IT JUST MAKES SENSE THAT WHO WE ARE IS MORE THAN flesh, blood, and bones. It takes someone or something to activate your physical structure. When you vacate your "dwelling," it slumps to the floor, devoid of its animation. The body, which is still alive (for nothing dies), begins to disintegrate and melt back into the earth from which it came. Recycling is a natural process of life.

The body is an electrochemical carbon unit serving as the opportunity for us to experience ourselves as life. But what we have done is give ourselves, our happiness, our needs over to a body to fulfill. What would happen if you decided that the car you drive determines how much love and happiness you could experience? How silly!

The world is set up at this time just like that. We have lost ourselves in a material game and forgotten who we are, where we came from, and where it is possible for us to go. Flesh cults are everywhere, and the worship of the body and material things has created a world filled with power trips, starvation, crime, disease, violence, sexual abuse, obesity, and drug addiction.

The masculine aspect of life devoid of the feminine has lowered itself into the role of destroyer of bodies, destroyer of nature, children, sweetness, and love. The patterns and beliefs of the flesh cults are deeply ingrained within each of us, so far beneath the surface that few may even recognize what I am saying. We are in a drugged state of a deep sleep lost in the patterns, designs, atoms, and molecules of our own creations.

In my opinion our only salvation as women and the only hope for our children and our precious Mother Earth is to shake off this unconscious cloak of forgetfulness and wake up and remember who we are. As we awaken and remember that we are spirit, our body's type, style, shape, size, age, and design will have no power to determine the quality of our existence or how we choose to love and express ourselves. This takes courage, for we must give up judgment of our bodies—and all bodies.

Within each woman and man's body is the genetic cellular memory of family life from the very beginning. Each individual's soul memory is also present, soul memory being each creature's collection of lifetimes and life experiences since the beginning that never was. Life has no beginning or end and this knowingness is imprinted in every cell and atom as well as in the etheric soul and emotional and mental bodies. We are multidimensional limitless creatures ever evolving, growing, changing into, and becoming whatever we desire to be.

We have grossly limited ourselves by identifying ourselves simply as a body that has either a vagina or a penis. We have different genitals for the purpose of proliferation and the reproduction of our particular form of life in this material world.

OUR BODIES ARE NOT FOR PLEASING MEN

I remember standing in my sixth-grade classroom willing my breasts to stop growing because I couldn't stand the pain of the boys laughing at my breasts and making comments about my body. I hurt so much from their ridicule that I hated the boys and willed myself to stop growing. Later on I had breast implants because a man in my life convinced me that he'd love me more if I had bigger breasts. I should have laughed at his penis and told him to have a penis implant, but a rejoinder like that was not possible in those days. I would never want to hurt his feelings! But it *was* okay for *me* to be hurt!

My body is the best teacher I have, for it doesn't have a mind of its own. It is my most perfect reflection, my most perfect universe that I can count on to give me feedback as to where I am in my mind, emotions, imagination, beliefs, and values.

For years I had deep pain, sadness, suffering, and fear—all body related. "Am I pretty enough for my family to love me?" "Am I beautiful enough to be in the nightclubs?" "Is my body too fat for any man to want to have sex with me and perhaps even marry me?" "What will people think of me if I have clothes on that aren't in style or don't look right?" "Will he leave me for a 'hardbody'?" "I hate that woman. She is so much more beautiful than I am. Surely my man wants her and not me!" "Look at my flab. I had better firm up or he won't want to have sex with me!" "I know, I'll buy that piece of lingerie that looks like one a prostitute would wear, he'll be excited and stay with me a while longer." "Oh, my God, I look like my mother! OH NO!!" "I'm afraid to talk about sex. His ego will get hurt, so I'll be quiet. I wouldn't want his ego to be bruised. He'll leave me and I'll be alone. So what if I'm not satisfied and we don't really communicate, share, or feel intimate. It is better this way than nothing." "I'm getting older. My body is changing. What can I do to keep him?" "Who wants a relationship anyway. I'm not beautiful enough for anyone to love me." "I'm afraid to enjoy my body and love myself because I'll attract too many men who may want to sexually use me, so I'll stay hidden." "If I let him have sex with me, he'll like me." "He's hurting my body, but if I say anything he'll hurt me more or he'll think I'm a jerk." "What will happen to me if my body isn't okay for men?"

We paint our bodies, poke holes in our ears, hang material and other stuff on them, and anything else we can think of to make them "attractive." We pour alcohol into our bodies, stuff them with food, drug them, and do anything we can think of to escape them.

LOVE, DON'T JUDGE!

We've done this in our attempt to feel good and end the pain. We've done everything except love ourselves and our bodies. Your body is a holy creation. Your body is your mobile home unit that goes everywhere you go on this physical plane.

We curse, abuse, poison, and attack our bodies with our judgments and beliefs that our magnificent bodies are ugly and not worth loving. We feel shame because of what we have done to our bodies and the bodies of others. We judge others as not worth loving because of the color of their skin or the number of pounds of flesh they are carrying. We ignore and avoid those whose bodies are deformed, crippled, or misshapen, forgetting that there are human beings with feelings living in those mobile homes.

We wear uniforms having to do with our life-style and occupation, bypassing those who aren't dressed for success. Little children wear designer clothes and feel competitive about their appearance in kindergarten, already conscious of their bodies, their faces, their weight, their clothes, and their life-style. They sit in front of the television being programmed as customers, as consumers. They want, they desire, and little by little they forget who they are and become robots programmed to be just bodies caught in the material trap.

I have played this game and tortured myself on this no-win flesh cult wheel of birth and death.

Who you and I are is so sweet, so delicious that there is actually nothing in this world that can compare. I'm not advocating leaving the world, but I am addressing the opportunity each of us has to step out of the insanity and step into harmony, balance, and love.

Here is a frightening thought. What if your worst fears come to pass? Your worst fears will manifest themselves anyway, and if you cling to those fears, all you'll do is postpone what you believe is inevitable. Release the fears and you are free!

Before I loved my body, my body was the cause and source of my pain and suffering. How does anyone win, especially women? People reinforce the idea that men become distinguished as they get older and that women simply age. As a woman you have two alternatives. You can have face and body lifts as long as you live or you can check out of the game and not play. I propose this option: Love yourself and your body as your temple with every breath and with the totality of your spirit, heart, soul, and mind.

We women perpetuate the whole game simply by

playing along with it. If you and I didn't play, the body game would not exist. Women judge other women. Women gossip about and compete with other women. Women play dirty pool when it comes to getting and keeping men and their possessions. Women see themselves as sexual toys to be used for attention, money, security, and power. Women call other women beautiful or ugly. We size each other up as to beauty and power over men. If you can't be beautiful, be smart and help men achieve their dream; they will need you and therefore remain.

As women we have been insecure and exploited ourselves and other women. We have betrayed our daughters, we have trained our sons to be the men who cause us pain, and we have undermined our sisters and our Goddess heritage.

Here's an exercise for you. Pay attention and be aware of how much you judge, compare, evaluate, and work on your body. Why? How can we find peace within ourselves and flourish as magnificent beings of love and light if we are caught in the trap of "What do people think of me and my body?"

TAKING RESPONSIBILITY

In order to not make waves or upset the men in our lives and therefore our socioeconomic status, we have allowed rape and sexual abuse of all kinds, children to be uneducated, war to continue, starvation to exist, and the continued exploitation of men and women. Why? We have forgotten who we are and have diminished ourselves into fear-ridden, security-minded, needy females. And what has been the male identity? Sexual prowess, the size of the penis, the amount of money in men's possession, and the degree to which they can make other people be responsible for their happiness, ego gratification, and success.

The full awakening of the female will create a cosmic event heretofore unexperienced. As women love their Goddess bodies and worship and adore the beings that they are, men will be able to release their burden of pain and become gentle, sensitive lovers and caretakers of the garden once again.

In my dream I envision all children in a joyful and safe environment to develop their talents, values, and abilities. In my dream I see all women feeling beautiful, loving themselves, and expressing their great wisdom, intelligence, intuition, and love. In my dream, men are sweet, loving, intelligent husbandmen who, together with the women, create a paradise of beauty, balance, harmony, and bliss.

Yes, I am an idealist, for I feel and sense the subtle innermost desires of our hearts. We can change our world into a safe and unlimited playground of the goddesses and gods. First, last, and always, it occurs within you and me.

Notice the women on the streets, at parties, in the market, in your churches and temples. Pay attention to what they talk about, how they feel, what their lives are about. Watch television and notice the roles men and women play. Watch commercials, read the ads in the magazines and newspapers. Look at the covers of magazines. What are the headlines, the stories? Pay attention to what we've been creating and then set out purposefully to create a new world.

Billions and billions of dollars are tied up in keeping you an insecure, fear-ridden, unhappy, greedy, female body. Billions of dollars are made from sickness, fear, and the belief in scarcity rather than the desire for our wellness, self-sufficiency, or happiness. Nothing can replace love but the original and real thing, self-love.

Our drug culture is a symptom, a reaction stemming from our deep pain and beliefs in the hopelessness and the inevitability of disaster, loss, abandonment, sickness, and death of the body. We pump up the body to feel better even if we become addicted to the substance. We've become addicted to shopping, to makeup, to "stuff," to attention, to crisis and drama. When our bodies don't feel alive and that's all we think there is to feel alive with, we get a fix of whatever makes us feel something—anything.

What I am advocating is the total awakening from the dream of bodies so that we as spiritual beings can play on earth in our most magnificent spacecrafts called bodies. What this requires, as I understand it, is for each of us to be 100 percent totally committed to loving ourselves and loving our bodies without any judgment, comparison, fear, guilt, or violence. This is an enormous commitment to oneself, and without it you and I can never pass into greater experiences.

BEGIN AT THE BEGINNING

How do you do this? You begin at this moment. You create priorities and place the love of yourself and proper love of your body above all else. Personally, I got tired of the pain and the roller coaster ride of feeling love only on those rare moments when someone else's attention made me feel special. I truly believed that marriage would end the pain and insecurity because it would be final and he loved me! I found out that insecurity breeds insecurity.

Security came to me as I began to love myself. The mood swings stopped when I decided to stop torturing myself and to finally find myself acceptable to myself. "I am worth my own love" became my affirmation.

It doesn't happen overnight; just like anything worthwhile, it takes commitment, reinforcement, and discipline. The discipline involved is the retraining of yourself and your patterns of thinking, feeling, believing, and living.

There is no greater joy than to be free of self-condemnation. The body is amazing in its ability to be as healthy as it is in spite of the mental, emotional, and verbal abuse that we subject it to. Can you imagine what lies ahead of us if we adore our space suits? It will be fun to have a body and more than fun, we can know, feel, and experience life through it!

The following paragraphs suggest some ways to approach this subject in your life. Use these to get in touch with yourself and the way in which you perceive and experience your body. Take this time to reframe and create anew the relationship you have with your body.

Pay attention to the ways in which you foster your "body madness" through your judgments of who and what is physically beautiful. Notice the words you use to describe your body and the bodies of other women and men. What are you doing, saying, thinking, and feeling that perpetuates the body game? What do you imagine would happen if you stopped degrading yourself?

How are you programming your little girls and boys as sex, power, success, money, and body machines? Why are you doing this? Our children will blossom and be able to fulfill their most cherished dreams and potential if they are loved and taught to love themselves first as spiritual beings and second as humans who possess and occupy a body. Out of fear we program our children with values that we believe will help them be popular, financially secure, respected, and admired. All it does is perpetuate the game of losing oneself in the trappings of the body game.

Just imagine what their lives would be like if they loved and respected themselves and their bodies not for their appearance and what it could get them but for the way bodies function as a means of experiencing life. Our children are precious, and what they need from us is our example and guidance, so that they may know themselves and be able to navigate their way safely and beautifully through life as they fulfill their purposes, ideals, and visions. It is never too late to begin a new way of being. My daughters and I are continuously evolving into higher levels of awareness and love in our relationship. Sometimes this occurs by way of an upset and challenge that unleashes an old, stuck program or wound. When you realize or discover a thought, pattern, or action that is unloving and harmful, instead of condemning yourself for it, congratulate yourself for realizing what you've been doing and change it.

Call all bodies beautiful. Try looking at each person's body as his or her space suit and art expression. Anyone I love is so precious and beautiful to me. Notice how you feel when you direct your attention to the beauty of the inner person and simply allow the body to be just a body. The people I love are beautiful to me.

Our society is not set up this way, so it will take some doing to change it. If we can start loving ourselves and others for the beauty and majesty of our essence instead of judging our worth based on the sex, color, size, shape, or design of our bodies, all people will have the opportunity to share their gifts, talents, and genius. We've done terrible things to people because we decided that their bodies made them fair game for ridicule, violence, humiliation, deprivation, and hurt. All people feel and all people are divine. As women let us love ourselves and all people as we love our children and as we have always wanted to be loved.

Stand naked in front of a full-length mirror and look at every part of your body. If you have judged any part of your body or compared it with another's, verbally ask that part of your body for forgiveness. If you have deprived yourself of your own love and acceptance for one moment because any part of your body was unacceptable to you, ask for forgiveness from your body and yourself. Go over your body again and touch each and every part with your own hands. Love and accept your body and call it beautiful. Feel worthy of your own love and adoration. Your word is law and your words are made into your flesh. Look at your face and with your hands lovingly caress it and fall in love with it. How could anyone else's love ever mean more to you than your own? You give yourself pleasure.

Give up making fun of or ridiculing your female genitals, breasts, or body odors. We laugh at our beautiful Goddess bodies and listen to people make jokes about female and male bodies, especially the genitals. Our genitals are beautiful. They are our pleasure and power centers.

Notice how you think and speak about your body. Raise your thoughts, feelings, and words to the level of divine and loving when you refer to your body or another's. Don't put yourself down or attack your sweet body in any way. If you do, quickly forgive yourself and acknowledge yourself for being aware of an old pattern and change it in the next moment.

Take care of your body. Treat your body with respect, treat it the way you'd treat a precious baby. Dress in a way in which your body can be comfortable, relaxed, and happy. Personally I wear the kind of comfortable shoes and clothes out in the world that I do in my home. Be loving and kind to other bodies.

Pay attention to your senses and allow yourself to enjoy your most wonderful treasures of sight, sound, taste, smell, touch, and feelings. I allow myself the gift of fragrances, foods, music, and visuals that I enjoy. Bubble baths are a favorite of mine; so are hot tubs under the stars on a clear, fresh, beautiful evening. Learn how to relax and release stress. Relax, be patient and take it easy. Be happy and have fun at whatever you do. It is the best health plan available to you.

Feed and nurture your body with the foods that are good for your body and help you feel and be healthy, energetic, and vital. We're not all alike so it is up to you to explore this realm and take care of yourself as you see fit.

Dance, run, walk, jump, stretch, climb, and play in your body. Know your body, feel your body, and get in touch with what your body is telling you. I've done hundreds of sessions of body massage and structural integration as well as many forms of physical therapy and fitness. The body holds the memory of your past experiences, including your pain, fear, and judgments. A qualified body therapist can assist you in feeling and releasing all that blocked emotion and pain from your body. The body is a treasure house of data, information, and gifts. Learn to massage, move, touch, and heal your own body. I personally have found great value in Joseph Heller's and Ida Rolf's body work techniques. Change your body patterns and you create new neuron connections in your brain.

Let your body be a source of pleasure and delight, not just something to attract or repel others. I used to exercise because I was afraid that I'd get old and flabby and therefore be unattractive to men. If fear is your motivation for anything, you'll find that you create that thing anyway.

Try moving in a way to become one with your space suit, so that your body becomes your partner, lover, and friend. Whenever you dance, it is hard to be unhappy. Your body is energy. Let your energy body be in a constant state of movement and flow and you'll never be rigid or inflexible. Your body will be your companion as well as your greatest teacher. Discover your body and let it give you gifts.

Make sure that you feel rested; get enough sleep so that your body and soul can let go of stress. At night as you sleep, you traverse the universe on a nighttime adventure. I know that at home on our farm, I sleep deeply and soundly and a great healing takes place. If you are tired, sleep, and when you awaken refreshed, get up and live the day as you desire. If my body is exceptionally tired I know something in my life is out of sorts. My body doesn't lie. It is a dependable barometer and feedback system that signals my conscious self as to whether I am on or off course for myself. A symptom of illness is a gift if you are willing to look for it and make the necessary corrections in your life.

If I am unusually tired or feel out of sorts, depressed, or sluggish, I ask myself these questions:

Is there anyone in my life with whom I have a problem?
What do I need to say to that person?
Am I doing what I want?
Am I feeling acknowledged and appreciated?
Do I need to get away somewhere in nature and just relax and play?

CARING FOR YOUR BODY

My body is my temple and therefore sacred to me; no one touches my body unless I allow it. I allow myself to touch and be touched only from love. "No" is a wonderful word because it allows you to say "yes" to yourself. Contemplate how to use your body and what you use it for. I used to believe that I needed to use my body to capture and keep the man I loved in my life. It was a great day for me when I realized that my body was mine and not something to use to attract and keep anyone. My body is my home and belongs to me and me alone.

Dealing with this issue has brought to the surface soul memory of having been violated and used for someone else's sexual stimulation. I have felt both fear and anger having to do with men who felt they could use my body as they wanted by force. I even bought a shotgun at one time—it was very freeing to me to know that if anyone attempted to harm me physically it was my right to protect myself. I know how to use the shotgun and I know I won't ever have to, because I feel comfortable with dispensing with anyone who invades my space with the intent to harm me or my loved ones. I was raped one time and didn't realize it until a couple of weeks later. I let a man force himself on me because I was afraid he would hurt me if I didn't. I had felt uncomfortable trying to get him to leave because I thought he would think I was a fool to even suggest that he was after my body. I was so afraid of men not liking me that I gave my power away. What I learned from that incident was to trust my intuition; I now do whatever it takes to remove myself from any situation in which I feel even the slightest chance of being violated, regardless of what any other person may say to me or think of me.

Men and women who live off of others' fears are clever at manipulation; they are experts at surprise, catching you unaware and vulnerable. Respecting myself and my body first, last, and always keeps me inviolate and out of harm's way because I don't create any incidents to prove anything one way or another. Our beliefs create our reality. Look to what is going on in your life having to do with your body to recall and remember the originating cause that created the situation. Change the thought and take the appropriate action necessary for you to love yourself and your precious temple body. Do this as safely as you can for yourself and others. Removing yourself from dangerous relationships and areas is a very positive step. In past lives, we've been sacrifices, sex toys, slaves, ornaments, and possessions. We did this to ourselves or it couldn't have happened. Release your anger and bitterness as quickly as possible and move on to a more beautiful life.

Are you continually sick, accident prone, or physically hurting yourself in some other way? Why? What are you doing that for? Are you willing to release this pattern and be good to your body? Kiss and hug your own body! Bless and praise your body!

Meditate and wake yourself up to the possibilities within your own chakra system, brain and central nervous system. Learn how your endocrine system operates, how it affects you, and what to do to enhance it and increase its efficiency. Learn about your genitals, your yoni, and let yourself feel the pleasure and power that belong to you as a woman.

Your body is more than a frame on which to hang your clothes. Your body is more than something to judge or to use to attract another body so your body won't be alone. There is nothing more wonderful than feeling comfortable, happy, peaceful, and loving within your own body temple.

Our female Goddess bodies are incredible pieces

of machinery as well as beautiful and delicate pieces of art. You can't love yourself too much, for the love you feel adds to the amount of love available for all life forms. If and when each of us loves ourself and our space suit (body), only joy, peace, and love will abound everywhere. It is possible because I've done it, and I'm continuing to increase the amount of love I feel. There is nothing as delicious as the cells of your body loving themselves and you. The body is made of love and, in recognizing that, the universe must rejoice that all is well in the creation once again.

EXERCISES

1. Fill in the sentences. This is not a quiz. It is a mirror to assist you in being clear about your deepest thoughts and beliefs, so that you can keep what blesses you and release what doesn't.

A. If I, _____, love my body and know that I am beautiful, then _____.

B. I forgive my parents for saying that my body was _____.

C. I forgive these men, _____, _____, and _____, for telling me that _____ was wrong with my body.

D. I am now willing to release my resentment or anger I have toward _____ for hurting or ridiculing my body.

2. I offer these steps as guidelines for loving your body as the temple of the living Goddess, _____. These questions are to help you get in touch with your inner scripts, beliefs, and games that are not serving you with love. Remember then was then, now is now!

A. List at least twenty-five energy blockages (fears, judgments, or beliefs) that make loving and adoring your body not all right. This is an opportunity to write down whatever comes to you about what is wrong with loving and adoring your own body. Keep brainstorming until every single, minor, itsy-bitsy thought is down on paper. List what your mother, father, and grandparents taught you about it not being okay to love your body. Write down what the church or your religion has taught or suggested was sinful, immoral, unspiritual, or wrong with your female body functions and sexuality.

B. List your ten worst fears about loving yourself and your body. List any that bubble up, no matter how ridiculous they may seem.

C. List at least twenty ways in which you have suffered, harmed yourself, or denied yourself the joys of living by judging, hating, or abusing your body in any way.

D. List everything you believe, think, or feel is wrong or less than perfect with your body (I mean EVERYTHING).

    a. Who told you this or where did you pick up these opinions about your body?

    b. What is your number-one fear that keeps

you from mentally and emotionally making every part of your body perfect?

E. Notice how you evaluate, judge, or criticize the bodies (space suits) that other women are wearing. Why do you do this? What is the point and what are you hoping to accomplish in this useless and destructive habit?

F. Do you try and drive off your mate and lovers because you believe yourself to not be beautiful enough? Why? What do you get out of this process?

G. List ten rewards or gifts you give yourself by deciding you are not beautiful or young enough to be loved by yourself or others.

AFFIRMATIONS

1. It is perfectly all right for me, _____, to love my body.

2. My body is my temple in which I, _____, worship life.

3. I, _____, forgive myself for judging my body or comparing it to another's.

4. My sacred body temple belongs to me only.

5. I, _____, forgive myself for ever hurting any part of my body.

6. Every cell of my body temple is beautiful because I say so.

7. It is safe for me to release death, age, anger, and bitterness from my body and emotions.

8. I, _____, love my body as much and more than I've wanted others to love me.

CHAPTER 11

The Loving Yourself Forever Diet

I STARTED DIETING AT AGE THIRTEEN AS A FRESHMAN in high school and finished the almost endless diet four years ago. Thirty-one years of "I'm on a diet; I can't eat that or I'll get fat" was finally over because I was tired of the torment, sacrifice, guilt, and fear. Fear is usually at the bottom of the desire to diet or exercise. "If I don't lose weight, no man will want me." "If I don't lose weight and exercise, I'll be sick and die." "If I don't keep my body slender, hard, and young, the man I want will trade me in on a younger, prettier model."

It's a pretty sad state of affairs when fear is the prime motivation for how we live and what we do with our bodies. Threatening and using guilt, abandonment, and rejection are effective tools in the manipulation of people, but they never solve anything. Fear creates fear, guilt perpetuates guilt, and rejection begets more rejection.

Four years ago when I decided one fateful day that I'd had enough of dieting and there was something wrong with this approach, I dared to start my experiment of love. I was finished with fear and guilt as motivators, and I committed myself to the discovery of what would happen to my body and myself if I was motivated solely by love, peace, and joy.

Four years later my body is balanced, my relationships are flourishing, and I am at peace with myself, my body, and food. The process is not finished but I am past the biggest rocks and my boat is going with the flow. The most difficult part leaving my fear-based body game was the "fear" that maybe my fears were justified and it was all true. Maybe I'd lose everything. Maybe no one would love me. Maybe love wouldn't bring my body to balance naturally. Maybe I'd eat myself into oblivion. Maybe, maybe, maybe . . .

Every major decision in my life has been followed by my exercising that existential art of courage called doing it! We can know something spiritually, mentally, and emotionally but if we don't move that awareness into the physical world, it doesn't materialize physically. Talk is cheap because it is just talk. Anyone can do that. It is the follow-through that separates wishful thinkers from those who realize their dreams. It's the application of our most profound and loving beliefs and revelations that makes those wonderful ideas real and tangible.

IF I LOVED MY BODY

I had heard that if I loved my body 100 percent and blessed every bit of food that went into it, my body temple would be healthy, vital, ageless, and balanced. Since I had tried fear as a control device to keep me thin and therefore loved, I thought it time to try love. Why not? I was tired of the pain and embarrassment attached to my body.

I had a long history of fat and flab fighting since my mom and her side of the family were usually what the Western world would call "overweight." As an American woman programmed from child-hood by advertising agencies and the media to buy this or that in order to be beautiful and therefore happy, I was 100 percent enrolled in the fear-based body game.

I must have followed just about every diet that was popular over a thirty-one-year period. Near the end of my torture I even followed the organic and natural vegetarian diets that were not only sup-posed to make the body beautiful but also provide enlightenment at the same time. I learned a lot about myself and nutrition, especially in the last few years of my "diet" stage of development, so I don't want to put down or invalidate food plans. It is all part of your "Body Education Home Study

Course." This chapter is about the body and that which is beyond the body. It's about bringing an awareness of yourself from the highest part of you into the intellect and emotions and then into the body and body-related activities. Any permanent behavioral change begins first in one's desire, the desire based on one's purpose in life.

Band-Aids and the healing of symptoms of an illness simply stops an effect, but it doesn't deal with the cause of the problem. Any healing that has been thorough for me has been one where I found the thought, notion, or decision that created the problem and then released the manifestation on all levels.

WHY DIETING ISN'T THE ANSWER

Dieting, because it is based on sacrifice and insufficiency, is not a final solution. I would fast and then indulge; for me it was always feast or famine. This pendulum pattern in eating was also apparent in other aspects of my life. I would swing from sweetness to anger, feeling totally alive to completely depressed, from everything to nothing with no in-between. A manic-depressive lives with mood swings and is tormented by "out of control" feelings and reactions. Looking back, I'm sure I had manic and schizophrenic tendencies. Now I choose to believe that balance offers me just as many wonderful experiences, lessons, and gifts as the fanatical swings of "all or nothing." Before, balance was boring; now balance is exciting. Before, enough was never enough; now enough is all there is! With moderation you can have everything you like without indulgence or denial.

STOP JUDGING YOURSELF!

The first step in my "loving yourself forever diet" is to release all judgment of your body, its size, shape, age, or condition. Remove the judgment of "wrong" about your nutrition, exercises, and body-related activity. Ask yourself, "Does this behavior help or hurt me?"

We tend to categorize everyone by body appearance, money (or its symbols), accomplishments, or sex. We grossly limit ourselves by selecting our friends based on surface patterns, thereby missing the true gift—their essence. The value of a book isn't found on the cover, but in the contents. Although the cover is what first entices us to open the book and read it, when we take a peek inside, we sometimes find riches beyond our greatest expectations.

We are at a point in time when it is appropriate to discover the other aspects and facets of self and nurture those qualities in the people of earth. If you can't or won't play the "fear-based body/sex game," then you are either judging and hating yourself because you feel like a failure or you are part of the "counterculture." To be "counter" is to be against and being against anything only gives the thing you are against more fuel with which to thrive. There are no enemies except those we create.

The world in which we live is alive with thoughts, beliefs, and emotions; like raindrops, some bounce off of us and some penetrate and become part of us. It takes a conscious person to stop, stand back from the game, and say, "Wait a minute. Is this how I choose to be and live or is it someone else's ideas that are controlling my life?"

The number-one killer of people is self-hatred and self-invalidation. To invalidate yourself is to make yourself nonexistent. The number-one secret to your survival and subsequent flowering is self-love, self-respect, self-worship, and self-validation. Worthiness is a prime factor in your energy if you are to flourish and continue being. "I am worthy and deserving of love" is an affirmation of self-validation. The more we recognize our value, the more humankind will flower.

Loving yourself and loving your body as you love yourself generates an energy field of health and wholeness. You can't love your body and judge it unworthy of love at the same time. You either accept yourself or not. I'm not saying that, given our programming, you can do this instantly or constantly—yet it is possible. I've been working for years on releasing the old "I'm not beautiful, slender, or young enough to be loved" programming of lifetimes. Thought by thought, feeling by feeling, word by word we can move our entire energy system into the frequency of love and self-acceptance.

Love is such an awesome and powerful feeling and energy that of itself it transforms your body, your relationships, your creativity, and every other aspect of yourself. Love, ecstasy, and bliss combined with strength, power, passion, and expression are the energies of this new time. We combine the best of both worlds, the feminine and the masculine.

I feel that we are each experience-seeking creatures. Once I was looking at a friend of mine and for a moment or so I saw layers of creatures in his face. I saw reptiles, birds, animals, humans, and even creatures I had never seen before that could have come from other solar systems or dimensions. He was all things rolled into one human creature. We are creating ourselves moment by moment by every experience we have; we always have been and always will be. We must be more of what is possible to us today than yesterday.

We know what it is like to be judged for our bodies, our money, and our accomplishments. The problem is that there has been a standard of right and wrong, success and failure that has denied "citizenship" to masses of people. This denial of entry into the realms of glory, beauty, and self-worth has caused wars, crime, disease, poverty, abuse, pollution, oppression, and even death. Why should people be denied entry into the regal realms just because they are unwilling to alter themselves to fit someone else's standards?

What would happen if all people were elevated to "magnificent, glorious, and divine"? WOW! The problem is it is an inside job! Each of us has to do it for ourself. We can assist others and create the environment and educational systems to facilitate the process.

YOU ARE ENOUGH

Again the first step of the "loving yourself forever diet" is the decision to remove all judgment of your body, its size, shape, age, or condition from your beingness. You are enough. Love yourself and your female/Goddess body as it is now—this moment, naked. "I love my body as it is." "I love every cell of my body, now and forever." These statements became and remain my mantra.

When a fear bubbles to the surface, breathe deeply and continuously release the old pattern, thought, or belief through the healing and creative power of the breath. Then think your most loving thoughts, breathe them in, and feel the feelings of love, peace, and self-acceptance. Raise your thoughts above the conditional mind and endless mind chatter and think a higher truth. "The more I love my body, the more I attract loving people into my life."

Experiment with the following suggestions and notice your reactions, feelings, and thoughts as well as the reactions of others. It is important in our evolution to detach from the programming of social control so that we can have a foundation of deep and profound love and appreciation for ourselves and others based on who we are, not just on what we appear to be. Many businesses thrive and earn billions of dollars off of our insecurities and fears that our bodies are not beautiful enough to attract and keep others with us.

Try this: wear simple comfortable clothes and shoes and no make-up out in public. You don't get much attention this way except from children and animals who only care how you feel about them. Look in the mirror at your face and body and project acceptance, love, and the feelings of beauty onto yourself. "My face is my ideal and every part of my body is beautiful to me" is a good affirmation. Look in the mirror until you love yourself and what you see.

This is a process of making yourself "perfect." You are all there is and all the rest is you reflected back that you may know yourself. The alternative is to be imperfect. "Perfect" to me means to be whole and complete within yourself, containing everything you need to be all you are capable of being, doing, and having. Love yourself and you are beautiful on all levels. True beauty is the feeling and essence of love. This step is really a reaffirmation of what I wrote about in the previous chapter on loving your Goddess body. I restated it because you "can't love yourself too much."

YOUR BODY IS YOUR FRIEND

The second step in the "diet" is to drop your fear of food and the fear that your body can hurt you or deprive you of love. Having a body that is your enemy, not your friend, is a painful way to live. Time is your enemy, food is your enemy, your face is your enemy, and ultimately life itself is a dangerous threat. Nothing is worse than living in a hostile environment where everything and everyone is potentially dangerous and threatening.

Fear projected on food creates food that hurts you. You feel the fear and feel attacked as you are eating it, even though you want it and need it and can't do without it. Food becomes the killer, the Grim Reaper, the enemy that you need to survive but the one that can "destroy" your chance at happiness. The ultimate killer is *you*, because at the base of all these fears is your lack of self-trust, self-control, and self-love. How can you stop this destructive belief system? By loving food and appreciating its gifts!

Bless your food. Every bit of it. If you eat a hot fudge sundae, love every morsel or don't eat it. Stop saying things such as, "This food is bad for me," "This will make me fat," "I would die for a piece of pizza," "I know I shouldn't, but . . ." Listen to yourself when you talk about food. Your words are your declarations and carry the power of your great essence. Change your words and speak with reverence and blessing for the nourishment and pleasure of food. Your food is spirit in form and therefore conscious and alive. It is here to offer itself to you. Honor your food. Don't waste it and be grateful that you have enough.

Guilt and judgment on yourself and food is more dangerous than any food. The prime approach would be to love and bless everything you eat and to eat only that which is without toxins, pesticides, free radicals, or anything harmful. The food offers itself to you as the fruit falls from the tree and the vegetables reach their peak. The animals and fish who offer themselves need to be appreciated. Native Americans considered animals sacred spirit guides and nature spirits. They ate them when needed and didn't destroy them for "sport." Food offers itself to you to be eaten but then becomes a part of you. For us to not recognize this most wonderful gift must be a sadness for the food. I don't eat many eggs, but when I do, I eat the ones from our chickens on the farm and they are rich and alive. I eat ice cream with only natural ingredients and I eat it slowly and savor each succulent, creamy, cool bite. Yesterday I ate a frozen banana dipped in chocolate and nuts and savored every morsel. YUM!

ON ALCOHOLISM

At one time I was an alcoholic. That meant I was drinking more than enough wine every evening and I was using alcohol to give me permission to dump my anger, blame, guilt, and self-pity. I stopped drinking any alcohol for three years and then I thought, "Why would I be afraid of alcohol? I've released my anger, grief, and self-pity, so I can trust myself with a glass of wine." Now I enjoy a glass of wine occasionally and appreciate it. Some of us torture ourselves with the fear of our powerlessness over food and alcohol. One glass of wine is valuable. A little is all that is needed to help digest food, relax us, and sharpen our taste buds. Too much wine or too much anything can be used to bury our feelings and deny parts of ourselves. The more we have, the more unconscious we become. If you are addicted, do whatever you need to do to break the addiction and throw away the crutch. Alcoholics Anonymous or Overeaters Anonymous are both fine disciplines to support you in moving through this stage of your evolvement if this pertains to you. They can also stop you from moving on if you think you need to label yourself an addict forever. An addiction is a disease that can be cured by healing yourself of the cause, your dependency on outside sources for your feelings.

Notice how you feel and what you think and say about food. Catch yourself and in the moment make your thoughts, words, and feelings be those of love, respect, worship, and gratitude for what you are receiving into your temple. These are the offerings to the temple of the living God-us in a body. Before any meal, relax, breathe deeply to help you release any stress or fear, and give a blessing of thanksgiving, appreciation, and continued abundance. Before eating, relax, take a moment to appreciate the food, appreciate its gift to you, and recognize the abundance of the universe that is pouring its blessings on you. Now eat, savor, taste, chew, and take into you this most delicious part of life. "Everything I eat blesses my body."

TAKE TIME TO LEARN ABOUT FOOD

Learn about food and the nutrients needed for your body. Each piece of food in whatever form it comes is conscious and alive and as such it deserves respect and appreciation. Food offers itself to us that it may merge with us and become part of us, just as we partake of its energy and become one with the food. Eating is communion or merging; food is a sacrament. Anything you eat becomes your body. What is even more important than the food is the attitude, the emotions, and the beliefs that merge with the food.

Organic food is raised in harmony with the earth, insects, bacteria, natural fertilizers, animals, nature spirits, and humankind. Why wouldn't you love your body so much that you'd only allow the foods with the highest vibrations to enter and become part of your temple? To pray is to offer up, to raise yourself to your highest vibration that you may be infused with your divine nature.

If you don't want poisons, radiation, and toxins in your body don't buy food with them in it. Your money is your vote! Read labels, ask questions, and make your preferences known. Much of what goes into the body as poison doesn't show up for years. Your children's lives are at stake. Research the ways to flush out your liver and lymphatic systems of chemicals. Oxygen products bring more oxygen into your body. Healing herbs are wonderful body-balancing devices.

Animals that are treated cruelly and then killed to feed you and your loved ones hold fear and sadness in their tissues. Do you want that? Why torture these precious living, feeling, and communicating entities just because we want to eat them? There are gentle ways to put them to sleep in order to eat them and not waste their gifts to us.

Filter your water, as its function is to cleanse, fortify, and feed your body as the second sacrament. Again your wallet talks. Use it. Seek those services and products that benefit you and your family the most.

Stop buying any product that contaminates our paradise. If we no longer play into the ego games that promote greed, lust, hierarchies, class distinctions, suffering, insufficiency, and power struggles, then what's left is harmony and sufficiency for all. Health is order, balance, and harmony that flows from love.

Be conscious and aware of what you put in your body, what you say, what you believe, how you feel about the food you eat. If we stop killing ourselves we'll have to develop our lives in a new, more exciting and fulfilling way.

I eat what I want when I want it and I want to eat

the best because I'm putting it in my temple as an offering and sacrament. Sacrifices to the gods were probably leftover rituals of a forgotten practice of offering foods to our own bodies in appreciation and love. There was probably a time in our her-story when humans from outer space first came to earth and landed in the Mesopotamian Valley. The primates were their slaves and farmers, gathering the best of the crops to be offered to the Goddess and her companions. They mated with the primates and here we are. Possibly we just stayed and forgot we were from outer space!

I love thoughts of far-out realities. We are creating stories and myths right now, so let's create in the highest, most magnificent fashion. Our future is being created in this moment; we have the choice to honor and serve or fear and destroy.

Food will be a sacrament, a blessing welcomed into your body temple with love and thanksgiving. The body will balance itself and adjust to its healthiest weight naturally out of your love for yourself and your body temple.

STOP WAITING—USE YOUR ENERGY

Step three in the "loving yourself forever diet" is to stop waiting and start moving. Your body is energy, and the more you sit the more that energy solidifies. Inaction causes stagnation, rigidity, constipation, and density. A friend of mine moved from Chicago to Los Angeles and gained a considerable amount of weight simply because she stopped walking everywhere and started driving. Recently she's been swimming every day and the weight is being used up. Her body is shrinking. Energy gathered and condensed is weight. Energy moving is fluid and light.

Fat is stored energy waiting to be used. This body energy in a more ethereal state is emotion. How and what you feel is made flesh. Who we are at the deepest part of self is fragile, tender, precious, and sweet, the essence of a newborn baby. In this precious state we are vulnerable, innocent, and naive and therefore easily influenced and affected by the beliefs of others. Each of us deals with these imagined or real attacks and threats on our precious essence in our own way. Some become tough and attack first. Some of us become shy, helpless, and weak so that others will feel sorry for us and leave us alone. Others build up armor in the form of fat, money, power, fame, or anger as protection for their sweet and innocent self. Some hide, hoping no one will notice their existence. Some conform and aim to please.

When we focus our energy on the fear by attacking and attempting to destroy it or by protecting ourselves from it, this gives energy to it and it becomes real. There are no monsters. They are only illusions and shadows of the dark within our own imaginations. The imagination is powerful, as it is the machinery of vision and fantasy out of which we generate our story and our adventures. We become what we fear. To become something else we need to focus on nourishing the something else.

If a woman fears sexual molestation because of either a past experience or the fantasy of a future situation, she will use her energy to avoid what she believes is inevitable. She can make herself undesirable to men, arm herself with weapons, or escape to an ivory tower protected from the bad people in her ugly nightmare. I was told about a man who left the United States because he was afraid of violence and moved to Guatemala. He now owns a gun and has to protect his farm from the violence there. Whatever you run from, you run into.

Waiting is an attitude of "someday I'll be safe and then I'll live." Waiting for the nightmare to be over gives one's power to the self-generated fantasy of evil. Waiting involves anger, blame, resentment, envy, and self-invalidation. I'm not saying that women shouldn't protect themselves if needed. It's essential for every woman to take care of herself 100 percent. What I mean is that women can use their energy to create a glorious life rather than building protective fortresses.

Weight is energy stored for future use and for present self-nurturing and protection. There is nothing wrong with that at all if you need to do that. The number-one rule of enlightenment is to always appreciate and validate yourself by creating a good purpose that is motivating your behavior. Once you've gained the wisdom, release the game and select another game that is more loving to yourself and all concerned.

When I stepped out of the television ministry and into my time of contemplation, introspection, and hibernation, I allowed myself to eat whatever I wanted and gave up all fear and judgment on my body. Yes, I gained weight, but I kept loving myself and accepted the process as a necessary part of my evolvement. No, you don't have to gain weight in your process. I did. Now I'm satisfied and I eat what I want when I want and my body is slender and balanced. I was "waiting" for my wounds to heal. I had also stopped communicating, as I was tired of risking. We stuff feelings by stuffing food. I did that and I tried to avoid my pain by eating.

My experiment was and is to love all my selves including my body without the slightest bit of fear, judgment, guilt, jealousy, competitiveness, or comparison. What I've discovered through personal experience and observation is that we are grossly underdeveloped and underutilized because we have limited ourselves by the judgment of our bodies and our actions. When you free yourself from the body game a new multidimensional cosmic person is born. It takes courage for a person, especially a woman, to take charge of her life, body, and every aspect of herself, but look at the dismal alternatives.

Waiting can be beneficial for a certain period of time but devastating to one's purpose if it lasts too long. You can dream, visualize, and fantasize all you want, but if you want these visions to happen in the physical realm, you'll need to do something physically. Instead of belaboring what you don't want, do what you do want. Little by little, you'll pick yourself up, get going, have fun, and gather your rewards.

The key to not waiting for the actualization of your deepest desires and visions is to physically take action in the direction of your intentions. Movement uses energy; waiting conserves. When you are in a holding pattern, you are waiting for permission to move on. I don't mean that you have to do "busy work"; pointless activity can be a way of avoiding self-contemplation. The question to ask yourself is, "Am I living my vision and dream, or am I afraid that if I did, I could be hurt, rejected, or made wrong in some way?" The power is within you and without using that power you are stuck in neutral.

My own creativity is blossoming at this time and I'm overflowing with ideas, fantasies, dreams, and visions. I had put them on hold waiting for the "right" time. Now is the "right" time. Now I'm moving ahead on my creations and visions and have stopped blaming those that I felt were holding me back. I'm also finished with trying to motivate others into helping me achieve my objectives. Now I find those who are going in the same direction and play with them! It is called teamwork!

TAKE ACTION

Get active. Move your body. Take walks. Dance. Hike. Get going. Discover how you most enjoy moving your body and then do that. Often! My driveway is about a quarter of a mile, so I walk a half mile every day to get my mail. I love the stroll and I make sure I breathe in the fresh air and enjoy the trees, flowers, and wildlife. Dancing and yoga are very satisfying and fun for me. I especially love doing a weekend workshop or a seven-day retreat, because every day we do yoga, hiking, and dance. I'm more flexible now than I was twenty years ago. The only aches and pains I get now are created when I move in a new way and I enjoy it.

Climbing uphill is excellent for the body and for the respiratory system. The oxygen you breathe in feeds your brain and every cell in your body temple. Don't torture yourself with exercise. The trauma you generate by hating something and pushing yourself to the brink of collapse isn't good for you. Find ways to enjoy your body through movement. Walking vigorously, jumping on a trampoline to your favorite upbeat music, and swimming and playing mermaid and dolphin are all fun and satisfying. Set your living environment up in a manner that demands physical activity. Your body is you, even though it isn't all of you. Health comes from participation. Children play, move, jump, run, and climb. If your life-style supports your health, movement, and participation, then your body isn't separate. It is your ever-present vehicle, temple, and form in which you live, move, and are.

The most important aspect of movement is the move in the direction of your projects, visions, ideals, purposes, and dreams. Why wait? Remember "Someday" is not a day of the week.

STOP TESTING OTHERS

Step four of the "loving yourself forever diet" is to give up testing others by hiding yourself in your body and placing the responsibility on them to love you enough to find you; when they have passed the torture test, then you'll come out of hiding and reward them greatly for their courage, strength, and love. Forget it! Why bother to test every person you meet? We all set up tests for ourselves and others as part of the games we play. It is up to you to decide if you've set up games that pay off in the rewards you want or that are simply robbing you of your own power.

I saw a man in the park one day who was filthy, dirty, and smelled to high heaven. Needless to say, everyone stayed away from him. He tested people at the level of, "If you are a loving person, you'll see who I am and be close to me even though I push you away and stink." Who'd want that challenge but a masochist?

I've found that the most difficult task as a counselor and facilitator at seminars and workshops is to get people to open up and share of themselves. They hide because they are afraid to come out. They test me as they test others. If you are good, they give you a little.

Men test, women test, children test, and so do animals. Plants may also test before they are willing to entrust themselves into the care of another enough to flourish, blossom, and bear fruit. I've heard it said that you have to invite parsley six times into your garden before it will grow. Humans love contests or games of wit. Hiding and games of camouflage are written into our folklore, fables, and myths. Only the brave and true find the real gift—you.

It is at this moment that I realize that "women" and "men" can be terms of separation rather than just body types. A woman's body or a man's body does not mean anything. They are just bodies, space suits in which to experience life on earth. Who cares what they look like? We are so much greater than our judgments of bodies. Why bother to torment yourself by believing you are a woman? Strange as it may seem, to identify yourself as a woman carries with it massive beliefs, games of separation, right and wrong. Get a group of women together and there is definitely an agreed-upon reality about men, women, relationships, and so on. "Men are so . . . !" "Women are . . ."

At first glance these concepts appear to be true and valid facts about the intrinsic nature of women, men, and their relationships. A further look and the question arises, "Who made it up this way, anyway?" Is it all made up and we take on qualities of being and call ourselves different, or are we actually different in ways other than just our bodies?

Who are you testing with your body? What games are you playing as a woman? Who is supposed to discover you? What happens to those who fail to recognize the you trapped inside of a woman's body? What curses have you put on those who succeed or fail?

Those who are hiding say, "Someone wonderful is in here. It is your responsibility to find me, if you dare." Legend has it that the princess must be found by the prince. He must first be tested and found worthy to receive her blessings. It is true! If we believe we are to be saved by our Prince Charming then we continue to play victim/victimizer. You don't need to be saved. You only need to be discovered and valued first by yourself and then by your inner male. There is a tendency for a rescuer to imprison the victim. I found myself attached to female roles, myths and legends by wanting to be saved, shielded, protected, and then enslaved. I found men who if they couldn't have sex with me or save "little ole helpless me" would try and sink my ship.

LET PROFESSIONALS TEACH YOU ABOUT YOUR BODY

Step five is to visit a holistic doctor or practitioner and test your body to see if you are out of balance nutritionally or physically. If so, put your body back into alignment and harmony. There are also people who are qualified and expert at working with your body's structure to bring balance and alignment. The stress in living takes its toll by creating physical problems that affect the way you digest food, assimilate your nutrients, and function. The body holds the memory of your past and any pain, anger, resentment, hurt, and so forth that you have felt and not released.

I like to work from the inside out and the outside in to achieve a healing. By changing your attitudes, beliefs, and emotions combined with a healthy respect and caring for your physical body and its electrochemical energy needs, you are covering all the bases.

Learn about your body, how it functions, and what it needs to be a healthy and strong vehicle that will give you joy and pleasure instead of pain and heartache. Rolfing and Hellerwork are both excellent methods of deep tissue body therapy that have been extremely beneficial to me. Seven years ago I could barely walk and was in constant pain. I decided I wanted to run and jump again as I did as a child and have freedom of movement. I called forth the fear-based beliefs and thoughts that were causing my illness and at the same time I went to a nutritionist, chiropractor, and had Hellerwork body therapy every week. I also did yoga, weight lifting, and jumped on the trampoline three times a week. It took two to three years, but time passed and now I'm totally flexible and enjoy my body.

The body is a whole-system reflection of your whole self. You can't just treat one aspect of yourself without considering the relationship between each of your aspects.

I just put my exercise bicycle next to my telephone by "accident" and yesterday rode ten miles while talking on the phone. I breathed well and perspired enough to release old energy, afterward took a great shower and scrubbed myself off with a gentle brush, and felt invigorated. Calories are measurements of heat and heat is energy. Heat up your body and calories are released. Only eat what you need for the work you intend to put out. Adjust your caloric intake depending on the task or lifestyle.

When you make the switch from looking good as your prime directive to feeling good, your rewards are personal, physical, and emotional. Chemical imbalances can create abnormal behavior just as an emotional upset of yesterday can still be affecting you as a hormonal, glandular, or organ imbalance today. Mood swings can be sugar related just as alcohol and drugs can have an adverse effect on one emotionally, intellectually, and physically.

So many of our solutions are simple and obvious, yet because they are unknown, the problems seem difficult to solve. We can feel overwhelmed, hopeless, and defeated when all it takes is more information and action—step by step, little by little in the direction you intend to move.

You don't have to tackle your entire life today, just this moment. Praise yourself at every opportunity as you remember you are on a forever treasure hunt and the challenges of today have treasures in them. You are learning and growing into a greater appreciation and knowledge of yourself every moment.

Our body temple needs to be taken care of just like any piece of machinery. Food is fuel and a proper program of nutrition designed for your specific metabolism and life-style will work wonders and pay off in high energy, happiness, and self-esteem.

The "loving yourself forever diet" offers an approach to a healthy, balanced body that operates at maximum efficiency and feels wonderful. A body that is healthy feels so comfortable that you won't even know you have one. Watch a child jump, crawl, leap, tumble, dance, and play. That is just an example of what your body can do. It is not a limitation but an experiential temple that gives you the ultimate physical experience.

You'll add to the diet your own discoveries. I have simply stated some basic guidelines. What food or exercise plan you enjoy is whatever suits your needs, life-style, and challenges. Comfort and flexibility are important to me and I like to feel and be beautiful. Your body is personal to you so it is up to you to determine the size and shape that serves you best. Support yourself in whatever ways will help you create habits and patterns of health and fitness that will assist you in living your dreams.

Once your body is acceptable and pleasurable to you as it is, you can visualize your body as you desire it to be. Be clear on your motives. Most important of all is to feel beautiful, feel regal, feel powerful, and feel healthy. In this moment, you are.

EXERCISES

1. Step back from your female body identity and observe all the games you play with it. Write down some of what you notice.

2. Lift yourself up to your observation tower and notice if you live in a category and place others in categories based on their bodies. Write down what you notice.

3. How do you use your body size to hide and what will it take for you to come out and play?

4. What part of yourself are you protecting with your body size and how do you feel your body size can do that?

5. Recall a time when you decided to hide. Who did you hide from and what did they do?

6. Have you decided that no man will ever hurt you again? If yes, who is suffering, you or the men of the world?

7. What are you waiting (weighting) for? What do you use your body size and shape to escape from, avoid, or deny yourself?

I escape from _____.

I avoid _____.

I deny myself _____.

8. Fast from negative judgment, critical and guilt-ridden thoughts and feelings about yourself. Create a new habit pattern of self-acceptance, love, happiness, joy, fun, creation, and play. Enjoy your body.

9. Get to know your space suit. Take a yoga class; walk two miles a day; dance to your favorite song; breathe into your body; feel your muscles; and learn about how your body functions and what it needs to be ageless, healthy, strong, and active.

10. Reward, nourish, and comfort yourself in ways other than food. List your alternatives and then do them. Little by little you'll create new patterns. Remember if you forget, acknowledge yourself the moment you remember for remembering and start again. Never use guilt or judgment to control yourself. It doesn't work! Use love, acceptance, acknowledgment, and appreciation.

11. How would you feel if your body was acceptable and beautiful to you? Feel the feeling now. Feeling creates circumstances; circumstances only give you more reason to keep feel-

ing whatever feelings you want. Feel what you've been waiting to feel now!

12. Give up self-pity, depression, sickness, and suffering as a way to deal with life. Acknowledge your immortal self and get into the flow of your ongoing forever adventure of being alive. The key here is to do what you want to do, live as you choose, and be yourself.

13. Notice how much of your life is about your body and others' bodies, what you think of your body and their bodies, and what they think about your body and their bodies. Is it worth it? If you weren't consumed with body energy, what would you be thinking, feeling, doing, being, and having?

14. Create a vision of your life if you were no longer overly concerned with your body and its size, shape, or look.

I'd be _____.
I'd do _____.
I'd have _____.
I'd feel _____.

AFFIRMATIONS

1. Here is a partial list of both the limited thought or belief and its suggested replacement by a more loving and freeing thought or

belief about your body and food. Get used to affirming a reality that offers more joy and flexibility.

LIMITED	UNLIMITED
I can't trust myself with food.	I trust myself to eat what I need.
Food can hurt me.	The food I eat is good for me and my body.
If I trust myself, I'll be out of control.	The more I trust myself, the more I am in control of myself.
If I am old, I'll be alone.	The more I love myself, the more I have loving friends. I am timeless, ageless, and forever in love with myself.
If I'm not beautiful, men won't love me and will leave me.	I am beautiful to myself and my feelings of beauty are what I have been seeking.
I need to lose weight.	I now use the energy of my body to empower me to live and feel as I choose.

I feel guilty for eating this food.	I enjoy what I eat and it blesses my beautiful, alive, and magnificent body.
This food is bad for me and will make me sick or kill me.	Whatever I choose to eat is pure energy of love and it nourishes and blesses every cell of my beautiful body.
If I don't exercise fanatically the men I want won't want me.	My body is for enjoying life, so the more I dance, stretch, and play, the more energy I have.
My mother or father had a weight problem, so I guess I do too.	I now command the cells of my body to be healthy, vital, youthful, and freely alive.
I am my body.	I am a spirit who has a body and I enjoy my space suit.
I hate my nose, face, hips, etc.	My body is my art form and perfect thought of myself—I love my creation and I bless every part of my body and call it beautiful.

I'll do anything to keep the man I love.	I love myself, know who I am, and give myself everything I was seeking from others.
	or
	I now consciously attract loving, gentle, and able men into my life.
If a man wants my body sexually, then I must be okay.	When I enjoy sex, it is me enjoying my own body. I satisfy myself, allow the man I love to satisfy himself, and together we create a loving relationship.
List any defeating thoughts you have about your body, food, weight, exercise, etc. in one column.	In a parallel column, write your new unlimited thoughts that are in alignment with how you now desire to feel and be.

2. I, _____, now give myself what I desire, I live as I choose now, and I no longer wait for anyone or anything.

CHAPTER 12

Expressing Your Anger Without Hurting Anyone

NOTHING HAS GIVEN ME MORE TROUBLE THAN MY anger. If I felt it, I was wrong. If I expressed it, I was bad. If I stuffed it, I was depressed. What to do with anger, an emotion of intense feeling, has been a challenge for me and I'm sure for most of us. We as women have stuffed our anger and covered it over with our smiles out of the fear that if we expressed those intense feelings, we'd devastate our relationships.

All anger is justified in the eyes of the one who is angry. We can be justified or we can be happy but we can't be both. What has worked for me has been to find appropriate ways in which to release and express those feelings when I feel them and to let go of the need to repress myself. I simply communicate how I feel in the moment.

ANGER WITHIN A RELATIONSHIP

What has created the most anger in me has been the consideration that I have to suppress myself in order to have and keep a loving relationship. I have noticed that I've taken on the "karma" or energy of every man I've ever lived with and denied my unique self to some degree. I've taken on his beliefs, life-style, values, and priorities. We all do this to a certain degree and it can be a valuable experience to actually learn through another, but it can also be disempowering. Anger is the feeling that comes when you believe you've been hurt, disappointed, used, threatened, attacked, or rejected. What is obvious to me now is that everything I did or "gave away" was done by my choice. I never "had" to do any of it.

Now as I move through my life, I can select a quality of being I desire. Of course I'm becoming more independent all the time and much happier. What I'm finding is that the consideration, "If I am myself and trust my own guidance system, I'll lose my mate" was just a self-fulfilling prophecy. I no longer believe that and it now has no power over my life.

People let their parents, mates, and co-workers repress them. It is no wonder that anger is either exploding and creating destruction or is seething beneath the surface and oozing out into illness, depression, or self-pity. Anger is created by the underlying belief, "I have to be less or not myself in some way if I want to receive your love." Children are stopped from expressing themselves as sovereign beings, even abused for it. Thus begin the roots of adult anger.

Take a look at the anger, frustration, resentment, or depression you feel and list the considerations you have that caused it. Look to see where you have created being stopped, repressed, abused, denied, punished, or kept from being, doing, or having what you desire in any way. As you write out these thoughts, you will realize that the obstacles are self-generated. Why? For me it has been for "love." As a woman, I was supposed to be a sweet, subservient, adoring support system. The payment for this behavior was "love." Ultimately, anger is our reward for giving our power away. Anger is what we feel toward ourselves for not being true to ourselves.

Of course, I love love and I love to be touched, held, and cherished. What occurs to me is that it costs too dearly if we repress ourselves in order to have that. Anger is what is left if you didn't get what you wanted. Anger is the payoff and becomes a companion to those who sold out and were rejected.

We feel and express our anger in a number of ways. The first step is to accept our anger as an expression of how we feel and not judge it as "good" or "bad." Anger is an automatic reaction when one feels attacked, stopped, or thwarted. When you express yourself in that moment you are taking care of yourself. Then move on to the next moment. If you judge yourself, then suppress because you believe you can lose by expressing your feelings, you will probably stuff your feelings. It takes more effort to relive your anger than to express your feelings in the moment they occur.

There are men and women who prey on those who want to "be nice." They use the "sweet" person for their own purposes knowing that this person is a "people pleaser" and won't express their anger or stand up for him- or herself. This is still something I deal with inside of myself. "I am a nice person and I also stick up for myself " and "It is okay for me to take care of myself first" are two affirmations I now use, so I don't set myself up as a victim. "It is all right for others to express their feelings around me as I am always safe and loved" is another affirmation that allows for win/win situations in relationships.

ANGER IS OKAY!

As I said earlier, the first step in releasing any pent-up anger is to make anger and yourself okay. Anger is just energy that has stopped flowing and is piled up, waiting to blow its charge. Repression is the tremendous amount of energy you use to pretend you are not feeling what you are feeling. If we trusted our intuition and knowingness at all times,

made our decisions, and carried on our relationships from these inner feelings and guidance systems, we would handle each situation and moment
from the point of personal power. This would prevent any buildup of anger. A child is angry, ex-
presses herself, and the anger is gone. An adult is
angry, bottles it up for years, and ends up killing
others and himself in an act of inner or outer violence. Health is a function of truth. When people
live true to and in harmony with themselves, their
bodies are healthy. It is a uni-verse, a song sung in
uni-son as a star system of light.

Take a piece of paper and make a list of everyone
toward whom you feel even the slightest bit of
anger, resentment, guilt, jealousy, blame, or judgment. Your closest family members and friends
should appear on your list unless you are being absolutely true to yourself each and every moment.
Are you playing the victim's game anywhere in your
life? Victims love to feel hurt, rejected, used, and
unacknowledged. I think it is a part of our sav-
ior/martyr syndrome. We feel the best when we are
misused, or maligned, or not understood. We can
then feel saintly and righteous in our misery. What
better way of controlling those around us than to
pretend we are not creating whatever is happening
in our life. What I've discovered is that we like to
give awards to martyrs, victims, and sacrificers.
Don't want an award for any of that. Simply live as
you desire and generate what is important to you.

I have been a blamer and the belief I have been
holding is, "If I am all that I am and be, do, and

have whatever I want and if I express my light brilliantly, I'll lose love especially the love of my man." This thought is degrading to men because it puts them in a category of suppressive. My new affirmation is, "My relationship with my lover is ever increasing in love, respect, and joy and I am expressing my light brilliantly with infinite joy and love forever."

"I am safe to feel all of my emotions" is a powerful thought to accept; it will allow you to open yourself up to your feelings. Take your "anger" list and write next to each name what happened, how you felt, and how you handled your feelings in that moment and since. Say, "It is okay for me to feel angry and it is safe for me to express my anger." As you permit yourself to feel what you feel even if you know it is your victim or blamer, you are releasing yourself from the judgment of it.

ALLOWING YOURSELF TO FEEL ANGER

The second step is to find a safe place in which to express your rage. I've used my bedroom where I could lie down and scream into my pillow as I pounded my fists into the bed and kicked my legs and feet. Another way is to get on your knees either on the floor or on your bed and place two thick couch pillows in front of you. Move your body back over your heels and make a fist with your hands. With the energy of your entire body, beat the pillows with your arms and speak your truth to the person or situation you are addressing. Exaggerate your feelings and allow yourself to feel your anger. Pound the pillows with all your might until you feel released. I've found that some people are afraid to express their anger forcefully, to yell, cry, or swear, even when it is just a pillow they are pounding. They are more willing to beat themselves up than the pillow.

Another way to express your anger and release your energy would be to get a friend to sit across from you and be a surrogate or stand in for the one with whom you are angry. The person role plays and the two of you can get into a dialogue. You can then say, feel, and release what you've been repressing, holding back, or pretending doesn't matter. You are releasing whatever is stuck and allowing yourself to communicate all the "stuff" you didn't, couldn't, or wouldn't before.

A key here is to discover the games you've been playing, what the payoff or "benefit" to you has been, and what those games are costing you. Male anger tends to be released in aggression and violence; women's anger is the kind that festers beneath the surface. You must make a choice here. Do you want to continue to blame, resent, be victimized, be angry, and repress your creativity, or do you want to be happy, free, alive, healthy, and creative? Once you are clear and feel comfortable with your anger, then ask yourself if this is how you want to live and if it is worth denying your freedom of self-expression, success, and happiness to be bitter and victimized.

Every victim is also a victimizer. At one point Reuben and I were playing that one. I'd be "less" in the relationship and in my career so that he'd feel equal and we could be together. In truth no one can be "less" for another to be "more"—we simply have to be who we are. When I gave up my victim number, I stopped being the bitch who was justified in attacking and blaming. Both of us had anger that held the game in place. Anger is the intense energy used to keep us stuck to avoid loss. What is produced is loss, pain, hurt, and more anger. Express your energy in work, exercise, dance, and in communication.

Our family has been doing some clearing recently (meaning talking and sharing our deepest feelings about how we affect each other). We've been angry, frustrated, defensive, attacking, and very emotional as deeply buried beliefs have been revealed. We live on top of emotional volcanoes and at some level we are afraid to release that energy, thinking it will destroy us, our relationships, and everything important to us. Contrary to that, though, we actually save our relationships by releasing and expressing the pent-up anger, especially through communication, even though it may be highly confrontational and difficult to do. It gets easier and sometimes it is best to have a mediator, counselor, or facilitator to assist in the process so that you complete it instead of walking away or "killing" each other. Remember it is all a dream and you are the dreamer.

DENYING ANGER

As women we are the cause and men are the effect. For me, women are the sun and men are the moon, the reflector of the sun's light. We've had it backward for a long time and therefore we've lived in the fear of loss, rejection, and abandonment. But we were the creators of it all along. We desired to be the effect so that we could know that aspect and have compassion for it. So we created every possible experience from that point of view. The woman creates and maintains her universe and everything in it as she desires it to be. There is no need to be angry about what has occurred because it was all our creation in the first place. We forgot and then denied the truth. Denial brings up resistance and the need to fight against our creations. The trouble with fighting our creations is that they remain and we disempower ourselves and feel more hopeless and defeated at every encounter.

A woman at a recent retreat of mine drew a picture of her life and how she felt. Next to her in her drawing was a bag of fat. When I asked her why she put the fat next to her she replied that it wasn't her and she didn't want it. She's tried to lose weight and nothing has worked. She is in a "heavy" state of denial. She has a fantasy wish to run away or escape from her life. Even though life is an illusion made real, it is difficult to have a fantasy within a fantasy within a fantasy. What she came to do during the retreat was to own her fat and the parts of her life that she did not like. To own and be responsible for creating and having what is happening in your life is what will return your power to you and let you get on with your life.

Denial creates anger. Hurt lies underneath the anger. Underneath the hurt is the refusal to remember that you made the decision to create it in the first place. Some of these suppressive kinds of decisions that I have made were done simply because I accepted another person's beliefs, point of view, or idea.

The more you create authority figures and experts in your life, whether they are men, teachers, bosses, other women, or parents, the more you set yourself up to be repressed and to lose. I have a habit of speaking with authority and as one who knows. I try to put power into my words and statements, although sometimes I've said things that are limiting to myself and others, even though at the time I was not aware of it. We're all learning and growing, so it is up to each of us to question authority and to question our own beliefs as well as those of others.

We are very susceptible to the input of others and in a moment we can make life-altering decisions and forget that we even did that for perhaps years or even lifetimes. A way to prevent this is to stay in touch with your feelings and remember that you are unlimited, so whatever you desire to be, do, or have, you can. If a person makes a statement to you that is limiting in any way, let it pass immediately. If it seems to be true, be with the idea for a while and do a "love test" on it. "Does this thought bring me more love, happiness, health, wealth, and wisdom?" If so, it is probably a wonder-filled thought. If not, why bother to assimilate it into your belief system? It is not worthy of you.

I was talking with a friend of mine from New England who is a minister. In the last several years this woman had become extremely successful in her work. She then became an assistant minister at her church. A male minister started telling her that God didn't want women to preach and that the reason her marriage was falling apart was that God was punishing her for being a minister. She believed him and she let all of her wonderful creations crumble. She went downhill from there and when I talked with her yesterday, I could feel the deep pain and loss of will she was feeling. She now realizes what she did to herself and has decided to get back into life and live her dream and vision once again.

She probably didn't set out to lose her dream, but because she made a male minister and Bible quotes more powerful than herself, she denied her own divine inner guidance system. The only thing you have that is real is yourself and your inner guidance system.

Anger is what we feel when we don't trust ourselves. When things don't turn out as we hoped they would, we're hurt and angry. The only one you should ever be angry at is yourself. Yet, it is not even appropriate to be angry at yourself, because "if you knew better, you'd do better!" We are all doing the best that we can based on our current consciousness level. We learn by trusting ourselves and by noticing what happens when we don't.

GO WITH YOUR GUT!

If I look back at the major hurts or "failures" I've had, I can see I knew deep inside of me that whatever was going on didn't feel right—but I overlooked and denied my feelings. I'd blame my gut reaction on fear or resistance. We receive warning signals if something isn't for our highest good and it is only when we ignore those feelings and signs that we get into trouble. When the difficulty is past, you can't wish you'd done it differently. You did what you did. Learn from it and find the good that was there. Next time you will choose differently and you will have gained wisdom from your experience. You are learning to trust yourself.

We're not taught to trust ourselves, especially as women. Our feminine intuition is laughed at, put down, and denied as worthless. Your intuition is accurate. It is up to you to know the difference between your intuitive feelings and your fantasies of loss and hurt. Your fears come from the head, your intuitive feelings come from the solar plexus and heart. Intuition is an inner sense of knowing. It does not leave you feeling fearful and uncertain. A fear-based nightmare comes from the mind; in it you are projecting some limited, worthless thought. Learn to use your mind for the highest purpose,

for love, health, happiness, wealth, and enlightenment, and learn to use your inner guidance system
as a link with the celestial and ethereal levels of consciousness. Ask for what you want from your mind
and open yourself to receive the answer in the form
of visions, feelings, knowing, body sensations, and
revelations.

"It's never too late to begin again." Believing this
thought gives you a limitless number of chances to
start over. Once you allow yourself to express your
anger and move the stuck energy up and out of your
emotions and body, it is time to choose again.

You can wallow in self-pity, rage, anger, depression, and blame or you can get out of the muck and
mire and create a new life for yourself. The question, "But will this happen to me again?" probably
comes to mind. The answer is "Do you want it to?"
What I've discovered is that if I am afraid that I'll
do that to myself again, I hide out and not play anything so as to protect myself from hurt. That is not
living! I have to be willing to jump into the water
and take wisdom with me. This time I'll spend time
with myself so that I can become my own counselor
and advisor.

You are never alone. You are plugged into the
universal energy network and have available to you
the resources, wisdom, and knowledge of the universe. Learn to access what you need when you
need it.

Giving your power away to another, even to the
universe, renders you impotent. What we usually
do to get our power back is destroy something—the

relationship, the love, whatever. Simply do not look outside yourself for anything and whatever comes will be a blessing.

Not looking outside yourself doesn't mean being the sole giver and worker and never receiving from anyone, however. Much of my past anger comes from my game of being provider. I do all the work. I do all the creating and provide money for everyone else so they will have it easy. "It's okay. I can handle it. I can bear the burden and shoulder the load." I then get upset because I am doing it all and "they" expect me to! This is a victim game if I ever saw one! "Poor me!" This game was set up out of the guilt I had for having so much in this lifetime. I felt it wasn't right to have the abundance I had and that it was up to me to help, save, and provide for others.

LEARNING WIN/WIN, NOT WIN/LOSE

I stopped this game by playing the game called "win/win." I now make it okay for me to thrive out of my own efforts and to pay others the going rate for what their most wonderful services and products provide to me in support of my goals, purposes, and intentions. Anger was my emotional payoff for "How dare you use me, after all I've done for you!"

If we want other games, we need to be clear on the ones we now choose to play, with whom we will play, just what each does, and the rewards involved.

It may take a while to release yourself from victim/victimizer and from codependent relationships. Be gentle with yourself.

If the answer to the question, "Am I getting back equal to what I am giving?" is no, look again. Do you feel used, abused, unappreciated, tired, overworked, and underpaid? You could very likely be playing the martyr game. "Look how much I give and how little I receive." The payoff is usually manipulating others through guilt and being in control. You are keeping others indebted to you and they keep playing because they are afraid they can't make it on their own. Reverse this and it is also true. You are afraid you can't make it and flourish on your own and so they control you by not taking responsibility for their own lives. You are stuck in a "no win," energy-draining game. Everyone is angry and everyone hides it under the pretense that "everything is fine."

Changing these games and going into a win/win life-style can create havoc initially. Be patient and continue toward your destination of joy, wealth, love, and health. Changing patterns requires that you step into a new pattern. Be patient with yourself. Becoming aware of what you've been up to can be demoralizing. To avoid this, be grateful for having realized what you've been creating, so that now you can forge a new and clearer path for yourself.

We are each on our own and responsible for ourselves. Anyone who tells you differently is not doing you a favor. This is the good news. The bad news is that most of us haven't ever really totally accepted this, so it may take some time and energy to have our lives turn in the direction of our most beautiful dreams.

Anger dissipates as we get what we want by creating, not by manipulating others to get it. Clean living is guilt free, stress free, and open. Honest choices empower us and others to live as whole people balanced in female and male energies.

Many of us come from dysfunctional families. We were taught to play the victim/victimizer game to get our love needs met. Our family members didn't know any better—they learned these games themselves in their childhood. Now is the time for a whole new way of being, loving, and working together based on first love of oneself and then on mutual respect for each other.

What keeps us tied to the old games is the fear of being alone and lonely. We will sometimes continue any game even if it is frustrating, damaging, and disempowering rather than play no game at all.

Boredom and being fed up with anger-producing games because the payoff in hurt, pain, and struggle is no longer worth it will release you from the game. Just ask yourself, "Is this worth what it costs me?" "Do I want to be happy, healthy, loving, rich, and enlightened or do I want to be miserable, sick, poor, fearful, and asleep?"

You'll probably need to communicate what you've been holding back with your closest players and they'll need to do the same. I suggest you find a professional that will help you clear the air. You can then set up a new game where the payoffs are the pleasures of life. The energy that repressed your anger and resentment and stopped you from flourishing will go toward producing a beautiful new life!

EXERCISES

These questions will give you greater clarity on your deepest values, ideas, and choices.

1. What are your ten greatest fears in releasing anger and no longer feeling angry toward men?

2. List five ways that you use anger to control and manipulate others.

3. Who are you angry with and what did they take from you? Is there anything they took from you that you want back again? What? Are you willing to put that back in your life and give up the resentment and blame?

4. What is it costing you to hold onto your bitterness, anger, and blame? List ten qualities of being in relationships or aspects of your life that you are denying yourself to keep your anger alive.

5. List ten safe ways for you to feel, express, and release your anger.

AFFIRMATIONS

1. I, _____, love all my emotions.

2. It is safe for me, _____, to feel and express my anger.

3. It is okay for me, _____, to be angry if I want to be.

4. I, _____, am now willing to release my expectations and dependencies having to do with men.

5. No one owes me anything. I, _____, can and do give myself whatever I need and want.

6. I, _____, enjoy taking care of myself. I am free to create whatever I desire.

7. No one can take from me what I do not freely give.

8. I forgive myself, _____, for ever hurting myself to get someone to love me.

9. I, _____, am a free agent and now release myself from the illusion of slavery and dependence.

CHAPTER 13

Love, Passion, and Intimate Relationships

RELATIONSHIPS ARE THE VEHICLES THROUGH WHICH
one living energy system interacts and merges with
another. This creates endless variation on the
theme of one plus one equals three. Your universe
added to my universe creates a third universe called
"us."

I think of people as an energy system rather than
a one-dimensional unit that lives inside a bag of
skin called a body. Who you are is a complex system
of simple energies called aspects or selves. You are
made up of an almost infinite number of cells
(selves) each fulfilling its own function as well as
working in union with all the other cells (selves).
All of these aspects are focused toward a particular

objective, the well-being of the organism. The challenge is for each of us to know all of our different "selves" on all levels and to align our "selves" so that we are working together as a healthy, happy, powerful team. The way to harness this team energy within us for a constructive purpose is to appreciate and organize all those parts into one highly developed, co-creative unit. We need to know the team members within and have a game to play.

Learn to dialogue with these aspects of yourself when they appear: the bitch, the little girl, the creator, the genius, the brat, the frightened person, the mystic, the mother, the star, the taskmaster, the arrogant person, and so on. Dialogue with your body sensations. What is going on with your throat when the words you are trying to speak get stuck or you feel choked? Ask yourself, "What am I feeling now?" Listen to what you are saying. Notice your reactions. Ask your senses, your anger, your feelings, "What do you want from me? What do you need?"

We are each a complex set of simple characteristics, energies, wants, and needs. We evolve not just out of the thoughts we hold of ourselves and the notions we project, but out of our willingness to communicate, investigate, discover, challenge, interact, and share. The relationship you have with another person is much like the relationship you have with yourself.

Relationships between people are the interaction of two enormous energy systems full of conscious and unconscious patterns, dialogues, programming, failures, hopes, and dreams. In the moment that your spark connects with another's spark, a spiritual, mental, emotional, and physical union occurs. An incredible opportunity suddenly becomes available to both of you at this point. You will either be awake and alert to it or not; it is always your choice. To not enter because of past heartaches is to cry for what could have been and this keeps you from living fully in the moment. You can move from heartache to ecstasy.

The phoenix is a mythical bird that consumes itself in fire and is reborn from its own ashes. Life renews itself as a continual cycle of death and rebirth, meetings and partings. Death, to me, is a moment-to-moment process; every time you exhale your breath, you release the toxins and residue of the moment just past. Life is also a moment-to-moment experience; you breathe in a new beginning, a fresh start, a new dream that comes on the heels of the last exhale.

The key to ecstasy is to live totally in the moment. Release all of your past. Allow the future to unfold. Focus on the present. That is the only place where joy, love, and ecstasy abide. They do not come from another person; they generate and expand from within you. When two people both live from a base of love, passion, and ecstasy, what happens between them makes their most sacred and precious dreams come true.

It takes courage, fearlessness, desire, commitment, and action for you and me to bring forth the treasures within us that we may know the multiple aspects of self and combine with the multiple aspects of another.

Go through your personal STOP signs. Heartaches are the result of people stopping, quitting, denying, avoiding, hiding, and so on. If you don't keep going, all your dreams will diminish and die. We are frightened little children, hiding under the covers so that no one will find us, spank us, or hurt us in any way.

Everytime we've been hurt, we close off, hide, go home, attack, or do whatever we believe will protect the vulnerable aspect of ourselves. The vulnerable aspect is the baby/child you were. That aspect still wants a mommy and daddy to take care of it so that it will feel safe. You need to indulge that aspect of yourself. You be its mommy and daddy so that the adult aspect of you can test your boundaries, explore your territory, discover your talents, and express your most creative self in harmony with all of your other selves.

When there is real danger, the primitive part of our brain triggers the fight-or-flight mechanism to ensure survival. The trouble is that the physical survival instinct is no longer serviceable in the mental, emotional, and spiritual realms; we have lost the ability to tell the difference between real danger and imagined danger.

WHAT TO DO?

Begin by establishing for yourself the difference between a survival-based, reactive response and a love-based, power-backed response. Each feels subtly different and you can attune yourself to the difference. For you to move past these STOP signs, these fear-based fight-or-flight survival reactions, you must ask yourself, "What do I want here?" The "I" refers to your higher self, that spiritual self that knows it is invulnerable and unlimited. Ask the Goddess you are for exactly what you want and then trust her response to you. Ask for your dreams to come true. First ask each aspect of yourself, "What is the outcome we desire?" This is the same question you would ask of your mate, your colleagues, your clients, your universe. "What is the outcome that would bless us, contribute to our highest good?"

It takes two to play a game. Before you begin any enterprise, whether it is playing a game, dancing, creating a vision, or setting a purpose, you must first know what you want. You need to have, at least at some level, a sense of the outcome you most desire. The other person you are interacting with must also have a desired outcome. When the two outcomes are similar, the relationship flows.

YOUR "MANIFESTATION" BASKET

Find a basket that feels and looks special to you. You may want to make it or decorate it so that it is a personal reflection of yourself. This basket will be your "manifestation" basket. Think about qualities that are important to you in a relationship. Write out or draw or cut out pictures representing everything you desire to have present and available in an intimate relationship. Cut each statement or picture into its single component parts. Hold each one individually, meditate on it, consume yourself with the experience of it, and place it in your basket. When the moon is waxing (the period right before the full moon), go into the night, lift your basket with open arms, and ask the Goddess energy to manifest your dreams.

This exercise assists you in realizing and focusing your truth about what you need and desire. The fulfillment of your desires will come rapidly. If you experience a blockage it could be that one of the aspects of yourself is feeling that what you are asking for would hurt you or be wrong for you.

RELEASE YOUR BLOCKAGES AND STOP SELF-SABOTAGE

Neurolinguistic programming is a name given to a process that assists you in dialoguing with those aspects of yourself that may be holding you back. It helps you find another way of taking care of yourself and fulfilling your needs by altering the meaning behind the blockage or fear. You can change the meaning of something and no longer be stuck in a particular frame of mind. You can "reframe" it.

To reframe a concept, fear for example, is to no longer let fear be a problem to you. You alter the meaning and you alter the effects on you. Fear at one time could be an unknown or known terrible thing that you anticipated happening to you or a loved one. Change the way you hold fear and have it be a warning signal that can cause you to pay attention to something in your life so that you can do something to avoid the difficulty.

Parts of yourself and aspects of your energy system are really necessary for you to be fully operational. Therefore it is important to pay attention and alter the way in which you perceive anything inside of you that you have called negative. Loving and appreciating is essential when it comes to your understanding and knowing yourself.

Finding new ways to meet your needs and thrive means that you look to see if something you do is working for you or against you. If you can give a new meaning to what you find yourself doing or feeling, it helps you drop what is destructive to you yet still listen to what you need. If we misunderstand and/or devalue the contributions of some part of self, for example fear, we are in conflict within and denying ourselves our full expression of self. Then that part of ourself feels frustrated and angry, thus we ourselves are frustrated and angry. "It" doesn't understand that we no longer desire that particular contribution to our lives. For example, as children we would throw temper tantrums when we did not get our way. Sometimes the tantrums would work and so a part of ourselves, one of our "inner children," learned that by throwing temper tantrums we could get what we wanted. As an adult, temper tantrums are no longer appropriate, but the little child within is still operating as a child. Therefore, we need to "reframe" the method that little child inside uses to get his or her needs met.

The other person you are in relationship with may also need to reframe. At some point in their growth, maturity, and integration they learned behaviors that worked in the past but may not be appropriate now. The desire for love, attention, and touching is so great within the human that the child will do anything to get them. It is at this level that fear-based game playing becomes all consuming.

Our prime energy and the prime energy of life is what we call feminine. It is the God-us or Goddess energy. What we call masculine has difficulty with this and therefore is terrified to discover and express the Goddess energy that is its other part. This fear represents itself in our denial and negation of our hurts, needs, wants, dreams, and visions. We repeat and repeat the patterns.

What unlocks self-defeating, fear-based ego games is to actually feel your feelings, share your thoughts, unleash your emotions safely, tell your truth, and commit to yourself and to your dreams with absolute and total love. Being in touch with your body responses, your feelings, your words and mostly the still, small voice within you can free you faster than any other way.

In relationship there must be first a commitment to a direction, an outcome, or purpose that both agree to. The commitment to always share the truth about where you are, how you feel, and what you want must be first and foremost if the relationship is to flourish. Both must be willing to operate from this agreement for the treasures to be found within the relationship. If you are withholding in one part of your life, say in your communications within the relationship, you will feel incomplete and unsatisfied with your relationship and your life as a whole. Without giving yourself fully to the relationship, all you can do is hold back, deny, punish, feel guilty, be angry, and deplete yourself of your vital energy.

REFRAMING

To move through your blockages, ask all the parts of yourself, "Which part of me is blocking me in being, doing, or having what I want in this relationship?" Reassure that part that you understand it is operating as you once requested and that you appreciate the job it has done in protecting and helping you get what you want. Feel the response of that aspect as a body sensation of some kind, a knowingness, a vision, or a feeling. If it is too subtle for you to notice, ask it to be more obvious in its response. Explain to it what you now desire in your life and ask it if there is another way for it to take care of the responsibility you have assigned to it. For example, if a part of you believes that your mother won't approve of you if you have sex, the part that assumed the responsibility for getting your mother's approval will ensure that you have many blockages to making love and your relationship may suffer. Ask it to take on another responsibility, say to help you feel joyful within your relationship with your mother. Once you have reframed your blockages, you and your partner can then share of yourselves, thus creating and co-creating yourselves, your lives, and your most cherished dreams.

Self-sabotage is the way in which men and women "protect" themselves and their "inner children." It actually stunts one's growth and denies one passion, ecstasy, vision, love, health, joy, and the gift of who one is. Nothing is worth not being all you are capable of being. Sacrifice is not what a loving relationship is about (yet there may be compromises or promises that empower each other and support the continued unfolding of the partnership).

Agreement creates reality. Agreement between our aspects or selves is how we are able to accomplish anything. Each part performs its special function. We co-create our reality and our relationships.

Attaining what we desire involves growth, agreement, commitment, communication, and the death of something. To have anything you have to release something else. To be happy, you have to let self-pity die. To have loving, powerful, and rewarding relationships, you have to let the "poor me," victimized, spoiled, self-centered child leave you. You have to realize that the old childish games are not giving you what you want. You have to know that they are actually robbing you of your life force.

RELATIONSHIP IS AN EVER-EVOLVING DANCE

There is no destination for a relationship. There is only the opportunity for what is possible each and every day. What does relationship mean to you and why do you want one? The question is what are you looking for and if you know it when you find it. We are in relationship all the time and the forms change. We call some intimates, some enemies, some friends, and some associates. Form follows function.

Take some time now and write out a description of your ideal relationship. I'll list some categories and you contemplate each aspect a few minutes and then write down what is important to you. Don't compare your relationship with anyone else's! This is a sure way to kill your hopes for a wonderful love life. You are unique and what is important to you may not be important to anyone else. If you ask another what is right for you in relationship, you will only be a reflection of another's beliefs.

It takes three to argue! There are you, your partner, and the "third person" who is agitating and saying things like, "Are you going to let him get away with that?" The third person can be a memory in your mind, someone you think is judging you or your mate. This third person can be the same one you think your mate wants more than you. If you simply allow yourself to be true to your own values and ideals and accept your relationship for what it is and call that wonderful, you'll be in great shape. Get in touch with your innermost desires and needs.

Take out your journal or notebook. What are your priorities in relationship (having fun together, feeling peaceful, going dancing, loving animals, and so on)? List the qualities, the feelings, the lifestyle, purpose, and activities in a relationship that are important to you. What is important for you to have separately? Each person in a relationship must have a separate identity and a separate work, even if careers are combined. List the spiritual values as well as the earthly or natural values that are important in your marriage. (On a spiritual level any intimate relationship is a marriage and you don't need a religious or governmental ceremony to sanctify the union unless you want one.)

WHAT IS IMPORTANT IN A RELATION-SHIP

What is important to me is a partner, friend, and lover who is committed to loving himself and me, telling his truth at all times, participating fully in the creation of the relationship, having his own separate vision, and being responsible for being, doing, and having what he desires.

Know yourself and know your priorities. Once you know what is important to you, use your knowledge to stay centered within yourself and to keep the relationship on track, going in the direction you desire to go. A wise person knows her values, knows when she has attained them, and cherishes those precious relationships that foster her priorities. Many throw away gems because they always think that what they have isn't enough. Humankind is programmed to "hide and go seek" not "hide and go find." A master is one who knows when she has found what she has been seeking and treasures it.

We've lost many of our myths and values upon which to build a platform for our lives. We can look into our past through the vehicle of ancient myths, legends, and stories of our ancestors to rediscover some important values and rites of passage that we can integrate into our modern day lives. Take from the past what you can use and call forth from spirit what is relevant now in the way of new qualities, standards, and ideals. We are in a transition into a new realm where we have few, if any, role models. To create your own foundation and reconnect yourself with nature, spirit, and your inheritance, you must find some stable anchors that will allow you to fly and still be grounded. Your ideals, values, and morals based on divine love will provide these anchors.

Your love will grow as you take care of it, nurture it, appreciate it, give it attention, and create purpose and games that include and encourage the love and sharing. It is all available and it takes a conscious act of deciding what is important to you and the setting out to become what you desire to be. You attract what you are, so *become* whatever you want to attract and bring into your life. In the past others told you what to be. Now you must decide it, create it, and become it. You are the dancing Goddess and the earth is your garden in which you can be who you are and give your gifts.

MIRROR, MIRROR ON THE WALL

Creating yourself as a cosmic earth woman in today's confused society is a monumental task. A relationship is a support system during this process and a reflection or gauge for your progress. In relationships, others always mirror back to us ourselves. This is the frustrating and challenging aspect of relationship. You are always in relationship with yourself disguised as another. What an awesome challenge!

The mirror effect always throws whatever you perceive in another back onto yourself as the generator of the reflection. What an ingenious Creatress to set up life as an illusion constructed of mirrors! We've always loved to look at ourselves. Everywhere you look, you are reflected back to yourself in every possible and conceivable form, design, and pattern. (Depending on your image of yourself, this can make life heaven or hell.) If people knew this, how simple relationships would be. Any relationship can be intense when whatever is going on inside of you is reflected back to you from the other. I knew a man who hated his father; the father was vicious and ugly in this man's eyes. When he decided to make peace with his father, he began to hate his wife and see her as vicious and ugly. He was simply projecting his feelings for himself onto those around him.

Whatever I want to see, know, feel, and experience I must generate, since what I give comes back to me multiplied. If I see ugliness, what am I judging as ugly within me? If I perceive beauty, then what is beautiful within me? As we evolve into more conscious, loving beings, whatever is involved in that process will be seen in the mirror.

If I judge others as angry, fearful, or insecure, again it is my attempting to perceive others through my anger, fears, and insecurities. The fear is that I'm as good as I should be in some way and the emotion behind the fear is unworthiness. Always a judgment first begins with a judgment of ourselves and then a projection onto the other. Without a spiritual, higher purpose for your relationship, there is nowhere to go. With the commitment within yourself to become what you are capable of being on multiple levels of spirit, an intimate relationship offers great opportunities.

Your mate is your most intense and accurate mirror. Your mate may look like your opposite. He may reflect your insecurities. He may show you the anger you are unwilling to recognize. You may feel "he" is repressing you. He may be loving everything about you and all this may change suddenly depending on how you are feeling about yourself in that moment. The mirror gives reflections; what you perceive must originate and be projected out from you.

The mirror effect may not be evident, since you and I are usually ignorant of aspects of ourselves. That is why we created a mirror that wouldn't lie. "Mirror, mirror on the wall, who is the fairest of them all?" The mirror in "Snow White" never lied! It merely reflected back to the "evil stepmother" (another myth still believed) her greatest fear, that Snow White was more beautiful than she. Comparison always leads to pain.

If you doubt yourself, you may have a mate who puts you down. If you need to learn to assert yourself, your lover may be a dictator so you can call yourself forth and express yourself in a situation that is repressive. The mirror is complex, with many possible variations; there are no fixed rules or formulas. If you desire to be taken care of, you will create a mate who will make your decisions and take care of you. When you decide you want to take care of yourself, you will resent and rebel against that same person. If the two of you aren't willing to make the necessary adjustments and allow the relationship to change form, it is doomed to pass into the mediocre and the mundane. Usually what occurs when you want more in relationship is the thought, "Why make waves? Why upset the apple cart? I can just continue as I have been." What is new in relationship is the woman's desire to reconnect herself with the Earth Mother and her spiritual, cosmic, eternal self, a part of woman that has been denied and closed off for a long time.

We pass through phases, rites of passage in our relating process. Instead of seeing every occurrence as a major event, as I used to, I know it is all temporary and we as people are continually changing, evolving, and mutating. I can't protect, shelter, or do anything for my mate except to be true to myself, love myself, and allow him to do the same. I have given my power over to men. I have given my power to gurus. I have given my power to money, my body, other people's opinions, and you name it. We must pass through and face whatever challenges we have created to get to the side of love, joy, bliss, and harmony.

A SEPARATE IDENTITY AND LIFE DEDICATED TO A GRAND PURPOSE

It is important to have a grander purpose in life for yourself beyond the relationship. The relationship itself must have a grander purpose if it is to empower and fulfill your individual destinies. You can make "the cap on the toothpaste" a major issue in your relationship if you have no grander purpose. By creating a spiritual purpose of transcendence and exploration, you will rise above the downward pull of fear-based relationships. You will be dealing with the day to day from a transcendent state of feeling and knowing that generates a wonderful sense of well-being, expectancy, and happiness. This wonderful feeling comes from sharing whatever comes up, even the toothpaste cap problem. An underlying issue or hidden agenda is creating the challenge and discussing it will help bring the real source of agitation to light.

You have to ask yourself, "Why am I upset? Is this worth losing my peace of mind and state of love and contentment?" Each moment is an opportunity to choose love or fear, whatever they may be disguised as. I'm not saying to overlook your feelings. I am saying to consciously decide if the issue is that important or if you are operating from your unconscious past programming of anger, blame, fear, guilt, resentment, and self-pity. You can transcend the past by asking yourself what you are really doing and consciously making the choice of how you will act in that moment.

Neurologists have discovered three "lower" brains and one "higher" brain. Each of these operates with relative independence. There is the "reptile" brain, survival at all costs, the "mammalian" brain, suckle and cling to each other, and the "primate" brain, which integrates the other two and itself and creates appropriate social behavior. The "new" brain is the frontal, love brain, the projector of love and beautiful thoughts. We can switch these brains on and off at will. Ask yourself, "Which brain am I utilizing in this moment?" The choice and the shift is instantaneous. The more we practice operating from the frontal brain, the more every aspect of our lives is moved into the quality of love. I feel that the human species is opening itself and mutating into a creature of a higher order than ever before. The activation of the frontal, love brain and the importance of right and left brain integration is a reflection of this evolving human. This choice of love actually moves us out of childishness and victim/victimizer into responsive adults who are still active in their healthy "child."

Continue to resolve the relationship you have with Mom and Dad. If you don't, you will find that you continually repeat "Mom and Dad" issues in your current relationships. Brothers and sisters, mom and dad, and you are all intertwined in family games. Some are life-giving, but many are self-defeating. It is hard to stand back and look at your relationship objectively when you are so intimately tied into the game.

For a long time I had so needed an intimate relationship that I didn't realize what it cost me to have companionship, hugs, snuggling at night, and someone to share my heart with. My relationship is undergoing some changes at this point, as it is time for Reuben and me to each pursue our own vision and express our gifts fully. If we can do this and live together, we will. If we can't, I know the Goddess is in charge and something better will be available for both of us. For a while our identities had become lost in each other because we both needed so much nurturing. Now a new energy is moving in our lives and we must continue to evolve. We are both open and both love each other. The question is whether we can thrive and flourish independent of each other while together. That two people can do this is obviously possible; we will see if we are those two. What is impossible is for anyone to make the other love himself and find his own path.

Rites of passage in olden times assisted young men and women to grow up, leave their parents, and create their own lives. Without these rites for both men and women, these issues can drag out and perhaps never be resolved. Often what looks like the end of a love affair is the end of an old way of being and the beginning of a whole new adventure, perhaps one not necessarily within the relationship. I have had a pattern of loving my work so much that I wanted my mate to work with me so we could be together. Now I need to work alone and be solely responsible for my self-worth, career, and vision.

For a while I retreated from the world I had known to discover aspects of myself and return to Mother Earth. Now I am needing to participate in my career and my world as much as I desired intimacy in the past.

My own mother and father issues have come up again for me to observe. Finding your own separate identity is an ongoing challenge. The woman in me is coming forth in such a way as to demand a whole man and not a child. Reuben's desire to and need to bring forth his man is also coming about. We are both excited about our opportunity, saddened by the thought of perhaps not being together, both knowing that we will always love each other. For any relationship to thrive we need to be at choice, which may mean saying, "I love you and I can take care of myself."

Your success as a woman is not determined by your relationships, your money, your body size, or anything else. It is determined by who you are as a person and the levels at which you know yourself, express yourself, and are in touch with your inner and outer worlds.

In a relationship create a purpose of love and the framework of mutual support for each other to blossom into all each of you is capable of being. This creation of a greater context in which to live your life and play in relationship will increase the activation of this new, more loving self and more active, whole-brain function. Then create some games to play that allow you both to grow, flourish, and express your individual talents, wisdom, and power. Problems and challenges are actually opportunities to bring forth what is inside of you that had been sleeping and dormant. If you don't have a greater purpose, you use the petty relationship issues to create problems to solve. After a while, boredom sets in and you feel that it is the same old thing. You are going nowhere. You never actually grow because you keep destroying the love so that you can re-create it. Let love be a constant, ongoing, never-changing attitude and feeling. Love becomes the platform, the launching pad for other adventures and creative opportunities for your genius. Love and respect for the divinity of each person creates an atmosphere in which you both tap into the infinite potential genius.

Take a few moments and write some possible purposes for your relationship. Get clear on your separate lives, for each needs to be whole, take a stand for what his or her life is about, and know that he or she is valuable, makes a difference, and is able to support and take care of him- or herself.

UNHOOK FROM RIGHT/WRONG GAMES

Ask yourself, "Do I want to be happy, right now?" Taking the blame or responsibility for other people's situations, feelings, thoughts, or results robs them of their power to deal with an opportunity for wisdom. Making another wrong or blaming yourself robs you of your power and diminishes your light.

Most of us will go to any length to prove that we are a victim, that another did "it" to us. The only problem is that whatever length we go to may be devastating to us and our relationship. Childish people play games like "get even," "just you wait," "come find me," "if you only loved me enough you would . . ." "you owe me," "you hurt me," "you made me do it," and "if it wasn't for you, I would . . ."

If we only knew that we are only hurting ourselves and delaying our joy, we would own the responsibility for creating our relationships and experiences. I cannot use, "You did it to me." I am a participant in the co-creation of that type of response, so I must look within myself to discover what that is about, share what I have found, correct my error, forgive myself, be happy, and keep living and evolving.

Dependency is blame. Self-reliance and partnerships between responsible people are powerful. I like playing with partners who know that they are the cause of their life experiences and are willing to succeed and be happy.

Being right and miserable is not a wonderful place to be. It doesn't empower me. Being happy and willing to do whatever it takes to be joyful does empower me. The agreement between two people must be that the relationship is about much more empowering things than who is right and who is wrong. Right/wrong games take any relationship into a downward spiral of decay and the loss of aliveness.

If you are trying to make things wonderful for your mate so that he will love you and stay with you, you are setting yourself up to "be-the-cause" in his life. I'm angry "be-cause . . ." You will be walking on eggs and crying the tune, "What have I done wrong and what can I do to fix it?" You will never be able to do anything right and after a while your self-esteem will be at an all-time low. Is it worth feeling like you have to grovel, beg, crawl, blame, moan, and groan to hope that someday you'll be worthy enough for someone to love you enough to stay? He may leave you because you are finished with that life-style and are ready to grow up and create a glorious life with yourself first and foremost. Nothing occurs without your agreement on some level.

Relationships of wholeness, love, and empowerment come about through awareness, choice, and repetition of the behaviors, thoughts, and beliefs you want in your life. Relationships are not static badges of honor we wear to show others how perfect we are. They are opportunities, and the more you risk, the more secure you become within yourself.

Religion and politics play big-time right/wrong games. The nuclear bomb is a great deterrent to "right/wrong" games; however, because there will be no winners in a nuclear war, alternatives must be found. We hope no one is so "stupid" that they would rather be "dead" right. Some people actually do die to prove a point, but that doesn't usually end the game. It restarts immediately between other players.

A way to "unhook" from "right/wrong" games is to ask yourself, "Is this really important or is it ridiculous to even be upset for a moment?" I ask myself, "Is this worth being unhappy over and losing my peace, love, and joy in the moment?"

If I feel that the situation warrants clarity, communication, and some sort of attention because it is actually very important to me and the quality of the relationship, then I do something. Most of the time it is trivial, so I go "front brain" into love; I feel my loving nature and rise above my three "lower," survival brains. I don't bother to get even, talk behind people's back, or spend my time analyzing other people's motives and state of mind. Once you have mastered the art of transcendence and being a woman on earth, pettiness disappears.

BOREDOM IS THE OPPORTUNITY TO BRING YOURSELF FORTH IN A WHOLE NEW WAY

Boredom is what occurs when you are tired of playing the same old games and tired of being the same old way. Boredom can be the pause between the completion of one aspect of the relationship and the beginning of the next. Often boredom is taken to mean that the other person no longer interests or excites you when it is actually the opportunity to look within yourself to discover where you are not being stimulated and excited about yourself and your own expressions.

It is also a time when you can feel a relationship is finished. It is actually the point at which you need to communicate and find your own path more than ever before. You are stagnated, probably not communicating, and ready for a new challenge in your life. Look to boredom as a signal to enjoy the moment; be interested in developing and expressing another part of yourself.

Relationships move through stages. These stages

aren't stages of deterioration but stages of unfolding. The first stage is the meeting and initial fascination. The second is getting to know each other while we are on our best behavior. The third is, "Well, so far so good. Let's get 'real' and reveal our true selves and see what happens." This is a time when you could become disenchanted and think that the other has lost his or her charm. This is a process of exploring past the entry and into the main part of the house. Any relationship that is to flourish must have as its foundation "self-acceptance." Self-love and self-confidence give us the freedom and permission to be ourselves.

The fourth stage is the acceptance and deep appreciation of one another. This is a sharing of those hidden aspects of self not revealed before. The fifth stage is the continual merging and blending on multiple levels of self. Some feel it is time for marriage or a deeper commitment. This step requires trust, honesty, and a willingness to operate beyond fear, loss, and the belief in scarcity. Make sure this step is taken not out of a need for security, but a desire to transcend fear-based, ego-centered existence. Here you have a perfect opportunity to go where most never travel—the fear of removing the fear is so great. The sixth is transcending the usual female and male roles, releasing the fear of love, and rising into the celestial playground for lovers and playmates. This is represented by the male "search for the Holy Grail," the chalice that is the feminine self, and his surrender into the Goddess. The few who get to this step have relationships that are light-years beyond most others'. It takes a courageous male to find his way through his fear, his father and mother issues, his warrior self, and his insecurities into the bed of a woman. The man who loves the Goddess within himself as well as his masculine nature does receive all the Goddess has to offer. This is terrifying to most men and this path is only for the brave.

It is tough to get through this one because you are at a crossroads, you are standing in the center looking at your options. One direction available is to continue as you have, stuff your feelings, block your vision, make do, and tolerate because, "Well, it's better than most and I don't want to upset the apple cart." Another path can be to dump everything, burn your bridges, cut your ties, move out, and move on. Another road may be to go separate ways, but continue as friends. Communications may still be exchanged but the new lives will be apart. Still another direction calls for you to reevaluate and look at what is wonderful, beautiful, and valuable to both people in the relationship and acknowledge that value as something precious and as the foundation of what is to come. Then you each call forth what is wanted and needed to the partnership. This path takes a lot of courage, communication, risk taking, desire, and willingness to do whatever it takes to move through this challenge into a new adventure.

Last night my Goddess friend Nancy rebirthed me for two and one half hours. Rebirthing is a breathing technique utilizing rapid, deep, connected breaths to attain a oneness with the breath of life. What came forth from me during this rebirth was a deep sadness about my father leaving me off and on during my childhood years. I set up a plan as a child to keep him with me by fulfilling his needs, being good, and helping him to reach his destiny and love of himself. If I did all these things, as I saw it from my little girl mind, I could be close to and loved by my father. This has been my plan with men ever since. I saw also how I really didn't trust women or men, for that matter, so I wanted intimacy but was afraid to let anyone in. I didn't know the difference between friends and acquaintances. As I let myself breathe, I regained my connection with the Goddess, letting her guide and direct me. I am one with the Goddess, as you are. We can trust that her loving plan for us is unfolding right on schedule.

When you awaken to old patterns that have directed your choices, you can release the scenarios of past pain and your attempts to avoid the losses. You can create fresh in this moment from conscious choice.

What I needed to do to release my plan for my dad was to grieve deeply and feel those feelings of loss I had held within for so many years. It seems to me that, in general, men have more difficulty with letting their true feelings surface than women do. They cover their deepest feelings and actually lose the chance to attain what is possible for them in a relationship. There is nothing to fear but our emotions. If men are to develop, they must become feminine by surrendering to the Goddess or they deny their connection with themselves, others, and their higher levels of consciousness.

Once a partnership or love relationship fulfills its objective, it stops evolving and begins to decay. A new purpose must be chosen to instill new life in the relationship. There is a part of us that acts like a computer and its job is to fulfill its programming, to achieve the objective that has been set for it. Once this is achieved it is finished and must recycle itself by destroying the achievement and beginning again. That is why a "greater purpose" for anything you do is important. It gives you an ongoing direction and context within which to operate. If the goal is to get married, the excitement builds, the big day comes, and you wake up the next morning without a goal. Now what? Acknowledge you have achieved your first objective and create another one. If your goal is to mow a lawn and you do that, you can't keep mowing the same grass forever. You must move on to something else.

What I see as a major issue is what we believe to be the qualities and distinctions between men and women, masculine and feminine. How many of the differences are the result of cultural conditioning that had its beginnings in our earliest years as humans? Spirit is neither female or male yet contains the possibility of both. I view all people as spirit that has taken on a body of a woman or man in order to be human, living on earth.

There are the obvious biological differences based on functions such as the woman bearing the children and the male providing the seed. These biological functions could possibly be our entire purpose on earth, but I don't think so. I feel and observe that there is more.

Some things we have labeled feminine and masculine have nothing to do with women's or men's biological functions. To call a quality of being, an activity, a role, or a career feminine or masculine is grossly limiting. Why is aggression a masculine quality and passiveness a feminine quality? Labeling limits and diminishes a quality. Each sex has everything the other has in terms of qualities, mental abilities, and fortitude; each gender is whole and complete within itself. Labeling men as this and women as that creates a false separation and allows us to use ignorance to remain just human. Who we are is spirit, the God-us.

The ego gets nervous when we define the whole as "she"—the Goddess, the essence of love—because we have lived with the attitude that men are superior to women for so long. The God-us is our mother but not a woman. She is the earth. She is the loving essence of all life. All of life is her offspring, even the "he." God the Mother is more accurate than God the Father.

What I prefer at this time is to hold myself and others as whole or holy and divine. This means that we can hold ourselves responsible for ourselves and be able to draw from the energies, abilities, talents, and wisdom of the whole at will regardless of our genitalia.

As a woman you may be closer to the essence of

the Goddess because you are the biological form that represents her. Again it is identification, and what you identify with you become.

Men were created to plant the seed within the woman and then to protect her and their offspring from wild animals and warring humans. He was a husbandman or the gardener and maintainer of her properties. She, being in touch with the Goddess through her cycles and biological connection, knew and was able to counsel, heal, reveal, and manifest ideas, visions, needs, and desires through the elements, the four directions of the world, and spirit.

Because the male didn't know he was also able to tap into this wisdom through his Goddess nature, he feared, worshiped, and later conquered and controlled the power of the woman. He used her for his own purposes to manifest for him. His function of planting seeds and protecting as a support to the creation became the purpose of life instead of an aspect of it. The purpose of life is not to have sex and plant sperm, attack the neighbors, and build a country on the basis of defense and offense. The purpose of life is to live, love, play, create, and be in harmony with our Mother, that which has given us life, that which I am and you are.

We have been stuck in this position for so long we've believed that it is the way it is. The feminine or creation aspect of ourselves is one of our powers to use consciously, lovingly, and with the good of the all in mind.

Women have disempowered themselves by believing that men are responsible for what happens to them and for what has happened in the past. If you knew that you were the creator of your own experience, always have been and always will be, would you be depressed and deny and hate yourself? Or would you be excited about the possibilities for yourself and your loved ones?

Women have loved being victims. If you don't believe me, try to take a woman's "victimhood" away from her. Tell her that she is the creator of her own experience and see what happens. Rape, war, crime, starvation, sickness, poverty, unhappiness are all "body trips." We as the Mother have trained and guided our children and we as women have allowed it to happen. To allow something to occur, whether it be to yourself, another, or our earth is to be a creator of that. Why do we permit it? We have been afraid to assume our position once again for fear that men will leave us, hurt us, ridicule us, and ignore us, and we will be alone. We allowed ourselves to be separated from our sisters, mothers, and grandmothers. We gave up the wisdom of the earth and her gifts to us. We traded it for the shopping mall, beauty salon, weight loss clinic, and plastic surgeon. We teach our little girls to do the same and our little boys to "be like men" rather than to love and empower the feminine within them as their primary function. If man can't create because he has denied his feminine, then he can only destroy. If woman cannot create because she has denied her power, she can only be angry, afraid, and full of self-pity.

If men do not like this view that is too bad. They

lose the opportunity to be feminine and whole. If women refuse to be responsible for their lives and for being creators, they end up trying to find themselves within a man, a store, a catalogue, a TV show, a drug, a glass of alcohol, or a plate of food. We have lost the ritual and ceremonies that keep us remembering who we are, our function, and our nature.

We can find that again by becoming friends with our sisters, mothers, and grandmothers. Men need to be with men to establish their essence not in a council of war but in a council of concerned citizens who are looking for ways to bring about ecological balance to our land.

We can merge the chalice and the blade, the feminine and the masculine as qualities upon which each of us can draw to use responsibly. "Do what you will, but harm no one" is an ancient agreement of those who love the Goddess and let her work in their lives. Men and women who agree can have miracles and magic happen as ordinary occurrences!

A friend of mine is in a new relationship with a man who is a gentle, caring, and loving man. He was upset because she didn't give him the attention he wanted. He is still feeding off the hurt and is now playing the game of going away, not calling, and getting even. At first she also played aloof and busy too. She caught herself in the game and told him, "I'm playing a loser's game here, and that is not what I want." Deal directly, openly, and honestly. If someone doesn't want to play, fine. As you move on, your old patterns are being replaced and a more conscious and fun-filled relationship awaits you.

A KEY INGREDIENT: AGREEING

A key ingredient in any relationship is called, "We enjoy each other and love being together." You are being yourself and he is being himself and together you are feeling wonderful being yourselves. You don't have to be with anyone unless you desire it. You don't owe anyone your life. You don't have to torment yourself and make yourself sick to prove you care. You don't and can't be less for someone to love himself. You can't give another what he hasn't already given to himself.

Sacrifice only teaches us sacrifice. Duty and obligation only teach us irresponsibility.

Create agreements, either tacit or spoken, that you both want to keep. Make conscious agreements that involve the finances, living space, children, and so on. The agreements may evolve as the relationship evolves. Clarity is power and there is less opportunity to play games of entanglement, fear, and separation because you are creating your relationship on holy or high ground.

GOING TO BED AND WAKING UP

Here is one last and most important gem in the crown of romance and love. Every night when you go to sleep, first ask that any problems and challenges of the day be cleansed and solved in the night. Release the day and its problems into the void; relax and enjoy your much-needed rest. Sleep is a great healer and often people are irritable simply because they aren't rested. Second, hug and kiss your sweetheart no matter what has happened. Don't go to bed angry unless you want your problems and distance to increase. Sleep can be neutral ground and a place of perfect healing. Breathe consciously before drifting off to sleep. Relax your whole body about fifteen minutes before sleeping as you let go of the day and drift into the arms of the Goddess. Every morning before getting out of bed, be with yourself first and then merge with your beloved.

WHAT ABOUT SEX?

I have not mentioned sex because sex is simply an effect of a loving, connected relationship. There are no rules; therefore no comparisons can be made. Sex is as natural as nature is in all of her glory. Sex is not for conquering and exploitation, nor is it a reward or punishment. It is an extension of love and a desire for intimacy, surrender, release, and pleasure. We've become preoccupied with an act that can never take the place of emotional lacks we feel. People have become symbols of their type of genitals instead of expressions of that which is beyond our bodies, beyond our earth, and beyond our thoughts. Sex can be a ritual that allows us to transcend our physicalness and experience the ultimate. Trust yourself. Breathe, love your Goddess body, and be present in the moment. The key to enjoying sex as I know the experience is to breathe and surrender into your own pleasure and the oneness and intimacy of the union with your partner.

Everything is always evolving, changing, moving, and merging, so be willing for both you and your romantic playmate to grow and continue to flower. We are past outdated moral and religious beliefs, but we've thrown out everything without something to take its place. We need to reconnect with what is valuable within our Earth Mother, Goddess selves and also connect with our cosmic, androgynous, transcendent selves. There aren't any role models other than yourself and a few others. You have to be courageous and call forth your spirit of adventure.

EXERCISES

1. Take a moment or two now and contemplate how much time you spend in "right/wrong" games. Is it worth it to you? What is your number-one fear of no longer playing the game of "right/wrong"?

2. List the beliefs and thoughts you have about relationships. (Brainstorm and just write down what comes to mind.) What do you believe, feel, and think about men? About women? About relationships, marriage, living together, and being alone?

3. What are five main ideas from this chapter that you will use for yourself?

4. Write the higher purpose for your relationship.

5. Write a clear statement about what you desire in a relationship.

6. List five areas of dissatisfaction in your relationship that you want to correct.

7. Select some ways in which your relationship can help our earth and its people, animals, and plants, so that nature can be restored to balance and harmony. (Some examples would be working to save the rain forests, running for public office, helping to organize volunteer child-care centers, and so on.)

8. Express in writing five ways in which you have withheld yourself in a relationship.

9. What do you do to get people to love you,

provide for you, or stay with you? Is it worth it to you?

10. My energy blockages (fears, judgments, or beliefs) that keep me from having a loving, empowering, and committed relationship are _____ (list the thoughts as they bubble to the surface).

11. Find three ways in which you could take care of your needs and also be in a relationship.

12. Notice if you have repeating patterns in your relationships and list what they are. Where and when did they start? Are you willing to release them?

AFFIRMATIONS

1. I, _____, am a fully functional, whole person creating whole loving relationships.

2. I, _____, am worthy of being loved simply for who I am.

3. I, _____, allow myself to be loved and respected by the person I love.

4. I, _____, allow no one's beliefs to affect me but my own.

5. I, _____, no longer desire to control others, as I trust my own creative process to always give me what is mine.

6. I, _____, now give all my relationships to what I call a higher power.

7. I, _____, deserve to be loved and valued as I love and value myself and others.

8. I, _____, now allow myself to receive love and support at the level at which I give it.

9. I, _____, am now ready for intimacy, passion, and romance.

10. I, _____, release myself from the limitations of past relationships and enter into the realm of my most wonder-filled, loving, and passionate relationship.

11. It is all right for me, _____, to have Goddess friends that are trustworthy with whom I can share.

12. The people I love, love me.

13. I, _____, no longer have to pay people to love.

14. I, _____, call forth the merging of my female and male energies.

15. I, _____, can now be who I am and as loving and powerful as I am in all my relationships.

16. The more I, _____, love and accept myself, the more satisfying and fulfilling my relationships are.

17. It is perfectly right for me, _____, to enjoy the sensuality of my body during sex.

18. I, _____, no longer need to help my father and mother through my intimate relationships with men and women.

CHAPTER 14

Children and Parents, Two Sides of the Same Coin

CHILDREN LEARN BY YOUR EXAMPLE, NOT BY WHAT you tell them. Our primate and mammal brains learn by imitation. We are all susceptible to training and programming and it is used constantly by advertising agencies and those who are interested in controlling your thinking, feeling, decision making, and subsequent behavior.

A child is a precious gift of the divine to this dimension called earth. Children are innocent, vulnerable, and dependent upon the adults they call parents and family. When you look at a child, realize that you are in the presence of the Creator. Behold before you a divine gift from the Source. Who you and I are is also that precious, innocent, and vulnerable child who deserves ultimate respect, appreciation, and treatment.

At some level each child will become as he or she desires to be, but children need love, guidance, values, and support from us. Parents are those of us who have volunteered to be guides to those brave souls who have also volunteered to be human, some for the first time. Parenting is a short-term role whose purpose is to create a loving environment that teaches through experience and example how to be a responsible, whole, self-sufficient person. Parenting ends gradually and the parent reverts to one who is a friend while following his or her own path.

ON TRULY WANTING CHILDREN

The more we can be responsible for our sexual actions, the more we can be responsible for having children and creating the environment that allows these divine beings to flower. What appears to be the number-one criterion of successful parenting is to want to have children. If you can't have them but want to, get them from parents who don't want them or don't think they can care for them. Not every woman is a mother, nor every man a father.

It is much easier to prevent conception than to deal with unwanted children. We need to teach our daughters and sons that they are responsible for their bodies and that sexual intercourse produces children. Times have changed and we no longer need to produce offspring for the survival of the species. Our old survival reproductive programming is passé and actually a detriment to the health of our planet. The ego-based need to reproduce is no longer valid or a measure of successful adulthood. In some countries parents have children so they will have someone to take care of them in their old age, but in impoverished countries, overpopulation and starvation are the result. These ancient customs are no longer necessary and it is time to set them aside.

A measure of a man's masculinity used to be how many children he could father. In order for a woman to keep her mate, please her religious leaders, and ensure a future of livelihood, she had to produce children. Poverty often demanded many children because many died of untreated illness and hunger. As we assist more people in living healthy, secure lives, there will be less need for more bodies and more of a demand for a sustained, high quality of living for those already here. We won't have children as a means of physical survival or in place of pension plans. We will have them because we desire to participate in their lives, learn from them, and be mutually supportive. There will be balance.

We will also return to a time of respecting our seniors; senior citizens will be participating more in raising, teaching, and caring for the children. Families will cease the negative, neurotic game playing. The clan will become a strong, empowering, love-based support unit from which to explore our inner and outer worlds. We'll create tribes and classes in an extended family way. We will live with some of our family and not with others. Friendship will return, as will the counsel, dialogues, sharing, and truth.

CREATING A COMMUNITY FOR YOUR CHILDREN

It is time for us to be role models of the highest order for our children. To be a role model does not mean that we have to be perfect. Perfection is a limitation. We have to be open, honest, responsible, and loving in relating with these short people we call kids. You can be divorced. You can fail. You can make mistakes. You can be upset and cry. To be a parent is to know yourself and be committed to what it will take to guide and provide for a young seed to grow into a flower. A parent is one who is true to him- or herself and who has committed to be the loving guardian of a new soul until such time as it is able to care for itself.

Create a consistent family or support unit for your child. Communities that seem to raise healthy children are the ones in which the child has a number of people who are willing to love and guide the child. Child raising is a community opportunity when each child is greeted as a valuable part of the life force of the extended family. When I visited the small villages of the Fiji Islands, I observed that the adults all seemed to be involved in each child's life. Of course you'd want to be involved—they are valuable gifts and what they do affects you and your piece of heaven.

We're finding in our cities the lack of community. No one cares and the results are obvious. We've made machines, technology, appearances, money, and sex more important than the quality of personal experience. We've lost family, community, ritual, and guidance. I don't mean we should go back to the old, unproductive forms of family control: "Do as I say or else . . ." There must be a place for each of us to fit, not conform but cooperate and commune.

We look to the schools, government, police, ex-mates, babysitters, day-care centers, and even strangers to handle our child problems. Little by little we need to create our own little heaven-on-earth communities. Build friendships, build trust, build a life-style that will empower people into greatness on all levels. It is going to take our turning away from instant gratification to the long-term process of cultivating a quality life-style for ourselves and our families.

We have been programmed to buy stuff, stuff we don't need that pollutes our bodies, minds, and environments, all to satisfy the greed of insatiable ego machines. Children need nature. They need a dependable community that cares about them and offers dependable rules and guidelines by which they can grow, play, test, and explore. It no longer works to hand children heaven and hell lines or to use guilt and fear as a way to control and make them conform to an archaic, patriarchal system. You can't give them rules that don't go anywhere and expect them to listen to you or respect you just because you are their parent.

I was a divorced parent who was just about the sole financial support for my girls. Now that they are women and friends, we have the honor of continuing our relationship on new levels and I get to play the roles of grandmother and mother-in-law. We have had some challenging times but times that also built our relationships. Rebecca, my younger daughter, amazes me with her courage, strength, and ability to be a mother, a wife, and a friend. My older daughter Suzanne's courage in being herself and not conforming to "my ways" gave me the push I needed to break out of my neat little box and open myself to the journey I've been on ever since. Sometimes we are close; sometimes we are distant. Sometimes we don't like each other; other times we do. But we are all being responsible for ourselves.

Children aren't just liabilities, deductions, toys, or a necessary evil, but real people who have major contributions to make to you and the world. Take the time and contemplate your own deepest needs and those of your young wards. Begin to create a community that will provide a spiritually, mentally, emotionally, and physically safe, healthy, and stimulating environment. In my early years of child raising, I was so miserable in my marriage and so desperate to be loved and accepted by a man, that I was often unhappy, preoccupied, and involved in my own process. With a parenting community, children have others with whom to identify, not just one parent (or two) who may be afraid to love and be herself.

Children are very forgiving. All they want is your love. All they want is your attention and to be worthy enough to be as important as anyone else in your life. The more we women look to ourselves for love and create loving relationships with various people, not just lovers, the more we build our own values and self-worth.

Times aren't what they used to be, and it is no longer right for you to devote every minute to your children and mate at the expense of yourself. This is a new time—you must first love yourself and do what you do from that center within as a choice. Children who are doted on often turn out much the same as those neglected. I often made the men in my life more important than my children, but I was with men who were insecure, jealous, competitive, and lacked self-love. Even with all of this, my girls and I survived and grew strong, wise, and enlightened in the process.

Children are forgiving, resilient, and awesome partners in creating their own needs and life-style. When creating a community for your children, ask yourself, "Would I want to be with these people to whom I am trusting my children?" Find and choose people who are also committed to building family, community, and beautiful lives.

Protect your children from molestation, cruelty, and emotional or physical abuse. Many women fear being rejected by their men if they refuse to subject their precious babies to abuse. Until women own their power, get up off their knees, and stop begging for love, our children will roam the streets and let themselves in for abuse in their unending search for love and self-respect. Children need boundaries as well as freedom. They need a safe base from which to explore the world.

In my counseling retreats and workshops I have found that a large number of women have been violated and abused. It is so difficult for them to forgive and trust themselves, to be vulnerable, to generate a new, healthy life on all levels. Women have got to stop begging for love, take a stand, and create a life for themselves. That way their children, male and female, will learn to be responsible for their own lives through mom's example.

Sexually abused children often grow up to be abusers themselves, or at least preoccupied with sex, unless the problem is dealt with. To be preoccupied with sex, whether from abuse or some other emotional problem, is to live in denial and avoidance. I know men in their fifties who are still preoccupied with sex when there is so much more life and living available. It is as if their growth is stunted and the brain never gets fully activated. A child must develop on all levels and feel safe to do that. You are the mother. It is up to you where you and your children and the world will go.

Children need to have a safe place in which they can count on the rules being carried out consistently and lovingly. And the rules should be kept to that number needed for a child's safety, health, education, and growth—not based on the whim or convenience of the parent. Too few rules creates another kind of slave, one who has no guidelines and therefore no constructive games to play.

Rules should be oriented toward assisting the child to be all that he or she can be. Don't bother to yell when rules are broken; just carry through with your insistence on children's following the rules. You train your children to treat you and others as you treat them, so take the time to plan what is important and let the unimportant go.

There are many wonderful books on child raising and many resources that can serve you in your education and efforts to guide your children. Use them. The most important source for guidance and understanding of these little light beings is your own knowingness, your higher self. Trust it. Remember when you were a child and let your own inner child emerge and play with your children. Together you will learn and grow. It is not about you sacrificing yourself for your children—it is a growth opportunity for all.

Teach your children by example. Live your values, ideals, and spiritual beliefs. What you allow them to watch and listen to becomes their value system and sets up their future. Children need to be occupied by what is interesting to them. Offer opportunities for them to be involved in challenging and worthwhile activities. Saying, "Why don't you get interested in something?" isn't it. We must participate in our children's education, and that education doesn't just go from Monday to Friday, September to June. Be involved in what they are learning. Help create the curriculum if you can and offer options and opportunities to them. The cheapest form of crime prevention is a school system that builds self-confidence, healthy, creative, responsible, and able youths.

Interested children are involved in life because life is interesting to them. If you and I live our lives at the beauty salon and the local shopping mall and make our identity and self-esteem based on clothes, popularity, drugs, alcohol, and so on, so will our children. As you and I come to terms with our deeper values and more lofty ideas and standards, so will they.

With the disappearance of the influence of church, temple, and family, children hang out in malls and their parents at Club Med. We are right in throwing out the old fear-based values of a patri-archal, angry, vengeful God, but in creating our new communities we need to keep the most wonderful aspects of religious communities. Now it is time to create communities built on our new identities, needs, and dreams. These are in the process of being formed and, as in most new endeavors, there are few precedents to follow. We must therefore create them ourselves.

I think it is exciting to create a whole new way of being in relationship, family, community, and world. Our children are the messengers of light who have come to assist us in constructing our new civilization of peace, sufficiency, and limitlessness.

We need to value who they are and give them every opportunity to enlighten us.

HELPING AND LETTING YOURSELF BE HELPED

Children need to be able to give to adults. Giving builds self-esteem. Children who only know what it is like to receive do not know they have anything of value to give. We adults may believe it is our place to give to children, but for children to become responsible, caring adults, they must know the satisfaction of being able. Ableness is the result achieved when a person has something to give and gives it.

I feel it is important for children to learn that what they give out is what they receive. This also refers to the principles of circulation of currency. Money represents an energy exchange. When children know that their income is based on their outflow, they are prepared to provide for their needs and desires. Children who know that they can provide a valuable function and make a contribution to others feel valuable. Self-esteem is connected with contribution.

I've found that helping and assisting is something little children love to do. Let them. Acknowledge their effort. "Good job!" or "Thanks, I really appreciate that!" Say what is real for you. Behavior that receives attention is reinforced. We all love at-

tention and honest appreciation. People wonder
why they can't get their kids to help. It is because
the kids have not been permitted to give meaningful help in the past. They have become frustrated
and angry and decided to stop trying to give.

All of us need the freedom to make errors and
mistakes. Failure is part of the learning process.
Without an opportunity to fail, one cannot feel free
enough to succeed. Scientific geniuses use labora-
tories to do experiments. Life is our laboratory and
children need to know that mistakes are okay and
ultimately lead to success. Teach your little people
to be responsible for their bodies, their actions, and
their creations. This is a natural outcome of your
being responsible for yourself and your creations.

Instead of telling your children exactly what to
do, what to think, and how to live, assist them in
realizing that choices have ramifications. Let them
know about cause and effect and that their actions
have consequences. The more they are treated as
equals with respect, the more you can actually
guide them in their process of growing up and be
there in that capacity as they emerge into healthy
adults.

PARENT/CHILD GAMES: AN AGREED-
UPON REALITY

Parenting is not an occupation but a guidance
service. It is one aspect of life, not an entire focus.
The child-parent relationship is an agreed-upon

game. "I'll be the parent and you be the child, okay?" Roles that we play are just that—roles on the stage of life. "Let's pretend that neither of us knows or remembers. Let's pretend that I am born to you, you take care of me until I can take care of myself, and then we'll play another game."

Herein lies an opportunity for massive transformation. If we change the parent-child game from one that is disempowering to one that is empowering to all concerned, our world will quickly heal itself of psychosis and neurosis. Health, happiness, wisdom, and prosperity will flourish because each person is in-dependent rather than outer-dependent.

My mother just moved about ten miles down the road. We have never lived near each other except when I lived in her house until the age of eighteen. There are no accidents. I had written the first part of this chapter on children and wondered why I hadn't been motivated to do the parent portion. Now I know!

Last night, after spending a couple of hours with her and her husband, I found myself tossing and turning in my sleep. I'm such a free being, and now to have my *mother* living close by . . . What does this mean to me and my life?

First, it will give me a chance to pinpoint and release any beliefs, attitudes, games, and emotional patterns I learned as a child that don't serve me. Second, it will be a wonderful opportunity to know and be myself freely in front of Barbara, not *"my mother."* I don't desire parents at this time in my life.

I haven't needed or wanted parents for years, although there is always a small part in each of us that wants to be taken care of, given presents, and not held accountable for actions.

I'm not willing to play any kind of codependent games of emotional entanglement with anyone, I don't care who it is. I have done this before and the cost is too great. It doesn't go anywhere except into a pit. Can you tell I'm feeling a lot of energy around this issue? This couldn't come at a better time, because I've shed my past, limited self and am as a butterfly unfolding my wings to fly as never before. It's time for me to release any last pieces of "stuff" having to do with me as a child or as a parent. I am now a "self-contained," whole energy system determining my life, direction, and creations. I'm excited about my new relationships with my daughters, my mother, my son-in-law, stepfather, and mate.

I love Barbara and Adam, formerly Mom and Dad, and will always be there for them as they were for me. The best that I can give them is what I truly feel in my heart, mind, and emotions. I will always be true to myself without waver. It is at this point that I can receive their best and highest, because I am not playing any games of emotional drama or mental manipulation that drain our ethereal bodies.

FEAR OF LOSS

I think the fear of the child in parent-child relationships is the fear of loss. "You'll leave me. I could die if I don't have someone to take care of me." That thought has triggered much pain and suffering. The thought then carries over into all of our other relationships. Instead of looking for playmates, lovers, friends, and business associates, we are looking for parents. In rebirthing it is called the parental dis-approval syndrome.

Whatever you want from mommy and daddy, be that for your own little child within you. Create your higher power as your ideal parent who always gives you what you want and never suppresses you. Whatever you want, just ask and you shall receive it.

RELEASING YOUR PARENTS

Releasing parents to be just people means shifting your perspective so you no longer see these wonderful people through the veil of dependency in any way. The games we have played can be destructive and many people never recover from the negative effects of the parent-child dance. Whatever role you are playing, child or parent, dive deep within yourself and come from your own experience as to what is wanted and needed. There are no rules except learn as you go.

Parenting is a temporary career in which true love can be learned. Healthy parents truly desire that their children be all they desire to be, do, and have in their lives as humans. As a child you are allowing yourself to be guided, protected, and loved into your adult or mature self.

Here on the farm, we need to hire people to help with the work load. Recently we hired a couple of eighteen-year-old "boys" who made it known to us that they were men who wanted to be treated as men. At first they showed some desire to do well but quickly fell into the pattern of working only when the boss was around, lying about taking the car, and other codependent victim/victimizer games. We talked to them straight and gave them a few chances to get it together and be the men they said they were. Finally we had to ask them to leave.

I wasn't interested in playing the parent or being "ripped off," or used by people who "knew everything" and nothing at all. Their lessons are cut out for them as they venture out into the impersonal school called life. Life is the purpose of life and the teacher, tests, grades, lessons, and rewards all in one.

VALUES, IDEALS, STANDARDS, AND PRINCIPLES

Many people seem to be missing values, ideals, standards, and principles to live by, guidelines they can use to flourish with love and abundance in their lives. Some powerful and useful ideas can be gotten from fables, fairy tales, myths, and legends, although we need to be selective because many stories were created by the authority figures at that time to control women and shape the men into being warriors for the king, religion, or government.

I'm so happy that all of that is past us if we want it to be. We can now take the best and leave the rest behind, as we move into this new life and world we are co-creating at this very instant. As I create my life now, I no longer desire authority figures in my life. Instead I desire only wonder-filled, inspiring people from whom I can learn and with whom I can partner and network. Anything else is a drain on all concerned and I am not interested. I may seem overly emphatic on this point, but it is because I have been such a victim/victimizer myself. I overreact at times because I want to remind myself to pay attention and stay in touch with my feelings. I am talking to myself and reinforcing the ideals, attitudes, and beliefs that I now choose to live and share.

Interactions with these people, your parents, were your closest encounters with others and those encounters can leave you empowered and enlivened or disempowered and drained. It is up to you to decide what the outcome will be.

I've found with myself and others who have been committed to loving, understanding, and communicating that the key to having supportive parent-child relationships is to look within oneself. As humans we are much more alike than different. We all desire to be loved. The most difficult people are difficult because they want to be loved and are choosing that path to find it.

I've found in both child raising and parent releasing that honesty and personal integrity combined with a base of love and respect bring the most rewarding results. Sometimes it is difficult to be honest and straightforward because we care so much. But if we aren't being ourselves now, when will we be? Many people wait until their parents have left the earth to say "I love you and I know you love me!"

We can't solve anyone's problems but our own. That is how it is supposed to be. We can only be there in love while others solve their own problems. The truer you are to yourself and the truer others are to themselves, the more life becomes a mutual adventure in love, laughter, and joy.

EXERCISES

Here are some suggestions that will work both ways in the child-parent dance.

1. Know that you've both chosen to be together to play, share, grow, and learn about love.

2. Know that love is who you both are. Love is not a codependent, victim/victimizer relationship. Love is acceptance of the genius, worth, and magnitude of oneself and others. It is being supportive of one's dreams, desires, visions, and purposes. Love is nonjudging, noncritical and yet honest, open, and communicative. Love is 100 percent acceptance of all aspects of oneself including your "mistakes," your body, your past,

present, and future. Love doesn't mean you *have* to live with, sleep with, work with, or play with anyone. Love is who and what you are. Step up from your limited and negative considerations and rise above the fear-based thought and belief system that has separated us from one another. From a higher perspective we recognize our oneness and our love as the truth of who we are. Parent and child become games and roles we play in our human drama, our comedy adventure—not absolute identity.

3. Consciously create yourself as you desire to be. As you consciously create yourself, you can rise above your conditioning and your past programming and decide which beliefs you desire to retain and which to release. You are an independent, free-willed energy system of love, light, and power. It is up to you to make your own decisions.

4. Be grateful for what you have learned and received from your parents. I feel that all people really do their best at the time. It is important to acknowledge how these magnificent beings have contributed to your life. Let them know that you are a successful human being and that you are fully capable of handling your life in all ways.

5. See your parents as people and not as inhuman creatures that you feel dependent upon. Ac-

cept them as they are and drop all your childish expectations. Let them be who they are and enjoy each other.

6. You may have to move away or separate yourself in some way if you and your parents and family are suppressive toward each other. When you are able to transcend your fear-based limited view of yourself and life you will be able to be with them again. We tend to bounce off the walls when we are so attached. We so want love from certain people that we have great difficulty in holding our own and being certain about our decisions and choices. When you are strong and being true to yourself, your relationship with your parents and children will grow.

7. Stay in love with yourself around your parents or any authority figures. Don't give your power to anyone. Keep it for yourself and use it wisely as you desire. You are just as able and trustworthy as anyone. Trust your own intuition, desires, and feelings. Remember parents are just people. Disconnect the umbilical cord gently and give yourself space to discover who you are.

8. You do not owe anyone anything. No one owes you anything. That does not mean that you can't help people or support them in whatever way fits your ideals, standards, values, and beliefs. "Choice" is the all-important word. Obliga-

tion and duty never breed love, only anger and resentment. When you act from choice, you are acting from your center of power, the realm of spirit. It is a wonderful thing to provide for, care, and love our parents when it creates a mutual blessing. No one was born to be a sacrifice for another and no one is worth more than another. Create your parent-child union from love, nurturing, sharing, respect, and friendship. Your parents can't take care of you or learn your lessons for you.

9. Let your father and mother grow and learn by being truthful, honest, and loving. We believe that we protect people from hurt by hiding something of ourselves from them. Instead we are simply preventing enlightenment. Let your family deal with their own feelings, attitudes, and beliefs. They too may wake up from the unconscious and move into the dream of love.

10. List ten things you are afraid to share with your children.

11. List ten things you are afraid to share with your mother or father.

12. What is the number-one thing you are afraid your parents will find out about you that you believe would cause them to be hurt, disap-

pointed, or lose respect and love for you? How about your children?

13. List five ways in which you manipulate your children or parents into being what you want them to be?

14. List five to ten values and strengths you have gained from your parents and children.

15. If you were your mother or father, what ten things could you do to support yourself?

16. How could you parent yourself in a nurturing way?

17. How can you let the child in you come out and play?

AFFIRMATIONS

1. I, _____, now allow myself to release my parents to love.

2. I, _____, now allow myself to release my children to love.

3. I, _____, let myself release any guilt or blame having to do with my parents.

4. I, _____, release any guilt or blame having to do with my children.

5. I, _____, recognize my parents as spiritual beings whom I have had the opportunity to know intimately.

6. I, _____, recognize my children as spiritual beings whom I have had the opportunity to know intimately.

7. I, _____, now give myself permission to be myself at all times, especially in the presence of my children/parents.

8. I, _____, allow myself to be my own parent and child.

Conclusion: Visioning the Future

LIFE IS A TREASURE CHEST FILLED WITH LUMINESCENT pearls. Each moment can be a pearl, unique and special and priceless in what it offers. Being with you during the writing of this book has bonded us in our woman aspects and brought me many pearls. I imagine and feel you reading this book and I feel great love and compassion. It has been my desire that you feel understood, loved, appreciated, and inspired in every way. I look forward to the time when I will meet you and we will know each other in a moment as we remember our connection throughout time and beyond.

Every completion is the beginning of something new, full of pearls and gifts. Before we both leave this part of our lives, let's pause for a while and imagine the future and some of its possibilities.

I'll share with you some of what I see in the future and what I desire to make manifest so that you may align with me (if appropriate) or that it may inspire your own vision and aspirations.

Those without vision have no future. Our future is born from our imagination and the deepest desires of our hearts. History does not need to ever repeat itself, because each moment is a fresh opportunity for you to be at the beginning of something new and grand. If we look backward for tomorrow's ideas, we deprive ourselves of possibilities and simply replay old movies.

The future is ours to design as we desire it to be. We design first by daydreaming, fantasizing, and imagining, "Wouldn't it be wonderful if?" What comes after the initial contemplation of, "Wouldn't it be wonderful if?" is "What do I need to do to bring this about?"

Remember back to a time not so long ago when much of what we have in the world in the form of technology was mere science fiction and the visions of eccentric inventors. We can apply the same philosophy to anything we want. As women, we are the creators of the family and the caretakers of the earth with our men. We are more than vehicles for lipstick, designer jeans, and trendy adornments. We are the women and men who hold the future of our earth and its inhabitants in our hands. Some say that, no matter what, the earth will heal itself and peace will prevail, but my fear is that humans won't be here to experience it.

In my vision earth is a paradise for our children and their children and even for us to return once again, if we choose to lay down these body garments. I love the earth and I love the opportunity to be human. So I for one use my powers to create a beautiful future.

You and I have more power together than separately and can accomplish so much more as a team. In order for us to envision our future and to begin to live that future now in our present lives, we as women need to join together in love and bond with the Goddess energy. We women need to become safe, loving, and "there" for others. Men must bond as carriers of the Spirit, the seeds of new life, and the husbandmen of our gardens and vineyards.

The warrior energy is dying as the age is turning its pages and a new story is presenting itself. I call this time the Golden Age because then the adventurer and the explorer can go where no one has gone before. The possibilities are limitless.

I'm excited as I see, hear, and feel the manifestations of peace and harmony coming forth in the world. We are realizing that we are a global family, and each member of the family is distinct yet equally valuable. The Golden Age will be a time for us to use our most undiscovered and unappreciated natural resource, the human being. Imagine creating environments for children where instead of being suppressed, violated, abused, or criticized, they are guided, respected, and taught to be responsible for themselves and their creations and their contribution to the whole.

Let's become activists as well as pacifists. Let's become quiet and still within the depth of our beings and bring forth the most beautiful fantasies and dreams. Let's then actively generate the fulfillment of these visions in our lives and in our world through our work, community involvement, and international care and concerns. Let's remove the labels that separate family members. Let's continue to press on for what we believe to be right and important while still being open to the needs and beliefs of others. I observe that multitudes of people do not know that they can solve their problems or even that a beautiful life is possible.

I feel that we as a people need to consider the following list and encourage others to do the same. These are guidelines, not rules, simply offerings intended to restore our ableness, vision, and power:

——Encourage yourself and others to daydream. Turn off the television, lie down on a warm, grassy hill, and dream of your heart's desires. Dream of how you would love to be, what you hope to do, and what would be wonderful to have. Since the advent of television and movies, we have given away our ability to imagine and simply sat back and watched. We've also become so left-brained and linear that computer training has been more important for a child than music, dance, art, and play.

——Contribute to your community and others. Get involved, go outside of your yard, meet your neighbors, and work and play together once again as a family. Move out of an ego-centered reality and into a global awareness so that you can make your world what you want it to be. Know that you make a difference and have something to offer. Assist your children by setting up opportunities for them to serve others and be involved in making a difference.

——Remember your successes and the times you achieved what you wanted. Reinforce these feelings and attitudes in yourself and in your loved ones so that they may be certain about their power to make their dreams come true.

——Develop the values and ideals that will build you into the person you want to be, not because others say so, but because you desire it. Teach values that build friendships, caring, neighborly love, and ableness. Integrity is being true to what feels right for you and keeps you in balance.

——Be kind to yourself and others in the process of learning experiences. At the same time, be discriminate in choosing your friends and colleagues. You are affected by others to some degree so be with those you admire and respect and who demonstrate the qualities in alignment with yours.

——Recognize your personal worth and value so that you can be all you can be. Discover how to do this and how you can encourage others to do this also. We are so fragile and tender that it seems as if in a moment we can be hurt. People need to believe in themselves and to know that they are capable of achieving their objectives and living happy and fruitful lives.

———Be open to what is possible beyond what you currently know or have experienced. Engage in the Divine Experiment and discover just what is possible through exploration. Let mistakes be simply lessons. Make your corrections and continue on toward your bliss.

———Teach your children by your example that they are loved for who they are and not for what they do, what they look like, wear, or have. Perceive people beyond the surface as you seek to discover the qualities and the richness of experience that they offer. As you do this you will find peace within yourself.

———Remember what you give out is what comes to you. Give what you want to receive and give yourself the quality of life you desire.

Add to this list from your experience. Meditate on and implement the ones that spark your attention. With this list of possibilities in mind, activate your imagination and project your visions into the future. In my vision of the future, I see:

• Longevity will be commonplace as more people will be happy with themselves and life will be a joy to live.

• We will each be true to ourselves as we share our talents with others. Each person will be considered a genius in his or her own right. People will help each other not out of dependency and helplessness, but out of love and admiration.

• We will join together and clean up the environment, restoring the earth to health and balance.

- Most people will be self-employed and responsible for themselves and the quality of their craft, profession, or work.
- Senior citizens will be recognized as wise and respected members of society.
- Our children will be in school systems that provide an environment of learning and discovery. Youth will realize how to use their talents, abilities, wisdom, and genius.
- Women and men will love themselves with all their heart, soul, and mind. They will interact with love, unafraid to be themselves.
- We will live in communities that are both self-sufficient and involved with the global community. We will think globally and act locally even as we extend our citizenship to the galaxy.
- Female and male issues will no longer exist and each person will simply be recognized for who they are.
- People will heal themselves and participate with health professionals in having the optimum physical bodies for as long as they want and need.
- Men will be comfortable with their feminine energy.
- Age will no longer be an issue nor will race, color, or creed, yet we will draw on the wisdom and special qualities of all.
- Each person will recognize and express the artist, dancer, singer, musician, and genius that they are.
- Homes will be self-sufficient biosystems that

support people's health, creativity, relationships, well-being, and play.

- Women will be restored to their full power, and peace and sufficiency will prevail.

- We'll each make our own music, and new forms of music, art, and design will emerge.

- Organic food will be the staple of life and everyone will be aware of their bodies and what it takes for them to be healthy, happy, and fully alive.

- Through genetic engineering, people who have body ailments and disabilities will be healed and restored to physical ableness if they desire.

- All countries will be distinct and yet will all share and create as friends and partners on our earth home.

- Hunger will be a thing of the past and all people will know how to provide for themselves.

- We will manage and farm the land in harmony with nature.

- There will be no more epidemics because we will know the cause and treatment of disease and how to be healthy and youthful.

- We will handle our waste products in a way that supports environmental harmony and balance.

- We'll have found ways to recycle our refuse and manage our natural resources.

- Many will be immortal and seeds of a new galactic society.

As I say so long for now, I feel it appropriate that you, if you choose, write out some of the visions, hopes, and dreams that are in your heart. What I listed are just a few basic ones. Let your imagination soar! Have some fun! Much love and power is yours. Use it!

EXERCISES

Using the following categories as guides, write your vision for yourself and our world.

Yourself:	Technology:
Relationships:	Health care:
Environment:	Space travel:
Wealth:	Food:
Travel:	Governments:
Education:	Women:
Art:	Music:
Men:	Communication:
Homes:	Children:
Extraterrestrials:	Spirituality:
Bodies:	Any others you might have:

ACTION ITEMS

List five things you can do now to bring about your vision in your family.

List five things you can do now to bring about your vision in your community.

List five things you can do now to bring about harmony and cooperation with your neighbors.

List five things you can do now to bring about ecological balance.

List five things you can do now to get yourself going in the direction of your vision.

Create your plan and begin with the first step.

Terry Cole-Whittaker's message of enrichment has been chronicled in her other bestselling titles, *What You Think of Me Is None of My Business, The Inner Path from Where You Are to Where You Want to Be,* and *How to Have More in a Have-Not World.* At the height of her ministry in La Jolla, California, she preached her message to millions of viewers each week on her syndicated television show. In 1985 she left her ministry to take charge of her own spiritual destiny. Currently she lectures throughout the world and holds workshops and retreats on her farm in Washington state.